Electronic and Digital Media: Past, Present and Future

Electronic and Digital Media: Past, Present and Future

Ted Sharp

MURPHY & MOORE
www.murphy-moorepublishing.com

Electronic and Digital Media: Past, Present and Future
Ted Sharp
ISBN: 978-1-63987-183-4 (Hardback)

MURPHY & MOORE
Published by Murphy & Moore Publishing,
1 Rockefeller Plaza,
New York City, NY 10020, USA

Cataloging-in-Publication Data

Electronic and digital media : past, present and future / Ted Sharp.
p. cm.
Includes bibliographical references and index.
ISBN 978-1-63987-183-4
1. Digital media. 2. Mass media. 3. Digital communications. 4. Online journalism. I. Sharp, Ted.
P91.28 .E44 2022
302.231--dc23

For more information regarding Murphy & Moore Publishing and its products, please visit the publisher's website www.murphy-moorepublishing.com

Table of Contents

Preface

The media that can be shared on electronic devices for viewing by audience is referred to as electronic media. It involves distribution of media using live broadcasting, online networking and storage mediums. Some of the commonly used devices for electronic communication are television, radio and magnetic storage devices. Digital media can be defined as data which can be represented using series of digits. It refers to those forms of media which are encoded in machine readable formats. It can be created, distributed, viewed and modified using digital electronics. Prominent examples of digital media are software, digital videos, social media, websites, databases and electronic documents. This book provides comprehensive insights into the field of electronic and digital media. Different approaches, evaluations and studies on this field have been included herein. Those in search of information to further their knowledge will be greatly assisted by this book.

To facilitate a deeper understanding of the contents of this book a short introduction of every chapter is written below:

Chapter 1- The field of media through which information can be spread with the help of electronic devices is known as electronic media. Digital media refers to the media which is encoded in machine-readable formats. This is an introductory chapter which will introduce briefly all the significant aspects of electronic and digital media.

Chapter 2- Mediums of electronic and digital media can be broadly divided into radio, television, mobile, internet, social media and blog. Radio are further categorized into different types such as AM radio, FM radio, HD radio, satellite radio and internet radio. The topics elaborated in this chapter will help in gaining a better perspective about these mediums of electronic and digital media.

Chapter 3- Some of the different tools and techniques used in electronic and digital media are computer graphics, morphing, digital content, digital data, digital image, digital audio, digital video and broadcasting. Science and technology have undergone rapid developments in the past decade which has resulted in the discovery of significant tools and techniques in the field of electronic and digital media; which have been extensively detailed in this chapter.

Chapter 4- The process of distribution of content to the audience through electronic communications medium is known as broadcasting. A few of the various techniques of broadcasting are radio broadcasting, digital audio broadcasting, commercial broadcasting, public broadcasting, remote broadcasting, microbroadcasting, broadcast syndication, etc. are discussed in this chapter in detail.

Chapter 5- All the materials and tools that are used by a composer, artist and designer to create an art are known as artmedia. Some of the significant topics studied in relation to artmedia are new media art and interactive media. The topics elaborated in this chapter will help in gaining a better perspective about the artmedia.

Chapter 6- Digital and social media have a significant impact on various sectors such as business, education and health. This chapter has been carefully written to provide an easy understanding of the impact of digital media on these sectors as well as the impact of social media.

I owe the completion of this book to the never-ending support of my family, who supported me throughout the project.

Ted Sharp

1

Introduction to Electronic and Digital Media

The field of media through which information can be spread with the help of electronic devices is known as electronic media. Digital media refers to the media which is encoded in machine-readable formats. This is an introductory chapter which will introduce briefly all the significant aspects of electronic and digital media.

Electronic Media

The world is in a fast development in communication technology and application of the Internet. It is known as the WWW (World Wide Web) that has been rising and growing since 1994. The way in doing businesses has been changed. A lot of strategies, policies and practices are implemented to attain the efficiency and effectiveness of Electronic Media. Thus, E-media is the modern concept that used by companies in order to reach the maximum E-consumers. Companies adopt Electronic Media to shop their services and products. Companies in all sectors use E-media in order to support their dealings and markets. For example, Electronic Media is "achieving media objectives thru how to apply technologies". Electronic Media is defined as "the use of Electronic Media and applications for planning then executing the distribution and the pricing and to create transactions that fulfil invidious and company's goals". The term Electronic Media is responsible for such big change in technology and made a big social effect. Many opportunities for individuals and companies are provided. Individuals can purchase a wide variety of services and goods. In one hand, Electronic Media is a door for consumers to select then buy definitely and freely. In the other hand, companies expand their markets and introduce new services and product with a big competition in global environments for many reasons:

- Electronic media build relationships between people and provide opportunities to share interests, goods and services.
- Electronic Media socialize the media communication in an open and connected market.
- Electronic Media represents how people can share information and provide users with new form of empowerment sharing.
- Thru Electronic Media (EM), people are able to communicate online and exchange without limits.

E-Media use contributes positively to firm performance through organizational innovation. Electronic Media is going in a fast transformation of all parts of the value due to the effect of chains, owners, marketers and advertisers. All these changes are being done by the revolution of technology and social change, Darren suggests that media channels are becoming more fragmented and the media consumer is more empowered than ever before. Some channels are becoming Medias in their own right through blogging and other tools. However, it is not yet known whether engagement with proliferating electronic social networks is similarly associated with increased emotional support. The problem of Media classification in this context becoming important in term of possibilities to prepare research methodology for quality and efficiency evaluation.

While E-media provide meaningfully to the developing countries, challenges may include a lack of telecommunications infrastructure, low Internet and credit card penetration, lack of skilled professionals and insufficient delivery systems to accomplish the role of Electronic Media in company's strategies and approaches.

Importance of Electronic Media

Companies have gained a big market share thru tools of Electronic Media. Recently, people started to trust the online markets and services there Electronic Media such as mobiles phones, e-mails and other electronics tools are in reach of all people and connected to all network social sites. Compared to other channels, Electronic Media is considered cheaper than other ways. It provides unique segmentation opportunities and is considered easy and cheap and it can allow companies to contact in a direct way with consumers. Information technology (IT) have affected every home, company and sector, so they can provide information regarding companies and customers in a preferred way to buy and collect information. Companies like investing, banking online, payment online and E-transfer. The current companies are applying technology are increasing by using E-Media (EM). Thus, E-Media has become a big part of media planning.

Electronic-Media (EM) is very important to increase consumer response. Companies adopt widely and rapidly the E-media solution in their distribution. Small, medium and big enterprises can afford E- Media because of the low cost, Electronic Media (EM) has become the good tool when a company wants to design strategy. Number of customers is bargaining intense and power by competition for sectors and companies in global markets. In order to respond efficiently to customer reviews companies, need to identify consumer reviews platforms, understand their characteristics and continuously assess their impact on consumer purchasing decisions.

E-media have great potential for companies and customers. But maybe consumer's behavior may vary depending on the adoption of Electronic media and Internet. The consumer perception is the main reason for this variance in adoption of all the linked technology. The information technology is providing sectors and all kinds of companies. Information are useful and valuable in good time to help managers in decision making. The integration of e-media strategies with customers can perceive useful information. Thus, when an enterprise is trying to build a perception regarding consumer with a precise role, E-Media can play a big role in companies.

E-media is a current businesses practice included data collection, companies' perspectives and consumer's behavior. It has become very important tool for the communication between companies and a very important perception among the world. In one hand, it alerts customers, update them; in other hand, they are engaged in negotiation with companies. It is the best instrument that can be used to well market production. It is considered as a "direct media" thru quality of services that can increase customers' awareness and attention.

Electronic Media (EM) is considered as a tool in low cost with high use from individuals and companies. It has a big potential to help businesses to increase and considered one of the best platforms that merge between all businesses and the remarkable growth. The specific aspects of nowadays is that electronic space reveals the growing importance of the communication and the relationship with the customer. Many researches allow the understanding of customers in real-time by observing what they do online. It is well noticed that the E-Media tools are considered a great potential and the study of E-consumer comportment is becoming very important due to the online connection and interaction. It also represents most of the challenges for companies and sectors. It effects on the relationship between Electronic Media and online consumer's behavior.

Lin blend electronic media innovation with market research including market Segmentation, promotions, advertising and the media information system. Companies found this challenging and believed that resellers prefer taking up the responsibility of accomplishing the demand generated by selling the products of a certain brand holding a leadership position in the market place. The manufactures of these brands focus on the other hand on building and combining the ability of the resellers with their resources and support. Hence, we can say that all markets and brands try to provide strategic management direction to abide to the strength of the marketers. Therefore, it is now obvious that electronic media provides its marketers with important tools which enable them to contact lots of consumers and where the individual platforms allow for creativity and innovation in the electronic media strategies. Thus, in such a situation marketer are able to fit the needs of people. Moreover, it is extremely important for all researchers to study social media platforms trying to focus and to make these platforms unique for media and branding and viewed by millions of viewers. In addition, internet marketing adoption was positively related to perceived relative advantage, compatibility, organizational innovativeness, and competitor and customer pressure.

From other hand, Consumer perception pointed that Internet and network related to services and product have the possibility to reduce cost as well as keeping a good quality and service. Consumer behavior and perception are increased by selecting good choices of vendors, delivering, serving and following. Recurrent online shoppers retain the good feeling regarding E-Media (EM) as compared to non-shoppers. The study of product and branding it offers new possibilities to the development process of the product. That several factors can influence behavior and attitude toward E-Media (EM). In all companies for example, commerce sector need and require more knowledge and skills to use E-Media and knowledge about Electronic Media efficiency and effectiveness in various aspects.

But, with the development of more technologies a new element of media practices known as Electronic Media (EM) which is a media tool that forms direct dialogues between a company and its customers based on trust and confidence. Despite that, electronic privacy protection behavior was related to hacking anxiety and privacy self-efficacy. Data hacking worries mediated relations between hacking websites and privacy protection.

Electronic Media Classification

The most popular E-tool used for communication is social networking. Social networks have experienced an evolutionary process, in the beginning was like-minded grouping, news exchange by mean of e-mail. Later on, developed social networks, which became a tool for E-business.

In media practices, different trends are operational to attract customers by using e-mails, interactive media, database media as well as e-Media applied through the internet. Richard and many others defined internet, mobile, intranet and extranet in different contexts. However, they presented four media practices: Transaction media (TM), Interaction Media (IM), Database media (DM), Network media (NM).

Trying to prepare research methodology for efficiency evaluation of E-Media the systematic understanding of it, the classification of E-Media types by distribution channels are presented in Table.

The global digital economy tends to grow up through the adoption of key technologies, mobility, cloud computing, data mining, artificial intelligence or the extension of social environments. For e-businesses, companies use these various media such as television, radio, internet, fax, mobiles and others that are possible by technology. EM plays a crucial role for promoting communication in the society in several and various ways. Thus, it can provide these contributions:

- The real advancement of the business environment and situation.
- Employees are able to collaborate and share information regarding project in a time and cost saving manner.
- Employees can easily exchange and discuss ideas in various forums further promoting their work.
- It stimulates and promote marketing for businesses by employing them as tools for communication.
- Facilitate interaction in communication and helps companies to adopt a different way to well conduct public relations.
- Electronic Media enables individuals to get news and information concerning the whole world instantly and immediately.

Moreover, electronic media promotes communication through entertainment. It creates diversity use of internet via e-mails, all tools of social media, video charts and others. Thus, in education institutions, universities and schools utilize electronic media tools for teaching online classes discussions. Furthermore, social media networking is essential and fundamental in communication by people and societies worldwide. It educates, informs, updates, notifies, teaches, and updates their participation in all perspectives. It is really very significant to use any types of Medias to make communication easy between people.

Table: Digital channels of media distribution.

Electronic media channel	Description	Different communications techniques
Search engine marketing (SEM).	Searching all results for pages, like google Bing, YouTube. Also includes advertising on third-party publisher sites which are part of the search display networks	1. Search Engine Optimization (SEO) listing in the natural listing which does not attract a fee per click. Based on on-page optimization and link-building. 2. Pay-per-click (advertising) sponsored listings using Google Ad Words for example.

Online public relations (E-PR).	To maximize mentions of companies and brands products. It includes monitoring and responding to all kinds of mentions and conducting all relations through websites and Networks.	1. Syndicating content (e.g. press releases), gaining positive mentions, managing reputation for forums and the social networks. 2. The using of owned media-own company feeds, blogs and feeds. 3. Blogger and influencer outreach for earned media.
Online partnerships including affiliate marketing.	Promoting online services on a "third-party" like websites also through communication and E-mail. Different forms of partnership for example how to link building, how to affiliate marketing. Thus comparison price between sites and the online sponsorship besides cobranding.	1. Commission-based affiliate marketing. 2. Creating long-term partnership relationships such as sponsorship, link-building or editorial.
Interactive display advertising.	Achieving the brand awareness and encouraging the click action through to the target site or address market.	1. Electronic Media selling and advertising. 2. Network advertising. 3. The behavior to get interactive marketing.
Opt-in e-mail marketing.	Using legal, permission based e-mailing to prospects or customers who have agreed to receive emails from an organization. E-mails to communicate with prospects can be rented from a publisher or other list owner or companies can build up their own "house list" containing customer or prospect details.	1. Acquisition e-mail activity including list rental, co-branded campaigns, advertising on e-newsletters. 2. Retention and growth activity, e.g. house list for e-newsletters and customer e-mail Campaigns. 3. Automatic or event triggered e-mail campaign activity.
Social Network.	Social network and sites facilitate the communication between users with common interests, affiliations, and benefits.	1. Micro blogs post is seen by all followers and users. 2.A message widely posted and reposted is called a "viral post".
Mobile use for text and instant messaging.	Text messaging uses mobiles airwaves and protocols in order to deliver text message. Messages are near instant communication and can be quicker than a phone call or any other tool that needs time and cost. It facilitates privacy and friability in communication and messaging.	The instant messaging is comparable to text messaging. But it carried over the internet rather than over cell phone frequencies.

One key innovation has been the development of social media platforms (e.g., Facebook, Twitter, blogs and others) which have allowed ongoing, "back-and-forth" online conversations among students, professors, and researchers around the world. In addition, electronic Media positively make advantage, compatibility, organizational innovativeness, competitor and customer pressure.

Electronic Marketing is at crossroads and emphasis on client satisfaction, it has fundamental implications for social marketing networks, and also has a built-in advantage on the trust and confidence. These benefits of satisfaction sustainability and trust support the possible for ideas like social enterprise and can help to attain the growth and popular engagement that is needed to deliver social change and transformation.

Digital Media

Digital media are any media that are encoded in a machine-readable format. Digital media can be created, viewed, distributed, modified and preserved on digital electronics devices. Computer programs and software; digital imagery, digital video; video games; web pages and websites, including social media; data and databases; digital audio, such as mp3s; and e-books are examples of digital media. Digital media are frequently contrasted with print media, such as printed books, newspapers and magazines, and other traditional or analog media, such as pictures, film or audio tape.

Combined with the Internet and personal computing, digital media has caused disruption in publishing, journalism, entertainment, education, commerce and politics. Digital media has also posed new challenges to copyright and intellectual property laws, fostering an open content movement in which content creators voluntarily give up some or all of their legal rights to their work. The ubiquity of digital media and its effects on society suggest that we are at the start of a new era in industrial history, called the Information Age, perhaps leading to a paperless society in which all media are produced and consumed on computers. However, challenges to a digital transition remain, including outdated copyright laws, censorship, the digital divide, and the specter of a digital dark age, in which older media becomes inaccessible to new or upgraded information systems. Digital media has a significant, wide-ranging and complex impact on society and culture.

Play Media

Analog computers, such as Babbage's Difference Engine, use physical, i.e. tangible, parts and actions to control operations Machine-readable media predates the Internet, modern computers and electronics. Machine-readable codes and information were first conceptualized by Charles Babbage in the early 1800s. Babbage imagined that these codes would provide instructions for his Difference Engine and Analytical Engine, machines he designed to solve the problem of error in calculations. Between 1822 and 1823, Ada Lovelace, a mathematician, wrote the first instructions for calculating numbers on Babbage's engines. Lovelace's instructions are now believed to be the first computer program.

Though the machines were designed to perform analytical tasks, Lovelace anticipated the potential social impact of computers and programming, writing, "For, in so distributing and combining the truths and the formulae of analysis, that they may become most easily and rapidly amenable to the mechanical combinations of the engine, the relations and the nature of many subjects in that science are necessarily thrown into new lights, and more profoundly investigated, there are in all extensions of human power, or additions to human knowledge, various collateral influences, besides the main and primary object attained." Other early machine-readable media include the instructions for player pianos and jacquard looms.

Digital Computers

```
01010111 01101001 01101011
01101001 01110000 01100101
01100100 01101001 01100001
```

Digital codes, like binary, can be changed without reconfiguring mechanical parts. Though they used machine-readable media, Babbage's engines, player pianos, jacquard looms and many other early calculating machines were themselves analog computers, with physical, mechanical parts. The first truly digital media came into existence with the rise of digital computers. Digital computers use binary code and Boolean logic to store and process information, allowing one machine in one configuration to perform many different tasks. The first modern, programmable, digital computers, the Manchester Mark 1 and the EDSAC, were independently invented between 1948 and 1949. Though different in many ways from modern computers, these machines had digital software controlling their logical operations. They were encoded in binary, a system of ones and zeroes that are combined to make hundreds of characters. The 1s and 0s of binary are the "digits" of digital media.

Impact

The Digital Revolution

In the years since the invention of the first digital computers, computing power and storage capacity have increased exponentially. Personal computers and smartphones put the ability to access, modify, store and share digital media in the hands of billions of people. Many electronic devices, from digital cameras to drones have the ability to create, transmit and view digital media. Combined with the World Wide Web and the Internet, digital media has transformed 21st century society in a way that is frequently compared to the cultural, economic and social impact of the printing press. The change has been so rapid and so widespread that it has launched an economic transition from an industrial economy to an information-based economy, creating a new period in human history known as the Information Age or the digital revolution.

The transition has created some uncertainty about definitions. Digital media, new media, multimedia, and similar terms all have a relationship to both the engineering innovations and cultural impact of digital media. The blending of digital media with other media, and with cultural and social factors, is sometimes known as new media or "the new media." Similarly, digital media seems to demand a new set of communications skills, called transliteracy, media literacy, or digital literacy. These skills include not only the ability to read and write—traditional literacy—but the ability to navigate the Internet, evaluate sources, and create digital content. The idea that we are moving toward a fully digital, "paperless" society is accompanied by the fear that we may soon—or currently—be facing a digital dark age, in which older media are no longer accessible on modern devices or using modern methods of scholarship. Digital media has a significant, wide-ranging and complex impact on society and culture.

Disruption in Industry

Compared with print media, the mass media, and other analog technologies, digital media are easy to copy, store, share and modify. This quality of digital media has led to significant changes in many industries, especially journalism, publishing, education, entertainment, and the music business. The overall impact of these changes is so far-reaching that it is difficult to quantify. For example, in movie-making, the transition from analog film cameras to digital cameras is nearly complete. The transition has economic benefits to Hollywood, making distribution easier and making it possible to add high quality digital effects to films. At the same time, it has had an impact on the analog special effects, stunt, and animation industries in Hollywood. It has imposed painful costs on small movie theaters, some of which did not or will not survive the transition to digital. The impact of digital media on other media industries is similarly sweeping and complex.

In journalism, digital media and citizen journalism have led to the loss of thousands of jobs in print media and the bankruptcy of many major newspapers. But the rise of digital journalism has also created thousands of new jobs and specializations. E-books and self-publishing are changing the book industry, and digital textbooks and other media-inclusive curricula are changing primary and secondary education. In academia, digital media has led to a new form of scholarship, called digital scholarship, and new fields of study, such as digital humanities and digital history. It has changed the way libraries are used and their role in society. Every major media, communications and academic endeavor is facing a period of transition and uncertainty related to digital media.

Individual as Content Creator

Digital media has also allowed individuals to be much more active in content creation. Anyone with access to computers and the Internet can participate in social media and contribute their own writing, art, videos, photography and commentary to the Internet, as well as conduct business online. This has come to be known as citizen journalism. This spike in user created content is due to the development of the internet as well as the way in which users interact with media today. The release of technologies such mobile devices allow for easier and quicker access to all things media. Many media production tools that were once only available to a few are now free and easy to use. The cost of devices that can access the internet is dropping steadily, and now personal ownership of multiple digital devices is becoming standard. These elements have had a significant impact on political participation. Digital media is seen by many scholars as having a role in Arab Spring, and crackdowns on the use of digital and social media by embattled governments are increasingly common. Many governments restrict access to digital media in some way, either to prevent obscenity or in a broader form of political censorship.

User-generated content raises issues of privacy, credibility, civility and compensation for cultural, intellectual and artistic contributions. The spread of digital media, and the wide range of literacy and communications skills necessary to use it effectively, have deepened the digital divide between those who have access to digital media and those who don't.

Web Only News

As the internet becomes more and more prevalent, more companies are beginning to distribute content through internet only means. Prime time audiences have dropped 23% for News Corp, the world's largest broadcasting channel. With the loss of viewers there is a loss of revenue but not as bad as what would be expected. While the dollar amount dropped roughly 2%, overall cable revenue was up about 5% which is slower growth than what was expected. Cisco Inc released its latest forecast and the numbers are all trending to internet news to continue to grow at a rate where it will be quadruple by 2018.

As of 2012, the world's largest internet only media company, The Young Turks, are averaging 750,000 users per day, and are continuing to grow, currently having over 2 billion views across all The Young Turks controlled channels, which covers world news, sports, movie reviews, college focused content and a round table style discussion channel.

Copyright Challenges

Digital media pose many challenges to current copyright and intellectual property laws. The ease of creating, modifying and sharing digital media makes copyright enforcement a challenge, and copyright laws are widely seen as outdated. For example, under current copyright law, common internet memes are probably illegal to share in many countries. Legal rights are at least unclear for many common Internet activities, such as posting a picture that belongs to someone else to a social media account, covering a popular song on a YouTube video, or writing fan fiction.

To resolve some of these issues, content creators can voluntarily adopt open or copy left licenses, giving up some of their legal rights, or they can release their work to the public domain. Among the most common open licenses are Creative Commons licenses and the GNU Free Documentation License, both of which are in use on Wikipedia. Open licenses are part of a broader open content movement that pushes for the reduction or removal of copyright restrictions from software, data and other digital media.

Digital Media is numerical, networked and interactive system of links and databases that allows us to navigate from one bit of content or webpage to another. One form of Digital media that is becoming a phenomenon is in the form of a digital magazine. What exactly is a digital magazine? Due to the economic importance of digital magazines, the Audit Bureau of Circulations integrated the definition of this medium in its latest report: a digital magazine involves the distribution of a magazine content by electronic means; it may be a replica. This is the out dated definition of what a digital magazine is. A digital magazine should not be, in fact, a replica of the print magazine in PDF, as was common practice in recent years. It should, rather, be a magazine that is, in essence, interactive and created from scratch to a digital platform (Internet, mobile phones, private networks, iPad or other device).

The barriers for digital magazine distribution are thus decreasing. At the same time digitizing platforms are broadening the scope of where digital magazines can be published, such as within websites and on smartphones. With the improvements of tablets and digital magazines are becoming visually enticing and readable magazines with it graphic arts.

becoming a phenomenon is in the form of a digital magazine. What exactly is a digital magazine? Due to the economic importance of digital magazines, the Audit Bureau of Circulations integrated the definition of this medium in its latest report: a digital magazine involves the distribution of a magazine content by electronic means; it may be a replica. This is the out dated definition of what a digital magazine is. A digital magazine should not be, in fact, a replica of the print magazine in PDF, as was common practice in recent years. It should, rather, be a magazine that is, in essence, interactive and created from scratch to a digital platform (Internet, mobile phones, private networks, iPad or other device).

The barriers for digital magazine distribution are thus decreasing. At the same time digitizing platforms are broadening the scope of where digital magazines can be published, such as within websites and on smartphones. With the improvements of tablets and digital magazines are becoming visually enticing and readable magazines with it graphic arts.

2

Mediums of Electronic and Digital Media

Mediums of electronic and digital media can be broadly divided into radio, television, mobile, internet, social media and blog. Radio are further categorized into different types such as AM radio, FM radio, HD radio, satellite radio and internet radio. The topics elaborated in this chapter will help in gaining a better perspective about these mediums of electronic and digital media.

Radio

Radio is very powerful because it reaches a huge audience quickly and because it allows the people in that huge audience to interact with one another more easily than television viewers or newspaper readers.

There are different types of radio stations: community, commercial and public. They have different types of owners and audiences and different programming, but they share a common goal: to connect with the listener in a way that is immediate and relevant. Radio is powerful because it has the ability to reach and influence so many people. Radio is powerful because:

- It is immediate. News can be reported more quickly on radio than in newspapers or on television, because the technology is simpler.
- It is accessible. You can tune in to radio wherever you are. You can take a radio to the fields, or listen to it in a car. You can also do other things while you listen.
- It is inclusive. Radio can reach most people, including the poor, the marginalized and those who cannot read or write.

Radio presents challenges because:

- It is temporary. Stories often air only once, so if the information is confusing or if you miss a point, it's difficult to get clarification. Radio reports need to be clearly and simply written. And radio presenters and reporters must take extra care to speak distinctly.

Radio is accessible to everyone, but getting people's attention can be a challenge:

- Radio broadcasting requires meeting tight deadlines.
- Radio allows listeners to respond and make their views known.
- Radio allows listeners to become a community.

Reaching the Public

Benefits of Radio

Reaching the public, Radio is the most accessible of media because it can accompany you in whatever you do, and wherever you go:

- Driving in a car.
- Working in the fields.
- Cooking dinner.

You don't need to be literate or rich to listen to radio or to take advantage of its resources. In fact, educators and organizations have found that radio is the best way to get important messages across - especially to women in rural areas who may not have access to newspaper or television.

Reaching the public now, Radio is immediate. It is the modern equivalent of the village story-teller. Through words, sounds and the human voice, radio talks to an audience directly. How? By inviting listeners to explore new experiences, new places, new ideas. It gives listeners the stories they need to know in order to better understand the world.

Challenges

Understanding how and where people listen to radio - Radio is accessible, so listeners can tune in anywhere and at any time. This is an advantage, but it also creates challenges. When people listen to the radio they are usually doing something else at the same time. Listeners may only have one ear on the radio, so it can be easy to miss important information, or to get an inaccurate or incomplete picture of what was said.

On radio, you have to be particularly careful about the way you communicate. This leads to another challenge. Getting it Right - Right Now - Because radio covers what is happening now, it places a lot of demands on you as the practitioner. For example, when you are under pressure to be first with a news story, often there isn't much time to check facts. This can lead to mistakes. You will need to take care not to report in a sensational way, confuse rumors with facts or show bias in your reporting.

Skills and Responsibilities for Radio

Radio stations have many people with different skills and responsibilities. There are those who voices are heard on the air, like talk show hosts and reporters, and there are also people who work behind the scenes like sound engineers, producers, marketing managers, researchers and call-screeners.

Sometimes one person may take on several roles. In smaller radio stations, a talk show host may also do research or a news reader may file reports from the field. Even at larger stations, producers are often involved in research and booking guests. Whatever the structure or size of the station, remember that successful radio depends on teamwork and all roles are equally important. This module focuses on the responsibilities and fundamental skills that a radio journalist needs to do her job.

Responsibilities

Professional journalists, whether they work in radio, television or print, are expected to adhere to basic principles. Journalists should be:

- Accountable
- Balanced
- Independent

Journalism associations or unions in many countries have established codes of ethics for the practice of journalism. Many media companies have also established their own ethical standards.

AM Radio

Amplitude modulation or AM as it is often called is a form of modulation used for radio transmissions for broadcasting and two way radio communication applications. Although one of the earliest used forms of modulation it is still used today, mainly for long, medium and short wave broadcasting and for some aeronautical point to point communications.

One of the key reasons for the use of amplitude modulation was its ease of use. The system simply required the carrier amplitude to be modulated, but more usefully the detector required in the receiver could be a simple diode based circuit. This meant that AM radios did not need complicated demodulators and costs were reduced - a key requirement for widespread use of radio technology, especially in the early days of radio when ICs were not available.

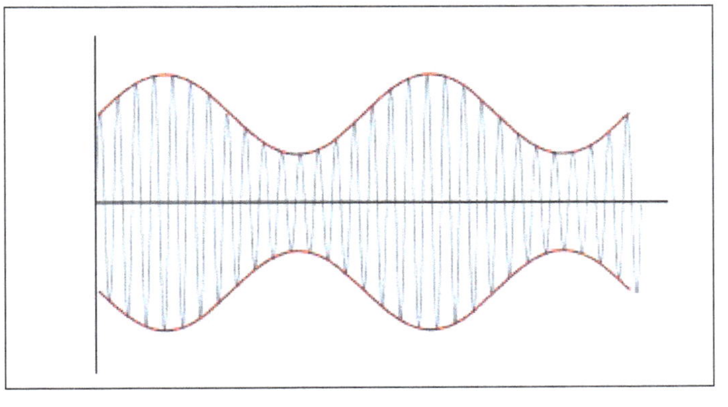

The first amplitude modulated signal was transmitted in 1901 by a Canadian engineer named Reginald Fessenden. He took a continuous spark transmission and placed a carbon microphone in the antenna lead.

The sound waves impacting on the microphone varied its resistance and in turn this varied the intensity of the transmission. Although very crude, signals were audible over a distance of a few hundred metres, although there was a rasping sound caused by the spark.

With the introduction of continuous sine wave signals, transmissions improved significantly, and AM soon became the standard for voice transmissions. Nowadays, amplitude modulation, AM is used for audio broadcasting on the long medium and short wave bands, and for two way radio communication at VHF for aircraft. However as there now are more efficient and convenient methods of modulating a signal, its use is declining, although it will still be very many years before it is no longer used.

Amplitude Modulation Applications

Amplitude modulation is used in a variety of applications. Even though it is not as widely used as it was in previous years in its basic format it can nevertheless still be found:

- Broadcast transmissions: AM is still widely used for broadcasting on the long, medium and short wave bands. It is simple to demodulate and this means that radio receivers capable of demodulating amplitude modulation are cheap and simple to manufacture. Nevertheless many people are moving to high quality forms of transmission like frequency modulation, FM or digital transmissions.
- Air band radio: VHF transmissions for many airborne applications still use AM. It is used for ground to air radio communications as well as two way radio links for ground staff as well.
- Single sideband: Amplitude modulation in the form of single sideband is still used for HF radio links. Using a lower bandwidth and providing more effective use of the transmitted power this form of modulation is still used for many point to point HF links.
- Quadrature amplitude modulation: AM is widely used for the transmission of data in everything from short range wireless links such as Wi-Fi to cellular telecommunications and much more. Effectively it is formed by having two carriers 90° out of phase.

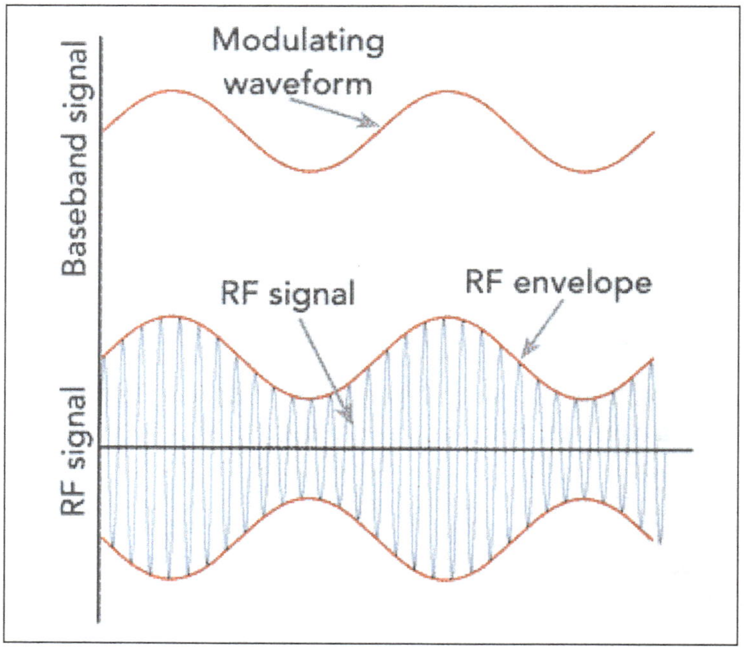

These form some of the main uses of amplitude modulation. However in its basic form, this form of modulation is being used less as a result of its inefficient use of both spectrum and power.

In order that a radio signal can carry audio or other information for broadcasting or for two way radio communication, it must be modulated or changed in some way. Although there are a number of ways in which a radio signal may be modulated, one of the easiest is to change its amplitude in line with variations of the sound.

In this way the amplitude of the radio frequency signal varies in line with the instantaneous value of the intensity of the modulation. This means that the radio frequency signal has a representation of the sound wave superimposed in it. In view of the way the basic signal "carries" the sound or modulation, the radio frequency signal is often termed the "carrier". It can be seen that the envelope of the signal follows the contours of the modulating signal.

Amplitude Demodulation

Amplitude modulation, AM, is one of the most straightforward ways of modulating a radio signal or carrier. It can be achieved in a number of ways, but the simplest uses a single diode rectifier circuit. Other methods of demodulating an AM signal use synchronous techniques and provide much lower levels of distortion and improved reception where selective fading is present.

One of the main reasons for the popularity of amplitude modulation has been the simplicity of the demodulation. It enables costs to be kept low - a significant advantage in producing vast quantities of very low cost AM radios.

Advantages and Disadvantages of Amplitude Modulation

As with any technology there are advantages and disadvantages to be considered.

Advantages

- It is simple to implement.
- it can be demodulated using a circuit consisting of very few components.
- AM receivers are very cheap as no specialized components are needed.

Disadvantages

- It is not efficient in terms of its power usage.
- It is not efficient in terms of its use of bandwidth, requiring a bandwidth equal to twice that of the highest audio frequency.
- It is prone to high levels of noise because most noise is amplitude based and obviously AM detectors are sensitive to it.

Although in the current technological climate, AM in its basic form is not nearly as effective as other modes that can be used, it is still retained in many areas like broadcasting, because of the number of users. However, it is likely that with time, its use will decrease still further and ultimately many AM transmissions will cease. However, its derivatives like quadrature amplitude modulation are widely used as they offer a very effective form of modulation, especially for data transmission.

Derivatives of Amplitude Modulation

Although the use of amplitude modulation is decreasing, it nevertheless forms the basis of other forms of modulation that are still being widely used, or their use is increasing:

- Single sideband, SSB: Single sideband is widely used for HF communications. It is formed by taking a signal that has the carrier and one sideband removed. In this way it becomes far more efficient in terms of both spectrum and power.
- Quadrature amplitude modulation, QAM: This form of modulation is essentially derived from two carriers that are 90° out of phase and adding information, either analogue or digital. Quadrature Amplitude Modulation is widely used for carrying many digital signals, everything from Wi-Fi to Mobile phone communications and very much more.

FM Radio

Frequency modulation (FM) has a long history of its application and is widely used in radio broadcast. To transmit stereo music, FM is enhanced by stereo multiplexing which carries both L and R audio channel content. With the digital age, Radio Data System (RDS) enables FM to carry text information such as traffic, weather, and radio station information which can be displayed on the end-user's device interface. Currently, growing number of mobile phones and consumer mobile devices will have an integrated FM receiver feature. The FM transmitter feature is also becoming popular for allowing users to transmit audio content from their mobile devices through their car radio. To make sure the FM-related functions work well, the FM mono, FM stereo, and FM RDS functions need to be tested in production.

Frequency Modulation

Frequency modulation is realized by varying signal frequency in accordance with the modulating signal or message, as in Figure below.

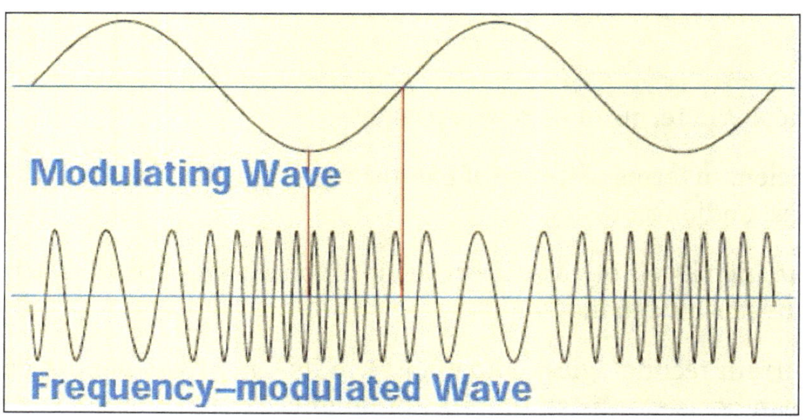

Frequency modulation.

An important concept in the understanding of FM is "frequency deviation". For a transmitter, the frequency deviation of the carrier is directly proportional to the amplitude of the applied modulating signal. Thus an FM transmitter has modulation sensitivity, K_f, which is frequency deviation/V. The relation between frequency deviation from the carrier (df_c) and the original signal is:

$$df_c = K_f * S_m(t)$$

where $S_m(t)$ is the signal before modulation, which can also be called the modulating signal, because this signal will modulate the carrier.

A somewhat complex mathematical analysis will yield an equation for the instantaneous voltage of an FM wave of the form:

$$s(t) = A_c \cos\{2\pi f_c t + m.\sin 2\pi f_m t\}$$

Where A_c is the carrier peak amplitude, f_c and f_m represent the carrier and modulating frequencies, and m is the index of modulation. This equation represents a single low-frequency sine wave, (f_m), frequency modulating another high-frequency sine wave (f_c).

As can be seen from the equation, m is equal to the peak deviation caused when the signal is modulated by the frequency of the modulating signal. Since in above equation the frequency deviation is integrated into phase deviation, m is a function of both the modulating signal amplitude and frequency. Furthermore, m can take on any value from 0 to infinity.

Pre-Emphasis and De-Emphasis

In FM, the noise increases with modulation frequency. To compensate for this effect, FM communication systems have incorporated a noise-combating system of pre-emphasis and de-emphasis. Pre-emphasis provides increased amplitude to the higher modulating frequencies prior to modulation under a well-defined pre-emphasis (high-pass filter) curve. This added amplitude will serve to make the higher frequencies more immune to noise by increasing their index of modulation. De-emphasis is just the opposite operation (using a low-pass filter) and it is done at the receiver.

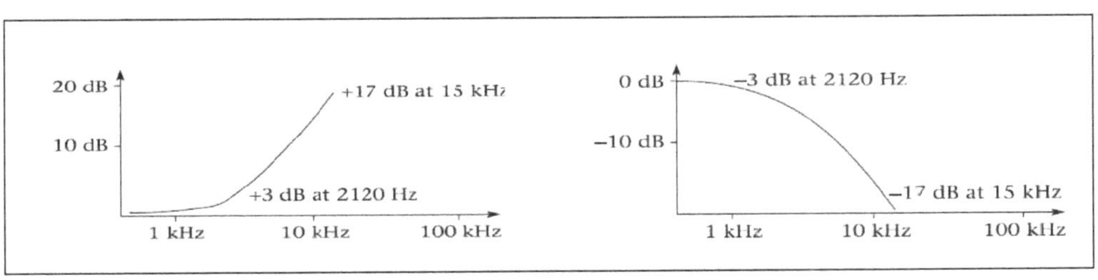

Pre-emphasis and De-emphasis filter.

FM Stereo Multiplex

FM stereo broadcasting was introduced during the early 1960s. The scheme that was adopted was chosen to be compatible with the monaural FM radios that were in existence at the time. Essentially, the system performs the multiplexing of two signals and further combines them into a complex baseband signal that modulates the FM carrier. Figure below shows a block diagram of the typical analog-stereo generator used to drive an FM transmitter.

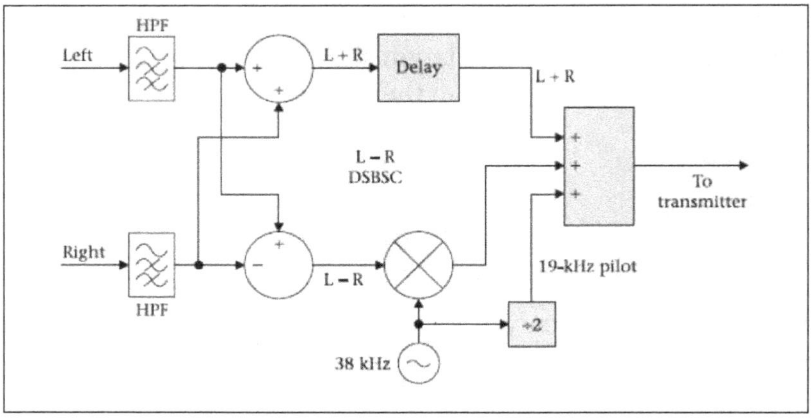

FM Stereo Multiplexing.

A Left and Right source of audio are first pre-emphasized (HPF) and then fed to adder circuits. The output of one adder is the sum of the two signals, or the L + R signal (the monaural signal), and the output of the other adder is the difference of the two signals, or L − R. The L − R signal is applied to a balanced modulator along with a 38-kHz signal. The output of the balanced modulator is a DSBSC AM signal centered at 38 kHz. A portion of the 38-kHz signal is divided in frequency to become 19 kHz, and all three signals are applied to a summary/adder circuit at the output of the generator. The resulting stereo-generator output-signal spectrum is shown in Figure below.

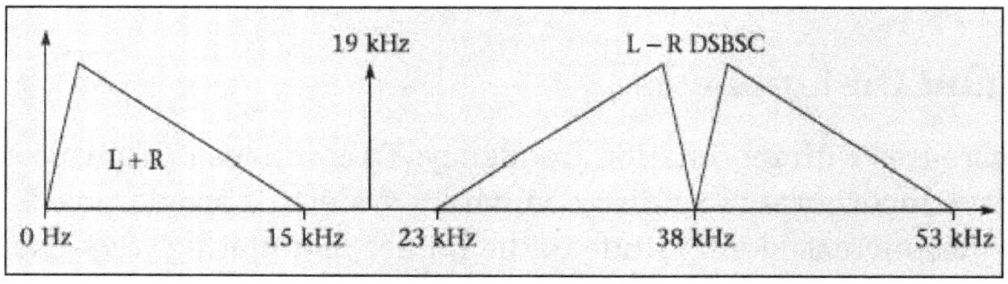

FM Stereo Multiplexing Spectrum.

The L + R signal, which contains baseband frequencies from near 0 Hz to 15 kHz, occupies that portion of the frequency spectrum. The 19-kHz tone is pilot sub-carrier signal, which will be used at the receiver to aid in the demodulation of the received signal. The L − R signal, which has been DSBSC amplitude modulated by a 38-kHz tone, occupies the frequency range from 23 to 53 kHz.

FM Radio Data System (RDS)

Radio Data System is a communications protocol standard from the European Broadcasting Union for sending small amounts of digital information using conventional FM radio broadcasts. The RDS system standardizes several types of information transmitted, including time, track/artist info and station identification. RDS has been standard in Europe and Latin America since the early 1990s and is now used throughout many parts of the world.

Baseband Modulation

RDS baseband modulation is a kind of differentially-coded BPSK as in Figure. The sub-carrier is suppressed. This method of modulation may alternatively be thought of as a form of two-phase phase-shift-keying (PSK) with a phase deviation of ± 90 degree. The basic clock frequency is obtained by dividing the transmitted RDS sub-carrier frequency (57 kHz) by 48. Consequently, the basic data-rate of the system is 1187.5 bits/second. The source data at the transmitter are differentially encoded.

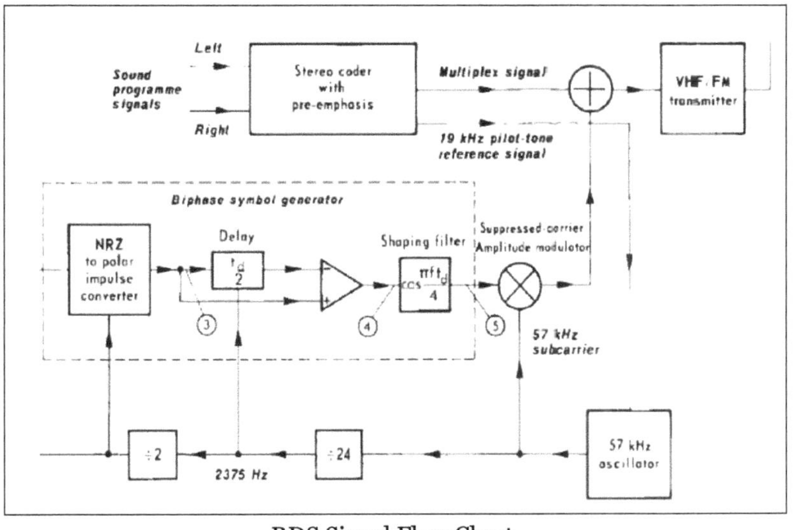

RDS Signal Flow Chart.

The power of the data signal around the 57 kHz sub-carrier is minimized by coding each source data bit as a binary-phase symbol. The principle of the process of generation of the shaped binary-phase symbols is shown schematically in Figure below. These impulse-pairs are then shaped by a filter $H_T(f)$, to give the required band-limited spectrum where,

$$H_T(f) = \begin{cases} \cos\dfrac{\pi f t_d}{4} & \text{if } 0 \le f \le 2/t_d \\ 0 & \text{if } f > 2/t_d \end{cases}$$

Coding Structure

The largest element in the structure is called a "group" of 104 bits each. Each group comprises 4 blocks of 26 bits each. Each block comprises an information word and a checkword. Each information word comprises 16 bits. Each checkword comprises 10 bits.

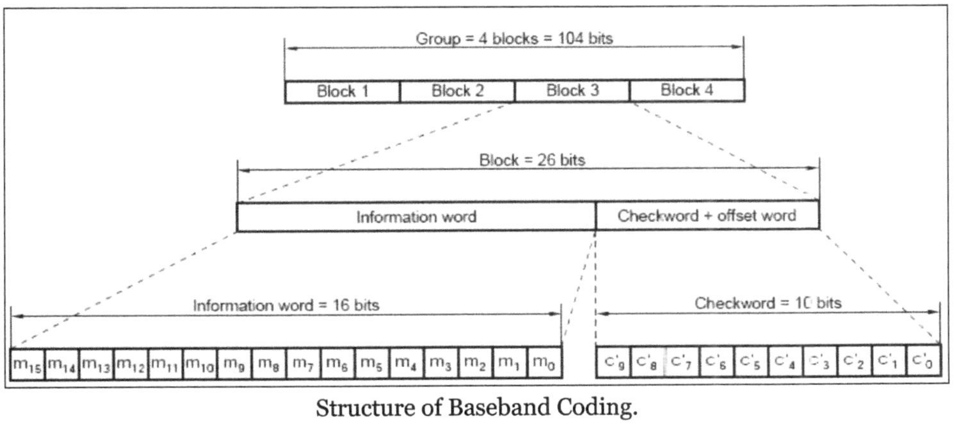

Structure of Baseband Coding.

Work with FM Stereo

Both use a 57 kHz sub-carrier to carry data at 1187.5 bits per second. The 57 kHz was chosen for being the third harmonic of the pilot tone for FM stereo (3 x 19kHz), so it would not cause interference or inter-modulation with it, or with the stereo difference signal at 38 kHz. This is shown in Figure below.

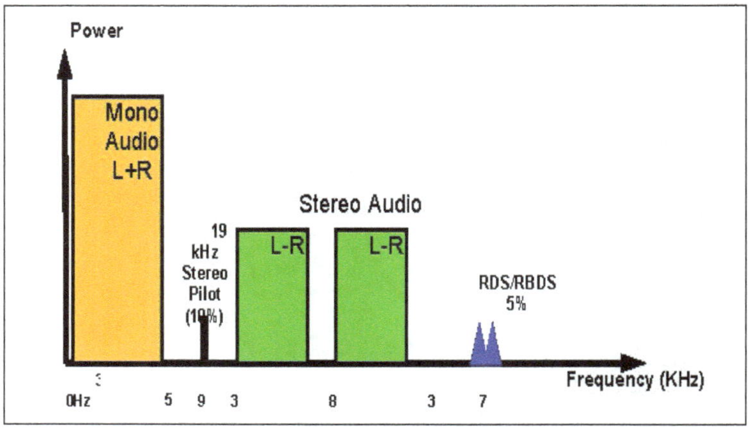

FM-Stereo-RDS Baseband spectrum.

Demodulation on V93000

This section presents the demodulation used in the Verigy V93000 software and demonstrates how to demodulate a FM Stereo signal. For TX tests, the RF output from the DUT is captured by the V93000 RF subsystem. The captured data are then fed into the V93000 demodulation engine. The FM-stereo part of processing flow of this engine for is as Figure below.

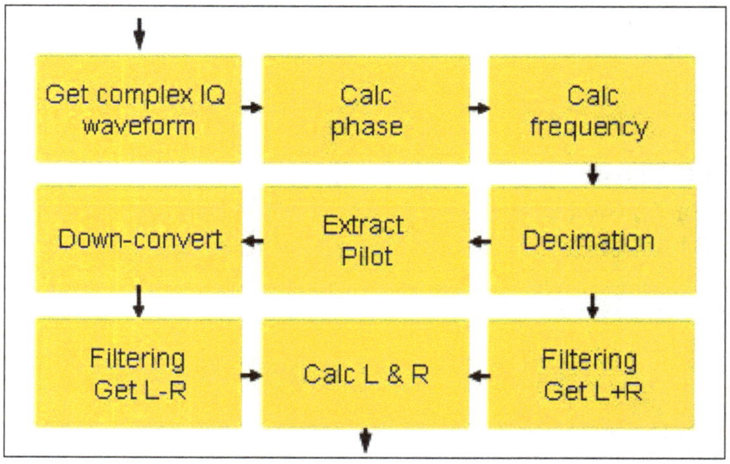

Signal processing flow.

Although we show some details of our signal processing flow, it can be used as a black box. The only input is just sample rate F_s and captured IQ array. FM demodulation engine outputs multiple results such as Stereo Multiplexed BB wave, L/R wave, modulation deviation, etc. the Figure above shows the FM spectrum, stereo spectrum, audio wave, and audio spectrum in V93000 Signal Analyzer.

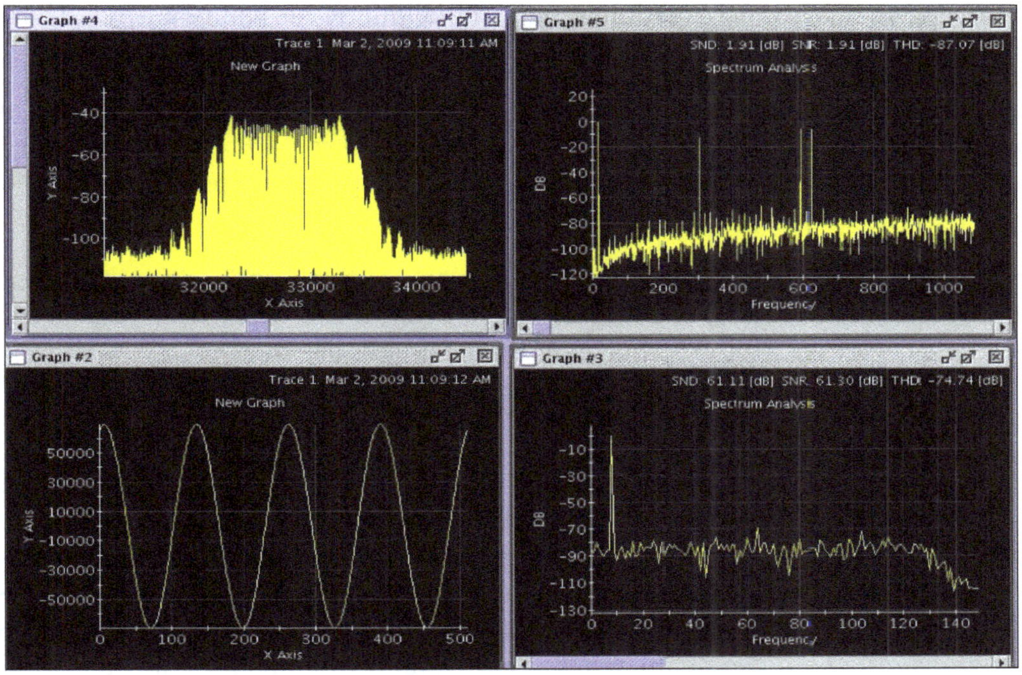

FM-Stereo Demodulation in V93000.

For FM RX testing, often the user needs to provide a Stereo FM RDS signal to the RF RX input of the DUT. Verigy has the SW engine to generate the FM Stereo RDS signal. Alternatively, custom waveforms from the DUT design department can also be used directly. Additionally, the V93000 RF and baseband AWGs have the ability to read Agilent Technologies Signal Studio encrypted waveform files. This allows the user to be able to use the same original waveform files that are used with many bench measurement setups.

HD Radio

HD Radio is a digital radio technology, but it differs from satellite radio. While satellite radio is received directly from satellites operating in the 2.3-GHz range, HD Radio operates on the same frequencies currently assigned to existing AM and FM stations.

Using orthogonal frequency-division multiplexing (OFDM) digital technology, HD Radio puts the new digital signals on either side of the existing AM and FM sidebands. On the AM bands (530 to 1705 kHz), the usual mode is to simulcast—that is, transmit the same programming in both analog and digital formats. Older radios ignore the digital content, while digital radios receive the digital signals.

Simulcast is the initial mode of operation on the FM bands (88 to 108 MHz) as well. An HD Radio will pick up the regular analog signal and the separate digital signals. FM HD Radio stations also have multicast capability. They can divide up their digital OFDM carriers and create as many as eight additional channels of broadcasting.

In essence, you get multiple additional stations at minimum cost. Moreover, multiple programs can be provided, just like satellite radio. Amazingly, no new spectrum is needed. This could potentially be a new source of ad revenue for a station, though initial multicasts will be ad-free. The additional content should attract new listeners with more focused music and talk venues.

HD Radio brings digital's benefits to broadcast radio. The high-definition nomenclature means that the audio frequency response is far greater than the 3.5- to 5-kHz bandwidth of typical AM radio and the 15-kHz bandwidth of FM. With improved frequency response, AM HD Radio now sounds more like FM, and FM radio has nearly CD quality.

Digital techniques significantly reduce noise and mitigate fading from multipath, as well as other effects usually experienced in a car radio. Overall quality is far better than that provided by current stations. And the cherry on the top is that all of these features are free.

How HD Radio Works

HD Radio sends more information over the same radio frequency by digitizing the signal. A digital signal can then be compressed by a computer, much like an MP3 is a compressed version of the much larger WAV file that is on a CD. Digitizing allows FM stations to broadcast with near-CD quality sound, and HD Radio AM stations will sound just as good as FM stations do now. An HD Radio receiver can also zero in directly on the digital transmission, eliminating interference and signal "reflections" off of buildings. The result is clear sound without any static, pop or hiss.

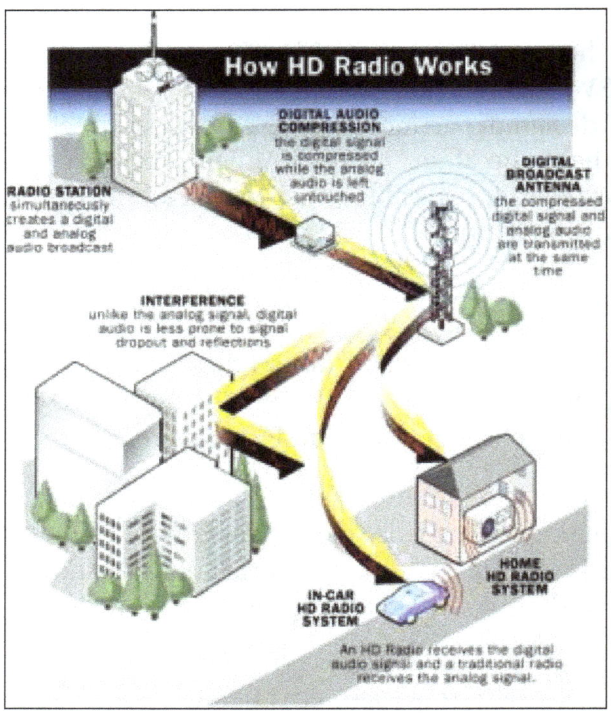

Another application of HD Radio is the ability to multicast multiple channels on the same signal. Multicasting also refers to a form of Internet routing architecture, so the multiple channel transmissions allowed by HD Radio might be more accurately described as multiplexing (iBiquity chose the term "multicasting").

The extra bandwidth of an HD Radio signal leaves room for completely separate channels operating on the same frequency. Here's how it works: Suppose your favorite radio station is 102.5 FM. When you tune in, you pick up the regular broadcast classic rock. Your HD Radio receiver indicates that the station is multicasting. You turn a dial to select the alternate channel, where they play nothing but blues. Or your favorite talk radio station might have separate, simultaneous broadcasts featuring news and weather, sports talk and political commentary.

Current HD technology allows the addition of one extra music channel and three extra talk channels before the sound quality begins to suffer. The extra stations are referred to as HD2 stations. If an HD Radio receiver loses the digital signal, it seamlessly fades back to analog FM until the digital signal returns.

An HD Radio receiver can display text data that is sent alongside the audio signal. This could take the form of artist and song information about the music being played or sports, weather or stock updates. No radio stations are planning to go all-HD. They'll continue to broadcast regular analog signals along with the HD signals, so old radios will be able to pick up AM and FM stations with no problems in the foreseeable future.

HD Radio Signal

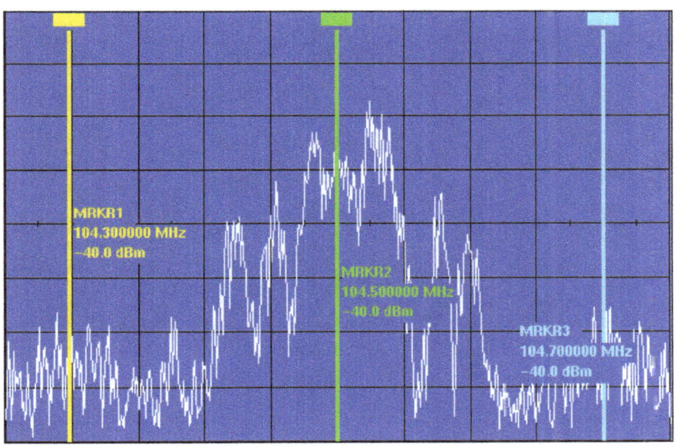

The RF spectrum of an FM radio station transmitting an analog stereo signal.

The radio waves that carry analog AM and FM signals are limited in the amount of information they can convey, both because of the nature of the waves themselves and the spacing of stations on the frequency band. FM stations are separated by 200 kHz, while AM stations have just 10 kHz between them. Alternate channel spacing of FM stations gives them 400 kHz to work with. The signals broadcast by radio stations are actually spread out on either side of the frequency into Upper and Lower Sidebands (USB and LSB).

The larger spacing between FM stations gives them enough room to broadcast higher quality audio in stereo, but not enough for true CD-quality audio. An FM signal could carry enough information for a higher-quality signal, but it would take up so much bandwidth that there would be room for far fewer stations on the dial.

HD Radio solves this problem by compressing the digital signal so more information can be sent along the same amount of radio bandwidth. Initially, iBiquity used a compression algorhythm called PAC (Perceptual Audio Coding). However, audio compressed with this method led to complaints about poor sound quality, so in 2003, iBiquity changed to HDC (High-Definition Coding), a different compression method that allowed for higher sound quality.

Although HD Radio is touted as providing CD-quality sound on the FM airwaves, the compression of the digital signal is a "lossy" method. That means that it discards some of the information in the signal, resulting in a reduction in overall fidelity to the original sound. Much of the discarded information is not perceptible to human ears, and the final product may sound very close to CD-quality, but technically it is not the same sound as on the CD.

The digital signal is sent out piggybacked onto the analog signal on the same carrier wave (the wave sent out by the transmitter that gives a radio station its frequency on the dial). A third signal can also be added -- this carries text data. It is an in-band on-channel (IBOC) system because the signal is piggybacked onto the analog signal and doesn't use up extra bandwidth. If the system was an in-band adjacent-channel (IBAC) system, the bandwidth would be increased by using space on nearby channels (and causing interference if another station was trying to broadcast there).

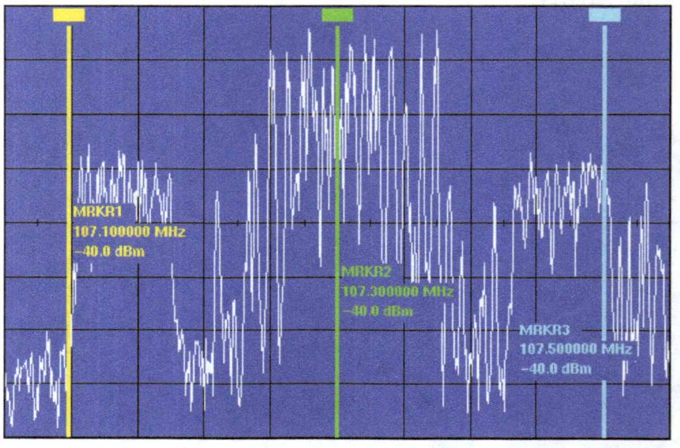

The RF spectrum of a broadcast FM radio station transmitting an HD Radio signal.

HD Radio Receivers

So far, the number of HD Radio receivers currently in homes or cars is low about 100,000 units. iBiquity hopes to sell four times that many before the end of 2006. One reason for the low market penetration was that first-generation HD Radio receivers were extremely expensive, costing more than $1,000. Today, you can buy car stereos that support HD Radio for about $200, and home theater receivers that can pick up HD Radio don't cost much more than other high-end receivers. There are also reports of a Kenwood home receiver that costs $100.

As of October 2006, HDRadio.com reported 609 stations in the U.S. broadcasting some form of HD Radio. About half of those stations were multicasting, and very few were using data casting. HD Radio has not had a smooth ride. In addition to compression method changes and cost issues, the technology has had to deal with controversy over the FCC's decision to name it the primary standard for digital radio in the United States, competition from other digital radio formats, complaints that the sound and reception quality don't live up to expectations and problems with interference with other signals.

Many people within the radio industry have voiced concerns that iBiquity's system was granted primary status by the FCC, because perhaps another digital radio format could perform better. Some claim that the people in charge of deciding that HD Radio should be the primary U.S. digital radio system are also the same people who have invested heavily in the technology, creating a conflict of interest.

Eureka-147, a digital radio format popular in Europe, uses a separate frequency band for digital broadcasts instead of piggybacking the digital signal onto analog broadcasts. There have been attempts to get the FCC to open that band to digital broadcasting in the United States. The development of a system to offer higher-bandwidth AM radio without many of the problems faced by HD Radio on the AM band, and without requiring new receivers to hear it.

While HD Radio is supposed to use the same amount of bandwidth as the original analog station, there have been complaints about interference, particularly with AM. AM waves travel much farther at night due to the bending of the waves within the ionosphere. Because of this, the FCC does not allow HD Radio broadcasts at night on AM stations. During the daytime, adjacent stations are not allowed to broadcast in HD because they create too much interference. Even on the FM band, the digital signal sometimes creates an audible sound on adjacent channels, particularly for hobbyists who try to tune in distant FM signals (known as DXing).

Those who have purchased HD Radio receivers have reported some problems. At times, the audio compression causes a noticable reduction in sound quality. Some radio stations are not properly processing their signal for digital transmission, causing distorted sound. At times, the volume level or timing of the digital signal is different from the analog version, resulting in problems when the receiver has to switch between the two. Other users have found that digital signals are difficult to tune in, that multicasting seriously impacts audio quality, or that stations broadcasting in HD Radio suffer a loss in quality of the analog signal.

An HD Radio Receiver.

Satellite Radio

Satellites have been a highly effective platform for multiform broadcasts. This has led to a revival of the radio era. The satellite radio is a natural choice to bridge the digital gap. It has several novel features like selective addressing and error control. The value-added services from such systems are of particular interest.

Man has always been fascinated by the 'heavenly voices' from the skies. This fascination has manifested itself in many mythologies where he has received divine messages, warnings, and forecasts from the heavens. It was this undiminished fascination that kept him working towards the radio system. It was one hundred years ago that Marconi first transmitted the letter'S' across the Atlantic Ocean. At that time, conveying information across such large distances was not as much a novelty as the new concept of broadcasting. While telegraphy was constrained by physical network of lines, radio reached a widespread, unidentified audience.

With the evolution of technology, today, man-made satellites placed up in the skies are able to deliver not just messages but crystal-clear music and news directly to the listeners separated by huge geographical distances. The reception of these programmes on ground is possible using special satellite signal receivers.

- Confluence o/Technologies: It is interesting to note that directto-home satellite television was introduced much ahead of satellite radio. This despite the fact that the television signal transmission demands more resources than radio. Radio is perceived to be an individual's possession because of its portability. It can be used even while one is moving. To do this from a satellite has been a major technological challenge. This has now been met by a true confluence of technologies - rock L etry, satellites, computing, compression, modulation, encryption and satellite receivers.

- New Demands: The demands on satellite radio are many. Besides mobility the other demands on the radio system are a diversity of formats, languages, genre, and a universal reach that cannot be met by terrestrial systems. For example, one may want to listen to a live classical concert of three hours duration without commercial breaks. A global traveller may want to hear his favourite channel irrespective of where he is located including remote and thinly-populated areas where a terrestrial choice is absent.

Satellite Orbits

A satellite's orbit is decided depending on the application. The geo-stationary orbit (GSa) is considered ideal for broadcast purposes. It is advantageous because of the ease of tracking - or rather the lack of tracking. In GSa, even though a satellite moves at a speed of over 10,000 km per hour, it appears to hang perfectly motionless in the sky. This is because for an Earth based observer, its absolute motion is annulled by the rotation of the Earth about its axis. In a GSa, therefore, the period of the satellite is one day. The unique relationship between the period of a satellite and the size of its orbit dictates that the satellite is placed at about 36,000 km over the equator with the correct magnitude and direction of velocity.

Gsa satellites are used for point-to-point communications as well as for point-to-multipoint broadcasting. In the latter case, the signals to be broadcast are sent to a satellite from an uplink station. These signals returned by the satellite to the Earth (downlink signal) can be received at any location falling within the footprint of the satellite transmit antenna.

Modulation

Modulation is the way information is imparted to the electromagnetic signal that is referred to as the carrier wave. In amplitude modulation (AM), the amplitude of the radio frequency (RF) carrier is made to vary in accordance with the audio waveform. It is obvious that in this mode, it would be quite sensitive to additive electrical noise.

Frequency modulation FM has a much better noise immunity, as it is the frequency of the carrier wave that is varied in a small range according to the audio waveform. However, noise free reception does not necessarily mean high fidelity (HiFi). HiFi refers to reproduction of all the frequency components correctly at the receiving end. In digital modulations one uses perceptual coding using auditory masking. This means the retention of only those components that the human ear can perceive. In this scheme, the human ear acts as a measuring instrument instead of traditional measures like signal to noise ratio (SNR).

The AM carrier frequencies can cover several thousand kilometres. The frequencies used for FM and satellites are such that the propagation is direct line of sight. Hence, the path between the transmitter and the receiver site must be substantially unobstructed. The bigger FM stations mount their transmitters on a tower of a few 100 metres high, covering radius of several tens of kilometres.

GSO is like an invisible tower of height 36000 km and hence the line of sight of a single satellite extends to cover about 40% of the surface of the Earth. However it must be noted that the signal strength from the satellite is much weaker as it follows inverse square law. The weakness of the signal explains why a satellite receiver, in general, is more expensive than a terrestrial FM receiver.

For moving customers in urban environment, it is possible that there are obstructions like tunnels or high rise buildings and in order to have continuous service, it is necessary to have ground based repeater network using what is known as multi-carrier modulation (MCM) techniques.

Digital Radio

Because of the tremendous advancement in digital technology in the recent years satellite radio is fully digital. In a digital radio, the transmitter processes sounds into patterns of binary digits and at the listening end, the digital radio reproduces the sound from the digits. By using techniques of forward error control, it is possible to make the reception virtually immune to interference.

Besides satellite radio, digital broadcasting can be totally groundbased as in the case of Eureka 147 that operates in L-band. Digital broadcasting can be done through the existing AM or FM band so as to use the existing stations and to receive the digital signal in the same analog dial position. This scheme is called 'in band on channel' (IBOC).

The transition to digital produces a number of other benefits too. It is possible to adopt encryption technology so that the programs can be delivered to whom it is intended. In the case of a satellite-based digital signal broadcast, it is possible to provide error control processing on the satellite to correct for errors in the transmission, thereby simplifying and downsizing the ground terminals.

Digital Compression

In broadcasting terms, bandwidth is the 'space' required to deliver a given signal. For example, current TV signals require as large as 30 MHz per channel, FM radio requires 0.2 MHz and AM radio needs only about 0.01 MHz. By conventional conversion from analog to digital stereo sound will require about 1.5 million bits per second that is indicative of a bandwidth of 1.5 MHz. By adopting advanced audio compression techniques, the bandwidth can be reduced by a factor 10-20. This is made possible by using perceptive coding that takes into account the characteristics of the human ear. It is the same technology that drastically reduced the storage and transmission requirements of music on computers. In the WAV format, a three-minute song will take about 30 megabytes of disk space and could take more than three hours to download on an average modem. In the case of MP3, 14 hours of music can fit into a single CD.

Frequency Allocation and Regulation

For the coexistence and mutual non-interference of various services elaborate schemes have been evolved under the auspices of the International Telecommunication Union (ITU). ITU allocates frequencies for various services.

As the satellite is located well above the ionosphere, the radio frequency of the carrier will have to exceed the ionospheric plasma frequency that is typically a few tens of MHz. For digital audio broadcast (DAB), a segment in L-band (1452-1492 MHz) is allocated in most of the regions except in USA and Canada where this service is available in S-band.

The Present Scenario

- Satellites for Radio Networking: Even though satellite radio is relatively a new phenomenon, satellites have been used to network the radio stations for a long time now. For example, All India Radio has been using INSA T for over fifteen years to carry network newscasts and syndicated programs. However these programs are not meant for the end user but are for rebroadcast via terrestrial transmitters.

- Satellites in orbit: With the launch of Afristar in 1998 and Asiastar in 2000, WorldSpace offers audio and multi-media broadcasts to the most-populous and under-served regions of the world. Very recently, Sirius radio and XM radio are offering a choice of more than hundred channels including music formats, news, talk shows and entertainment programming to mobile customers in the US. For the first time the concept of subscription based radio has been introduced in these systems.

Value Added Services

In addition to a variety of crystal-clear music programs, any digital radio can easily be configured to display information such as song titles, traffic information, weather data, stock market quotations, etc. It has tremendous potential for being used in distance education, telemedicine and other off-beat applications. For example, WorldSpace satellites offer a unique mode of synchronous, instructor-led training by exploiting the feature of multiple service components in the same broadcast channel. It is also possible to download pre-fixed websites directly onto the user PC without an Internet connection or a telephone line. This will be an important factor in bringing 'infotainment' to such regions where Internet is either unavailable or is too expensive. At this time, there are two space-based radio broadcasters:

- Sirius XM Radio
- 1worldspace

Satellite radio companies are comparing the significance of their service to the impact that cable TV had on television 30 years ago. Listeners aren't able to pick up local stations using satellite radio services, but they have access to hundreds of stations offering a variety of music genres. Each company has a different plan for its broadcasting system, but the systems do share similarities. Here are the key components of the two satellite radio systems:

- Satellites
- Ground repeaters
- Radio receivers

Satellite radio works a lot like satellite TV; you purchase a receiver and pay a monthly subscription fee for a certain number of channels. For the moment, there are slight variances in the three satellite radio companies' systems.

XM Radio

While XM Radio and Sirius have merged into a single company, the two services aren't fully integrated yet. Part of the reason for this is due to differences in hardware and software.

XM Radio uses two Boeing HS 702 satellites, appropriately nicknamed "Rock" and "Roll," and two BSS 702 satellites it calls "Rhythm" and "Blues," placed in parallel geostationary orbit, two at 85 degrees west longitude and the other two at 115 degrees west longitude. Geostationary Earth orbit (GEO) is about 22,223 miles (35,764 km) above Earth, and is the type of orbit most commonly used for communications satellites. The first XM satellite, "Rock," was launched on March 18, 2001, with "Roll" following on May 8 of the same year. A design flaw in the HS 702 satellite caused its solar panels to function inefficiently. XM launched "Rhythm" on February 28, 2005, and "Blues" on October 30, 2006, to replace the older satellites. Then XM Radio powered down "Rock" and "Roll." The older satellites remain in orbit and can serve as backups, if necessary.

XM Radio's ground station transmits a signal to its two active GEO satellites, which bounce the signals back down to radio receivers on the ground. The radio receivers are programmed to receive and unscramble the digital data signal, which contains more than 170 channels of digital audio. In addition to the encoded sound, the signal contains information about the broadcast. The song title, artist and genre of music are all displayed on the radio. In urban areas, where buildings can block out the satellite signal, XM's broadcasting system is supplemented by ground transmitters.

Each receiver contains a proprietary chipset. XM began delivering chipsets to its XM radio manufacturing partners in October 2000. The chipset consists of two custom integrated circuits designed by STMicroelectronics. XM has partnered with Pioneer, Alpine, Clarion, Delphi Delco, Sony and Motorola to manufacture XM car radios. Each satellite radio receiver uses a small, car-phone-sized antenna to receive the XM signal. General Motors has invested about $100 million in XM, and Honda has also signed an agreement to use XM radios in its vehicles. GM began installing XM satellite radio receivers in selected models in early 2001.

Currently, subscribers can receive the regular XM channel lineup for $12.95 per month. For that price, listeners get more than 170 channels of music, talk and news. They also get access to XM Radio online, a streaming audio service with more than 80 channels. Many of the channels have no commercials, and none of the channels have more than seven minutes of ads per hour. XM's content providers include USA Today, BBC, CNN, Sports Illustrated and The Weather Channel. The service bolsters that lineup with its own music channels.

This graphic illustrates how the XM Radio system works.

Sirius Radio

Sirius originally used three SS/L-1300 satellites, instead of GEO satellites, to form an inclined elliptical satellite constellation. Sirius said the elliptical path of its satellite constellation ensures that each satellite spends about 16 hours a day over the continental United States, with at least one satellite over the country at all times. Sirius completed its three-satellite constellation on Nov. 30, 2000. A fourth satellite will remain on the ground, ready to be launched if any of the three active satellites encounters transmission problems. In 2006, Sirius purchased a GEO satellite because of its superior signal delivery. The GEO satellite will supplement the elliptical satellites, not replace them. It is currently under construction.

The Sirius system is similar to that of XM. Programs are beamed to one of the three Sirius satellites -- the satellites then transmit the signal to the ground, where your radio receiver picks up one of the channels within the signal. Signals are also be beamed to ground repeaters for listeners in urban areas where the satellite signal can be interrupted.

Just like XM Radio, Sirius currently offers its regular subscription for $12.95 per month. Sirius produces car radios and home entertainment systems, as well as car and home kits for portable use. The Sirius receiver includes two parts: the antenna module and the receiver module. The antenna module picks up signals from the ground repeaters or the satellite, amplifies the signal and filters out any interference.

The signal is then passed on to the receiver module. Inside the receiver module is a chipset consisting of eight chips. The chipset converts the signals from 2.3 gigahertz (GHz) to a lower intermediate frequency. Sirius also offers an adapter that allows conventional car radios to receive satellite signals.

1WorldSpace

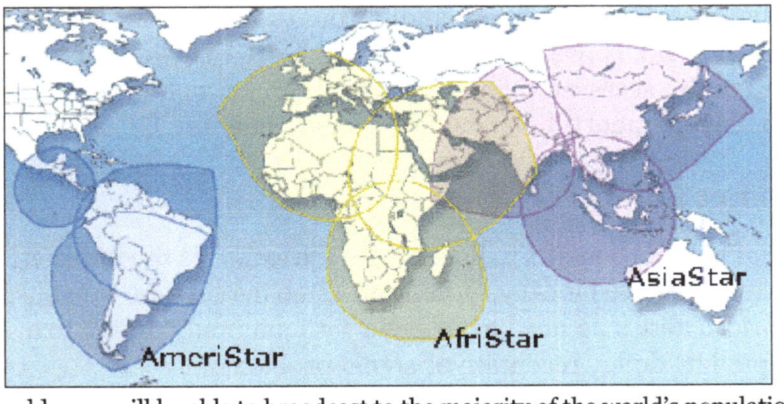

1worldspace will be able to broadcast to the majority of the world's population when its AmeriStar satellite is launched.

So far, 1worldspace has been the farthest-reaching company in the satellite radio industry. It put two of its three satellites, AfriStar and AsiaStar, in geostationary orbit before either of the other two companies launched one. AfriStar and AsiaStar were launched in October 1998 and March 2000, respectively. AmeriStar, which will offer service to South America and parts of Mexico, has not yet been launched. Each satellite transmits three signal beams, carrying more than 60 channels of programming, to three overlapping coverage areas of about 5.4 million square miles (14 million square kilometers) each. Each of the 1worldspace satellites' three beams can deliver more than 50 channels of crystal-clear audio and multimedia programming via the 1,467- to 1,492-megahertz (MHz) segment of the L-Band spectrum, which is allocated for digital audio broadcasting.

The United States is not currently part of 1worldspace's coverage area, although the company has invested in Sirius XM Radio and has an agreement with the company to share any technological developments. 1worldspace is going beyond one nation and eyeing world domination of the radio market. That might be overstating the company's intent a bit, but 1worldspace does plan to reach the corners of our world that most radio stations can't. There are millions of people living in

1worldspace's projected listening area who can't pick up a signal from a conventional radio station. 1worldspace says it has a potential audience of about 4.6 billion listeners spanning five continents.

1worldspace broadcasters uplink their signal to one of the two operational satellites through a centralized hub site or an individual feeder link station located within the global uplink beam. The satellite then transmits the signal in one, two or all three beams on each satellite. Receivers on the ground then pick up the signal and provide CD-quality sound through a detachable antenna.

1worldspace satellite receivers are capable of receiving data at a rate of 128 kilobits per second (Kbps). The receivers use the proprietary StarMan chipset, manufactured by STMicroelectronics, to receive digital signals from the satellites.

Internet Radio

Internet radio is accessed online, so you need a broadband connection and home wi-fi network rather than a traditional aerial to receive it. Alternatively, you can connect your radio to the internet using an ethernet cable, but that's only useful if you plan to have your radio near to your router.

Some, but not all, digital radios can stream audio from the internet. They tend to be pricier than the average FM or DAB radio. However, you don't even need to own a conventional radio to listen to internet radio. It can be accessed using a media player or web browser on your computer or laptop or via an app on your smartphone, tablet or smart-enabled TV.

Benefits of Internet Radio

There are a number of notable benefits to listening to the radio via the internet. Firstly, it's not limited by what signals are broadcast locally, so you can listen in real time to thousands of radio shows from all over the world. There's no need to struggle with manually tuning to a station or have your programme interrupted by dodgy reception or signal problems.

It's also possible to catch up on programmes that have already been broadcast, and many major internet radio stations allow you to listen to shows from the past week. In some cases, such as with the BBC, you can listen to any radio programme that has aired in the past month.

Signal strength is not an issue because the high-speed power of the internet enables fast and reliable signals to be transmitted, so it's possible to stream flawless high-quality recordings – as long as you have a decent wi-fi connection of course.

Most internet radios, for example the Pure Evoke F3, Roberts iStream 2 and Roberts Stream 93i, not only allow listeners to access internet radio stations, but they all link with the music streaming subscription service Spotify. They also allow you to stream music from your PC through the radio's speakers, giving you a multitude of different options in terms of what you can listen to.

Data use with Internet Radio

Everything you do on the internet uses a certain amount of data and, unless you've got unlimited broadband, the amount you use will be taken from your monthly data allowance.

The amount of data used will depend on the quality of the radio stream, but if you're listening to the radio using your smartphone, it's preferable to make sure your device is connected to the internet via wi-fi; otherwise, you'll quickly burn through your mobile-data allowance listening to internet radio.

If you want to listen to internet radio when you're out and about, it is possible to download some radio programmes and podcasts for offline listening. There is the option of connecting to public wi-fi, but the signal may not always be robust enough to cope with streaming audio from the internet.

Using a Web Browser or Media Player

Internet radio can be accessed using your web browser, or you can use a media player if you prefer. Windows Media Player and VLC are both suitable programs for streaming radio from the internet, and you can bookmark your favourite stations for easy access.

To stream internet radio stations through your chosen player, you need to first find the URL of the stream and put that into the box titled 'Network URL'. The broadcast URLs of online radio stations generally end in.m3u or.pls and can easily be found using Google.

Free Internet Radio Apps

These radio streaming apps are free to download and provide access to tens of thousands of internet radio stations on a variety of different devices.

Radio Player

Radio player is a non-profit partnership between the BBC and commercial radio in the UK. It contains more than 450 UK radio stations and can recommend stations based on where you are, what's trending right now, and what else you've listened to. It's easy to save particular stations and shows for quick and easy access.

It works with all Apple and Android smartphones and tablets, as well as the Amazon Kindle Fire, Windows Phone 8, Amazon Echo and Apple Watch. It has a car mode, so you can even play it while driving, or activate the sleep timer if you want to nod off to a broadcast without worrying about running your device's battery down.

TuneIn Radio

With a global audience of more than 60 million, TuneIn Radio has something for absolutely everyone. It has the largest selection of free sports, music, talk and news radio from around the world. You can even upload your own radio station to add to the 100,000 it currently has on the app.

The TuneIn app is compatible with Apple and Android smartphones and tablets, as well as Blackberry and Windows phones. It also works on the Amazon Kindle, Xbox One, Sonos speakers, Google Chromecast and Roku internet TV streamers, as well as Samsung and Panasonic Smart TVs.

Audials Radio

You can search for radio stations on Audials Radio by entering the names of your favourite artists or by selecting a music genre, country or local station near you. It's the only radio app that allows you to save songs and broadcasts as MP3 files for offline playback whenever you fancy. If you've just heard a hit on the radio but forgotten to record it, you can still save the track as an MP3 by finding it in the radio station history.

The Audials app is available on most Apple and Android devices, as well as Windows phones and tablets, and Google Chrome browsers. It has a sleep timer and an alarm function (with a snooze button), so you can fall asleep and wake up to your favourite radio station.

Television

Television (TV) comes from the (tele), meaning "distant" or "far," and the Latin visio, meaning "sight" or "vision." It is a mode of (tele) communication typically used for transmitting moving (color) images (and potentially sound) to audiences. Although the technology was commercially available since the late 1920s (in very limited amounts and at a very high price), television has since become a common household good. It is also used in businesses and institutions particularly as a vehicle for advertising, entertainment, and news broadcasting. From around the 1950s onward, television increasingly became the primary medium in the Western world for shaping public opinion because of the saturation of television in society. Color televisions became widely available from the 1960s, and because of the availability of media such as video cassettes, laserdiscs, DVDs, and high-definition discs, viewers have been able to use the television to watch prerecorded material. Recently, there has been a rise in Internet television services, with services such as BBC iPlayer, Hulu, and Netflix broadcasting their material onto television screens via the Internet.

In 2009, approximately 78 percent of the world's households owned at least one television set with 87 percent of TVs sold being color liquid crystal display–screen TVs. The most common medium for broadcast television is modeled on the radio broadcasting systems developed in the 1920s, it uses high-powered radio-frequency transmitters to broadcast the television signal to individual TV receivers such as antennae or satellites, which are then linked to the television set. The technology is also used in other forms such as closed-circuit television. The broadcast television transmissions are typically disseminated via designated channels in the 54- to 890-MHz frequency range. A visual display device that lacks a tuner is called a video monitor, which distinguishes it from a television. In its most basic form, a color broadcast can be created by broadcasting three monochrome images, one each in the three colors of red, green, and blue. When displayed together or in rapid succession, these images will blend to produce a full-color image, as seen by the viewer. Televisions are also used for surveillance, industrial process control, and guiding of weapons.

The first transmission of images occurred in 1881 using a device called the pantelegraph. Scanning in one form or another has been used in nearly every image transmission to date this includes television. "Rasterization" is the concept used to describe the process of converting a visual image into a stream of electrical pulses. In 1927, Philo Farnsworth made the world's first working television system with electronic scanning of both the pickup and the display devices; it was demonstrated to the press on September 1, 1928. This laid the foundation for the world's first electronically scanned television service that started in Berlin in 1935. In August 1936, the Olympic Games in Berlin were carried by cable to television stations in Berlin and Leipzig, where the public could view the games live. On November 2, 1936, the BBC began transmitting the world's first regular publicly available service in North London. It therefore claims to be the birthplace of television broadcasting as we know it today. In 2012, television revenue was growing faster than film for the major media companies.

TV programming is usually broadcast in one of two ways: original run or broadcast syndication. For an original run, a producer creates a program of one or multiple episodes and shows it on a station or network, which either has paid for the production itself or to which a license has been granted by the television producers to broadcast it. Broadcast syndication is the term used to describe usages beyond original run. It includes not only secondary runs in the country of first issue but also international usage, which may not be managed by the originating producer. The alternative producer(s) are allowed to and able to sell the product into their broadcast markets after signing a contract from the copyright holders. First-run programming is increasingly becoming available on subscription services, with few programs available on domestic free-to-air channels. To protect their income streams, subscription channels are usually encrypted to ensure that only subscription payers are able to receive the decrypted broadcast. Around the globe, broadcast television is financed by governments, advertising, licensing, some form of tax, subscription, or a combination of these. Most subscription services are funded by advertising.

Because of the broad reach of television, it has become a powerful and attractive medium for advertisers. Television networks sell blocks of broadcast time to advertisers in order to fund their programming. Television adverts have become effective, persuasive, and popular methods of selling consumer goods as well as utilizing the technology for spreading ideological and political interests. Research from and about the less-developed world has been a response to and a critique of the modernization or developmentalist theory that attempts to emphasize the role of the media in economic and social development. The paradigm holds that the media is a resource which, along with urbanization, education, and other social forces, would mutually stimulate economic (especially neoliberalism), social, and cultural development. As a result, media growth was viewed as a sign of development. According to this view, societies became modern when they demonstrated a specific level of media development and consumption of newspapers, broadcasting stations, and so on.

The rates for advertising costs are determined primarily by viewer ratings. The time of the day, the popularity of the channel, and the day of the week determine how much an advert can cost. For example, a slot during highly popular show can cost hundreds of thousands of dollars for a 30-second block of commercial time. However, the same amount of time during the Super Bowl or another big media event can cost several million. Time slots that often have fewer viewers are generally sold in bulk at lower rates to maximize profitability; this explains why at certain times the advertisements are often either for the same product or for different products from the same company that fits the needs of the viewer demographic. Some companies and businesses produce items for broadcast such as video news or press releases and pay program directors to use them. Some broadcasts weave advertising into their broadcast; this is known as product placement. For example, a character could be drinking a certain kind of drink, going to a particular restaurant, or driving a certain brand of car.

In the 20th and 21st centuries, television has come to play a pivotal role in the socialization of people, especially children. Although some aspects of television include negative aspects as the effect of media violence on children and young people, current research is still discussing if there is a direct effect between viewing material and acts committed by people. Others have suggested that individuals suffering from social isolation employ television to create what is termed a para-social or faux relationship with characters from their favorite television shows and movies as a way of deflecting feelings of loneliness and social deprivation. Some other studies have suggested there is a link between infancy exposure to television and attention deficit/hyperactivity disorder. Several studies have found that educational television has many advantages and that television can be a very powerful and effective learning tool for children if used wisely; this is largely reliant on the interactivity of the programming and the environment of the child. It has been found that simply placing a child in front of the television is more likely to be harmful than helpful in its development. However, if a child engages with the programming together with a parent or a sibling, for example, then the effects are enhanced and the educational aspects are increased and more likely to be remembered.

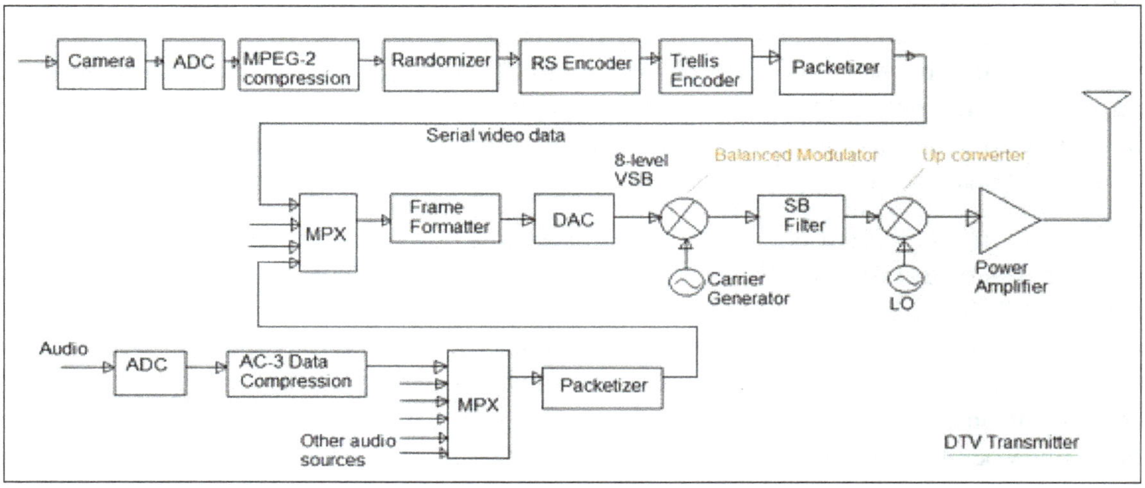

There is growing concern about electronic waste from among others discarded televisions as their high lead content and the rapid diffusion of new flat-panel-display technologies, some of which use lamps that contain mercury, are harmful for the environment and those employed in the recycling and destruction of these products. The occupational health concerns exist for disassemblers as removing copper wiring and other materials from televisions are a threat to their health. Further environmental concerns existing as a consequence of televisions is that the design and saturation in society mean that the use of the devices increase electrical energy requirements as well as provide an extra strain as the older models need to be disposed of.

There are two main systems in the TV system viz. transmitter and receiver. The transmitters are nothing but TV broadcasting stations and receivers are TV sets available in the household premises. The TV sets are connected with disc antennas or Yagi antennas or interfaced with cable service providers with the help of set top boxes and coaxial cables in order to receive the TV signals. TV remote control helps in selecting appropriate channel as per user intension or desire.

Advantages of Television (TV)

Following are the benefits or advantages of Television (TV):

- Television helps us to learn more about the world and things happening around us. This has become possible due to relaying of news, geography and other TV channels.
- Television presents information in very effective way. This makes things memorable easily.
- It is one of the great tools for entertainment as it relays movies, reality shows, serials etc. It also helps alleviate depression of mentally suffering patients.
- It is one of the ways to enjoy, relax and pass the time while at home or during the journey.
- It increases popularity of sports and other games among people.
- It helps us realize our responsibilities among the society to create better environment on the earth for the people to live long and healthy life.
- When children annoy parents, they provide them to watch cartoon serials such as Disney, nickelodeon, Pogo etc.
- It has also become luxury tool due to availability of costly LCD, Plasma and LED TVs.
- Television can be used by government agencies to relay vital information related to disaster, weather forecasts, demonetization etc. This helps in spreading immediate awareness among people. This is due to the fact that cheap TV sets are available in both rural as well as urban areas almost in each and every household.

Disadvantages of Television (TV)

Following are the drawbacks or disadvantages of Television (TV):

- TV can make us passive. This makes our brain lazy as we do not apply our mind.
- TV advertisements encourage us to buy things which we do not need. This incurs additional cost to us.
- It takes our time away from useful activities such as reading and writing. This ruins our education if proper attention is not given.
- Certain TV programmes may make people violent with the relaying of crime and vulgar movies/serials. This has huge impact on our society.
- Television interferes with social family life and communication among family members.
- It damages eyes and makes people obese or fatty if watched for longer duration and with inappropriate positions.

Mobile

Mobile as 7th of the Mass Media, identifies some characteristics that differentiate mobile as a medium from all the others (print, radio, television, internet and so on) that have come before. A mobile phone is an electronic device used for mobile telecommunications over a cellular network of specialized base stations known as cell sites. A cell phone offers full Duplex Communication and transfer the link when the user moves from one cell to another. As the phone user moves from one cell area to another, the system automatically commands the mobile phone and a cell site with a stronger signal, to switch on to a new frequency in order to keep the link.

Mobile phone is primarily designed for Voice communication. In addition to the standard voice function, new generation mobile phones support many additional services, and accessories, such as SMS for text messaging, email, packet switching for access to the Internet, gaming, Bluetooth, camera with video recorder and MMS for sending and receiving photos and video, MP3 player, radio and GPS.

We take these characteristics for granted too, but it is in the best interest of marketers and others to consider the value of these factors when considering how to integrate mobile into a campaign.

- Mobile is a personal mass medium: This seems contradictory, at first glance, but it is true. While it has the broad reach of broadcast media, mobile is personal first and foremost. When a consumer looks at his or her mobile phone, the message is going to him or her alone. This is not a mass consumption media (like film or television) – mobile reaches out to individual consumers on a one-to-one basis.

- Mobile users are permanently connected: The mobile user is permanently connected, and many have come to rely on their mobile phones as a source of information. A survey of 5,013 US owners of smartphones by Ipsos for Google, found that 70% of US smartphone owners will use their phones when shopping, while in the stores. Other research has revealed how the majority of people will use their devices during other activities, including dining, meetings with friends, and so on.

- Mobile devices are always carried: No other medium is quite as ubiquitous as the mobile phones that are in the pockets and bags of so many people. That may be the reason why people use their mobile phones as alarm clocks. Nokia reported at MindTrek 2010 that, on average, people the world over check their phones 150 times per day, which works out to once every 6.5 minutes when we're awake.

- Mobile enables augmented reality: Although augmented reality is still in its infancy, the ability to overlay information on visuals in real-time is only possible with mobile devices. Applications already exist to utilize augmented reality in games (overlaying UFOs over cityscapes, for example) as well in combination with location awareness, so that (for example) augmented reality can indicate the direction and distance of the nearest convenience store or toilet.

- Mobile devices include a built-in payment channel: In Kenya (population 38 million), 7.6 million people have bank accounts – compared to ten million people who have mobile-banking accounts. The Central Bank of Kenya values daily m-banking transactions as 1B Kenyan shillings, equivalent to US$10 million. This set up is unique to Kenya at the moment, but may become more common as near field communication and other technology make it easy to use our mobile phones as credit cards, or to access our bank accounts. Many smartphone users have some experience of this, downloading and paying for applications over the air directly from their devices.

Signal Frequency in Cell Phone

The cellular system is the division of an area into small cells. This allows extensive frequency reuse across that area, so that many people can use cell phones simultaneously. Cellular networks has a number of advantages like increased capacity, reduced power usage, larger coverage area, reduced interference from other signals etc.

FDMA and CDMA Systems

Frequency Division Multiple Access (FDMA) and Code Division Multiple Access (CDMA) were developed to distinguish signals from several different transmitters. In FDMA, the transmitting and receiving frequencies used in each cell are different from the frequencies used in the neighboring cells. The principle of CDMA is more complex and the distributed transceivers can select one cell and listen to it. Other methods include Polarization Division Multiple Access (PDMA) and Time Division Multiple Access (TDMA). Time division multiple access is used in combination with either FDMA or CDMA to give multiple channels within the coverage area of a single cell.

Codes in the Mobile Phone

Mobile phones have special codes associated with them. These include:

- Electronic Serial Number (ESN): Unique 32-bit number programmed in the phone.
- Mobile Identification Number (MIN): 10 digit number derived from the phone's number.
- System Identification Code (SID): Unique 5 digit number that is assigned to each carrier by the FCC.

ESN is a permanent part of the phone while MIN and SID codes are programmed in the phone when a service plan is selected and activated. Mobile phone is a Duplex device. When we use one frequency for talking, a second separate frequency is used for listening. So that both the people on the call can talk at once.

The Mobile phone can communicate on 1,664 channels or more. The Mobile phones operate within the cells, so that it is easy to switch on to different cells as they move around. A person using a cell phone can drive hundreds of kilometers and can maintain a conversation during the entire time because of the cellular approach.

Activation of SIM Card

SIM card (Subscriber Identification Module (SIM)) is a type of Smart card used in mobile phone.

The SIM is a detachable smart card containing the user's subscription information and phone book. This allows the user to retain his or her information even after switching off the handset. Alternatively, the user can also change service providers while retaining the handset simply by changing the SIM. SIM card Securely stores the service subscriber key having 15 digits. The digits of the key are:

- First 3 digits: Mobile country code.
- Second 2 digits: Mobile network code.
- Third 10 digits: Mobile station identification number.

Subscriber Identification Module SIM

When the Mobile phone is used for the first time, it sends a number called International Mobile Subscriber Identity – IMSI present in the SIM card to the network, which looks it up in a database to ensure the card is registered. If the IMSI is recognized, the network creates another number called a Temporary Mobile Subscriber Identity (TMSI), which is encrypted and sent back to the phone. In all subsequent calls, the phone identifies itself by broadcasting the TMSI.

What Happens when we make a Call?

- When we switch on the mobile phone, it tries for an SID on the Control channel. The Control channel is a special frequency that the phone and base station use to talk to one another. If the Mobile phone finds difficulty to get link with the control channel, it displays a "no service" message.
- If the Mobile phone gets the SID, it compares the SID with the SID programmed in the phone. If both SID match, the phone identifies that the cell it is communicating is the part of its home system.
- The phone also transmits a registration request along with the SID and the MTSO keeps track of your phone's location in a database. MTSO knows in which cell you are when it wants to ring the phone.

- The MTSO then gets the signal, it tries to find the phone. The MTSO looks in its database to find the cell in which the phone is present. The MTSO then picks a frequency pair to take the call.
- The MTSO communicates with the Mobile phone over the control channel to tell it what frequencies to use. Once the Mobile phone and the tower switch on those frequencies, the call is connected.
- When the Mobile phone move toward the edge of the cell, the cell's base station will note that the signal strength is diminishing. At the same time, the base station in the cell in which the phone is moving will be able to see the phone's signal strength increasing.
- The two base stations coordinate themselves through the MTSO. At some point, the Mobile phone gets a signal on a control channel and directs it to change frequencies. This will switch the phone to the new cell.

Mobile Network

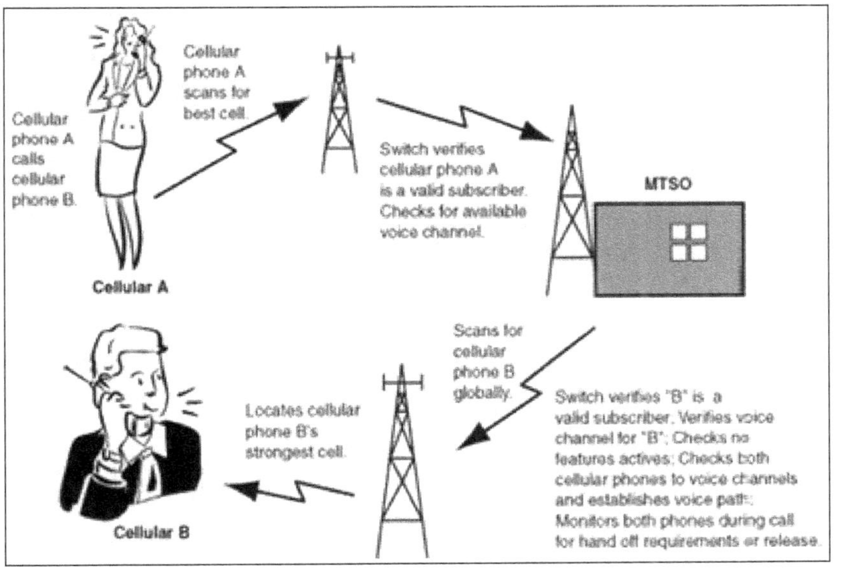

The GSM System

Global System for Mobile Communications is the standard for mobile telephone systems in the world. In GSM, the signaling and speech channels are digital, therefore GSM is considered a 2G (Second Generation) system. This helps wide-spread implementation of data communication applications. There are five different cell sizes in a GSM network. These are macro, micro, pico, femto and umbrella cells.

Macro cells are cells where the base station antenna is installed on a mast above average roof top level. Micro cells are cells whose antenna height is under average roof top level. Pico cells are small cells whose coverage diameter is a few dozen metres. These are mainly used in indoors applications. Femto cells are cells designed for use in residential or small business environments and connect to the service provider's network via a broadband internet connection.

Umbrella cells are used to cover shadowed regions of smaller cells and fill in gaps in coverage between those cells.Horizontal radius of the cell varies depending on the antenna height, antenna gain and propagation conditions. Maximum distance the GSM supports is 35 kilometers. Most 2G GSM networks operate in the 900 MHz or 1800 MHz bands while 3G GSM in the 2100 MHz frequency band.

Time Sharing

Time Division Multiplexing technique is used to share eight full-rate or sixteen half-rate speech channels per radio frequency channel. There are eight radio time slots grouped into a TDMA frame.

Mobile Network

Mobile phone converts voice, text, multi-media messages or data calls into Radio Frequencies (RF). Mobile phone base stations transmit and receive these RF signals and connect callers to other phones and other networks. Mobile phone network is divided into thousands of overlapping, individual geographic areas or 'cells', each with a base station. The size of a cell depends on the area of coverage and the number of calls that are made in that area. The smallest cells are in crowded urban areas with large buildings and heavy population density, while the biggest cells are in rural areas, where people are dispersed. There are two types of channels used in GSM. These are Control channels and Traffic channels.

- Control channels: These are responsible for housekeeping tasks such as telling the mobile when a call is coming in and which frequency to use. To ensure this handover works, the phone constantly monitors the broadcast control channel of up to 16 neighboring cells. In normal operation, phones continually adjust the power of the radio waves they send out to be the minimum needed for the base station to receive a clear signal. If a phone moves far away from its base station and if the signal is weak, the network consults the list and triggers a handover to a neighboring cell with best signal.
- Traffic channels: It is used to carry calls or other data from the mobile phone to the base station and vice versa. In the Traffic channel, voice or text data is carried in bursts. Each burst comprises two consecutive strings of bits (a series of signals representing 1s and 0s), each 57 bits long.

Range

The range within which mobile devices can connect is not a fixed figure. It depends on a number of factors like the frequency of signal in use, the transmitter's rated power, the transmitter's size etc.

Inside the Mobile Phone

Mobile phone is a sophisticated device using SMD components, Microprocessor, Flash memory etc. In addition to the Circuit board, Mobile phone also has Antenna, Liquid Crystal Display (LCD), Keyboard, Microphone, Speaker and Battery. Below is the Block diagram of Mobile phone.

The circuit board is the heart of the Mobile phone. It has chips like Analog-to-Digital and Digital-to-Analog conversion chips that translate the outgoing audio signal from analog to digital and the incoming signal from digital back to analog. Following are the Chips present in Mobile phone.

- Digital signal processor: It is generally rated as having 40 MIPS (millions of instructions per second) to conduct calculations of signal manipulation at high speed. This chip deals with both compression and decompression of the signals.
- Microprocessor: It handles all the housekeeping tasks for the keyboard and display. It also deals with command and control signaling with the base station, and coordinates the rest of the functions on the board.
- Mobile Microprocessor and Flash Memory: The Flash memory and ROM Chips of the Mobile phone act as a storage location for the phone. These chips store the customizable options of the cell phone, as well as the entire operating system. The power and radio frequency sections of the phone, phone recharging and power management etc are controlled by this chip. It also controls several hundred FM channels. The RF amplifiers focus on signals that go in and out of the phone's antennae.

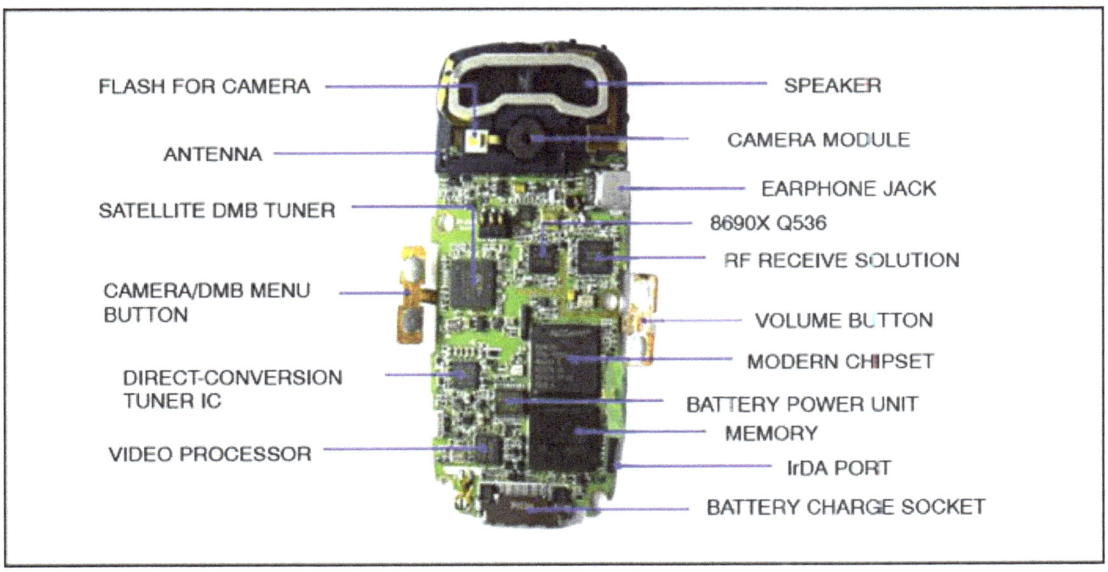

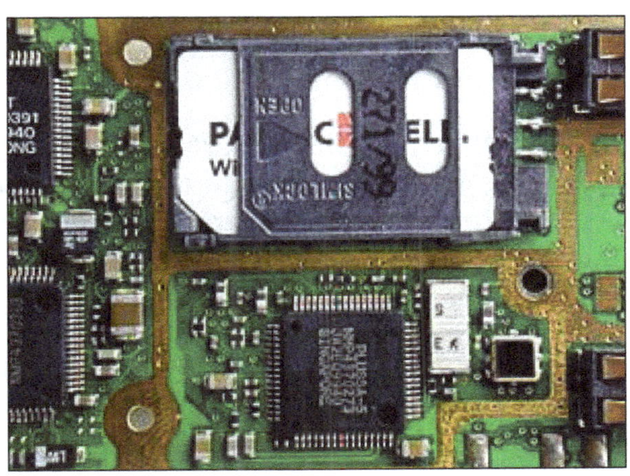

Mobile Phone Maintenance

Mobile phone is a delicate device and needs care for its proper functioning. Here are the common measures to keep the mobile phone in good condition:

- Do not keep Mobile phone in wet area or use it with wet hands. Moisture can cause non-repairable internal corrosion of parts.
- Do not drop the phone or damage the connection points.
- Do not over stress the phone. It may damage the display.
- Do not keep the phone near heat generating devices. High temperature in a car can damage its electronics.
- Do not over charge the battery. Charge the battery only its charge status goes below 50 percent.
- Prevent Cloning.

A phone is "Cloned" when someone steals its ID number and is able to make fraudulent calls on the owner's account. When the phone makes a call, it transmits the ESN and MIN- a unique tag- for your phone to the network at the beginning of the call. When the phone transmits its MIN/ESN pair, it is possible to capture the ESN-MIN pair. Using a Scanner device it is easy to modify another phone so that it contains your MIN-ESN tags. This allows the person to make calls on your account. Cloning may also occurs when the phone is repaired in an unauthorized service centre. It is possible to copy the data including images and video present in the phone.

Internet

The Internet is a worldwide, publicly accessible network of networks. Through interconnected computer networks, the Internet enables individuals and businesses to share information, resources, and services. Because no single individual or group of individuals controls the Internet, it is imperative that certain rules and guidelines are adhered to so that it can function efficiently.

The Internet and Standards

In the beginning, the Internet was used strictly for scientific, educational, and military research. In 1991, regulations changed to allow businesses and consumers to connect as well. Since that time, the Internet has grown rapidly and now covers the globe. New technologies are continuously being developed that make the Internet easier and more attractive to use. Online applications are available to the Internet user, including e-mail, web browsing, streaming music and video, online gaming, and instant messaging.

The way people interact, share information, and even do business is changing to keep up with the continuous evolution of this global network. The Internet is creating a wider audience and consumer base for whatever message, product, or service can be delivered. For many businesses, having Internet access has become critical, not only for communication, but also for day-to-day operation.

E-Commerce

Electronic commerce (e-commerce) is any business activity that can be conducted over the web. This includes using web space for advertisements, brochures, and catalogs, as well as ordering and distribution services. Companies can sell products and services over the Internet from their own websites, through auction sites, or through affiliated websites.

Communications

Communications refers to any electronic method of communication, such as the use of e-mail, instant messaging, and online chat. In addition, many businesses use internal phone systems that operate over the Internet using IP phones and voice over IP (VoIP) technology to reduce phone costs.

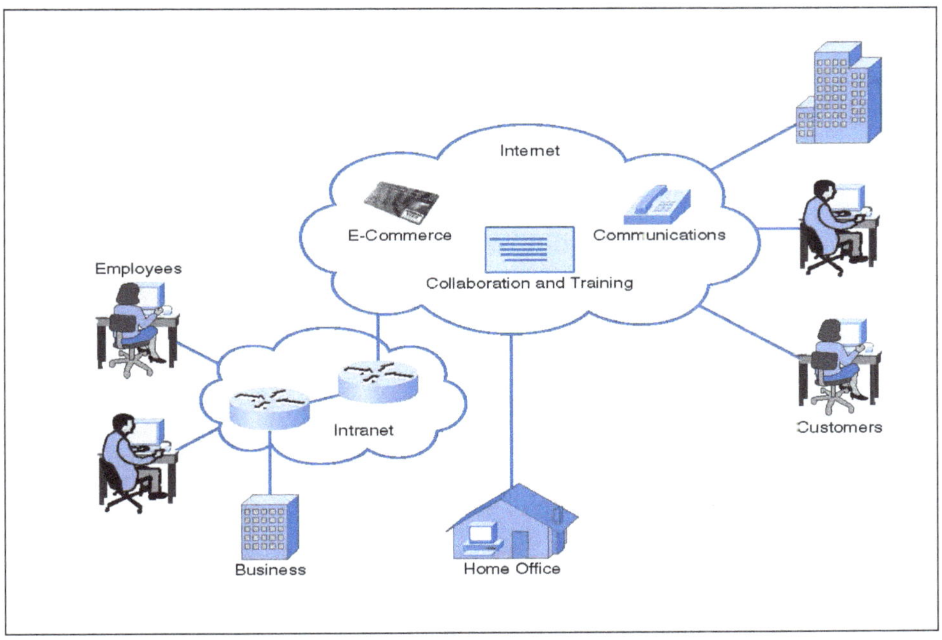

Common Uses for the Internet.

Collaboration and Training

The Internet enables the sharing of documents, presentations, and spreadsheets among users around the world. It allows teams of people to work together virtually from remote locations for business and training purposes. Examples include videoconferencing, virtual meeting places, virtual classrooms, online learning, online bulletin boards, FTP sites, and password-protected databases and applications.

With the increasing number of new devices and technologies coming online, it is important that all users and technologies adhere to a set of rules or guidelines. This allows services such as e-mail to be reliably delivered to all users. These rules and guidelines are known as Internet standards.

A standard is a set of rules for how something must be done. Networking and Internet standards ensure that all devices connecting to the network use the same set of rules. By having standards, different types of devices can send information to each other over the Internet. For example, an e-mail message is formatted, forwarded, and received by all devices in a standardized manner. If someone sends an e-mail via a PC, someone else can use a mobile phone to receive and read the e-mail as long as the mobile phone uses the same standards.

An Internet standard is the end result of a comprehensive cycle of discussion, problem solving, and testing. When a new standard is proposed, each stage of the development and approval process is recorded in a numbered Request for Comments (RFC) document so that the evolution of the standard is tracked.

Thousands of Internet standards help define the rules for how devices communicate on networks. These different standards are developed, published, and maintained by a variety of organizations. These include the International Organization for Standardization (ISO), Institute of Electrical and Electronics Engineers (IEEE), Internet Corporation for Assigned Names and Numbers (ICANN), Internet Assigned Numbers Authority (IANA), and Internet Engineering Task Force (IETF). Because these organizations create and maintain standards, millions of individuals can connect to the Internet using a variety of devices, including PCs, cellular phones, handheld personal digital assistants (PDA), MP3 players, and even televisions.

ISPs and ISP Services

Regardless of the type of device an individual or business uses to connect to the Internet, the device must connect through an Internet service provider (ISP). An ISP is a company or organization through which a subscriber obtains Internet access. A subscriber can be a business, a private consumer, a government body, or even another ISP.

- FTP hosting: The ISP provides the server and application software for a business FTP site.
- Applications and media hosting: The ISP provides the server and software to allow a business to provide streaming media such as music, video, or applications such as online databases.
- Technical support: Many businesses do not have the in-house technical expertise to manage large internal networks. Some ISPs provide technical support and consulting services for an additional fee.
- Voice over IP: A business can save on long-distance telephone charges, especially for internal calls between geographically distant offices, by using VoIP.
- Equipment co-location: A business may opt to have some or all internal network equipment physically located on the ISP premises.
- Web hosting: The ISP provides the server and application software for storing web pages and web content for the business website.

Internet Service Providers

Although ISPs offer their clients many different services, their main role is to provide a connection to the Internet. The actual type of connection varies according to the region. Not all connection types are available in all areas. Some connection options provide continuous connection, and others provide connection only when required. Bandwidth, both upstream and downstream, varies between the different options and must match the requirements of the individual or business. Bandwidth is measured in bits per second (bps), kilobits per second (kbps), megabits per second (Mbps), or gigabits per second (Gbps).

Delivering Internet Services to End Users

ISPs offer various connection options for home and business users. The main connection methods used by home and small business users include dialup, DSL, cable, and satellite connections.

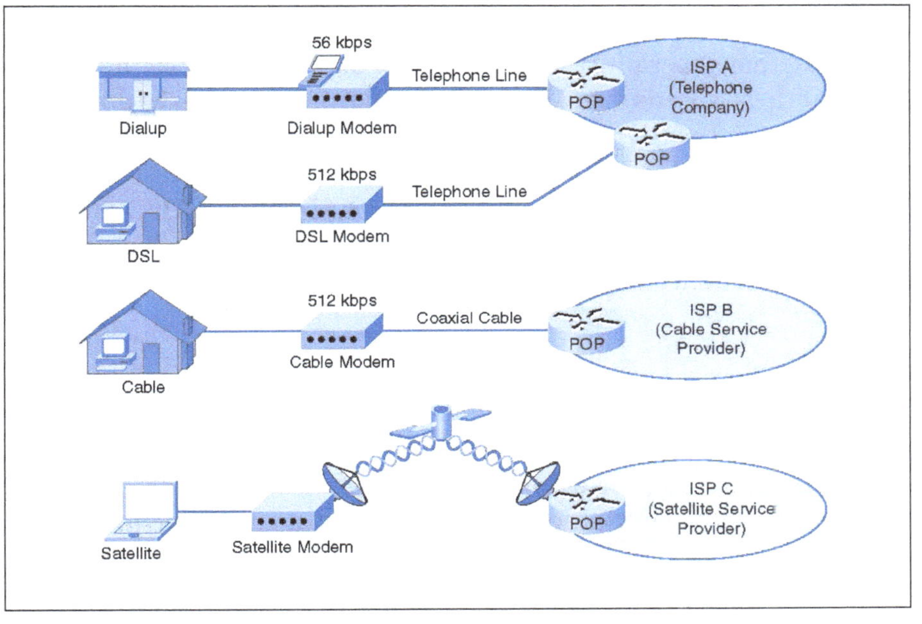

Dialup Access

Dialup access is an inexpensive option that uses a phone line and a modem. To connect to the ISP, a user calls the ISP access phone number. With connection speeds of about 56 kbps, dialup is the slowest connection option. At this speed it would take approximately 12 minutes to download a 5-MB file. Dialup is typically used by mobile workers and in areas where higher-speed connection options are not available.

DSL

Digital subscriber line (DSL) is more expensive than dialup but provides a faster connection. DSL also uses telephone lines, but unlike dialup access, DSL provides a continuous connection to the Internet. This connection option uses a special high-speed modem that separates the DSL signal from the telephone signal and provides an Ethernet connection to a host computer or local-area network (LAN).

Speeds of 512 kbps and higher are common with DSL services. At this speed, a 5-MB file would take approximately one minute to download. Upload and download speeds vary based on geography, distance from the ISP, and the type of service offered by the ISP.

DSL comes in several flavors. Typically, a home user uses an asymmetric digital subscriber line (ADSL), in which the download speed is faster than the upload speed. Because most home users download significantly more than they upload, this type of connection is sufficient. In a business environment, the amount of data uploaded may be equal to or even greater than the amount of data downloaded. For these users, an ADSL line is insufficient; a symmetric digital subscriber line (SDSL) service is more appropriate. SDSL offers the same upload and download speeds.

Cable Modem

A cable modem is a connection option offered by cable television service providers. It offers faster connection speeds than that generally provided by DSL. Cable Internet connections offer speeds of 5 Mbps to 10 Mbps. At these speeds a 5-MB file would take only seconds to download. The Internet signal is carried on the same coaxial cable that delivers cable television to homes and businesses. A special cable modem separates the Internet signal from the other signals carried on the cable and provides an Ethernet connection to a host computer or LAN. Unlike DSL, the distance from the ISP does not affect the performance of the cable connection. Cable is a shared-bandwidth service, so as more customers in an area connect and use the Internet, the speed is negatively affected.

Satellite

Satellite connection is an option offered by satellite service providers. The user's computer connects through Ethernet to a satellite modem that transmits radio signals to the nearest POP within the satellite network. Satellite Internet access speeds range from 128 Kbps to 512 Kbps, depending on the subscriber plan. Satellite connection may be the only available technology in many regions of the world.

Dedicated Bandwidth Options

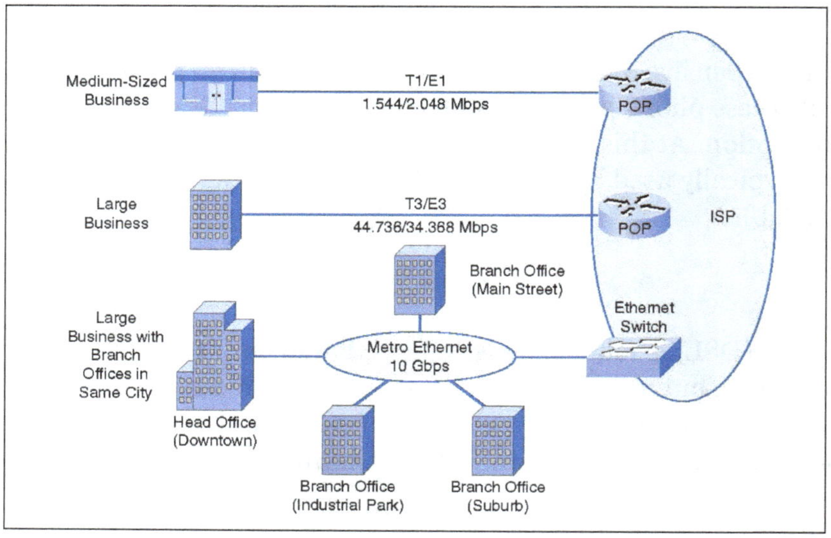

High-Speed, Dedicated-Bandwidth Internet Connections.

Business customers often require dedicated, high-bandwidth connections to the Internet. Figure shows the three main types of dedicated, high-bandwidth connection options that are used by businesses: T1/E1, T3/E3, and Metro Ethernet.

T1/E1 Connections

T1 connections transmit data at rates of up to 1.544 Mbps. They are symmetrical, meaning that the upload bandwidth is the same as the download bandwidth. A medium-sized business may need only one T1 connection for all its connectivity requirements. T1 connections are common in North America and some other parts of the world. E1 is a European standard that transmits data at 2.048 Mbps.

T3/E3 Connections

T3 connections allow data to be transmitted at rates of up to 45 Mbps. Although T3 is considerably more expensive than a T1 connection, a larger business may need a T3 connection to accommodate all its employees or business volume. Large businesses with multiple locations might use a combination of T1 and T3 lines. Quite often the main office or data center has a T3 line, and each branch office has a T1 connection. E3 is a European standard that transmits data at 34.368 Mbps.

Metro Ethernet

Metro Ethernet offers a wide range of high-bandwidth options, including Gbps links. Large companies with many branches in the same city, such as banks, often use Metro Ethernet. Metro Ethernet connects the main office location and all the branches using switched technology. It allows the transfer of large amounts of data faster and less expensively than other high-bandwidth connection options.

Point of Presence

After the type of connection is established, it is necessary to connect to the ISP to get access to the Internet. Individual computers and business networks connect to the ISP at a point of presence (POP). POPs are located at the edge of the ISP's network and serve a particular geographic region. They provide a local point of connection and authentication (password control) for multiple end users. An ISP may have many POPs, depending on the size of the area it services.

Within the ISP network, high-speed routers and switches move data between the various POPs. Multiple links interconnect the POPs to provide alternative routes in case one of the links becomes overloaded with traffic or fails.

Internet Hierarchy

The Internet has a hierarchical structure. At the top of this hierarchy are the ISP organizations. The ISP POPs connect to an Internet Exchange Point (IXP). In some countries, this is called a Network Access Point (NAP). An IXP or NAP is where multiple ISPs are joined to gain access to each other's' networks and exchange points exist worldwide.

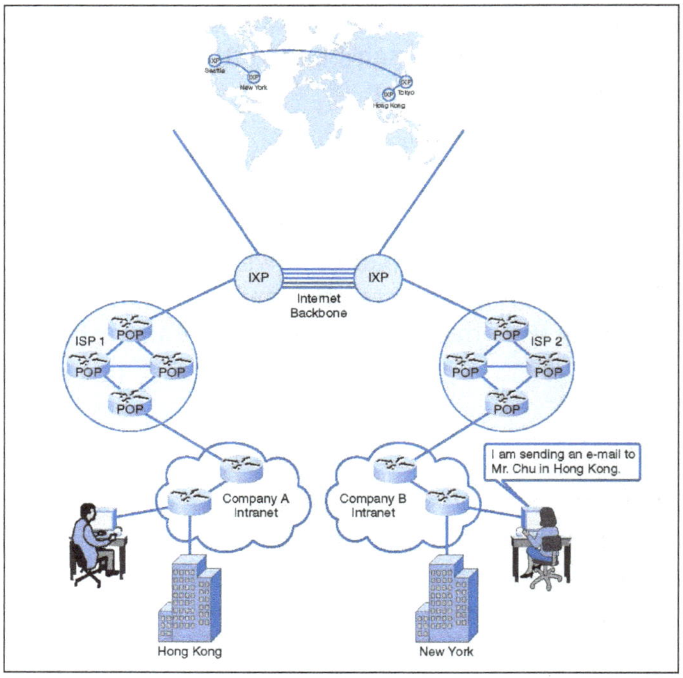

Internet Hierarchy.

The Internet backbone consists of this group of networks owned by various organizations and interconnected through IXPs and private peering connections. The Internet backbone is like an information superhighway that provides high-speed data links to interconnect the POPs and IXPs in major metropolitan areas around the world. The primary medium that connects the Internet backbone is fiber-optic cable. This cable typically is installed underground to connect cities within continents. Fiber-optic cables also run under the sea to connect cities between continents. ISPs are classified into different tiers according to how they access the Internet backbone. Three tiers of ISPs are identified.

Tier 1 ISPs

Tier 1 ISPs are at the top of the hierarchy. Tier 1 ISPs are huge organizations that connect directly with each other through private peering, physically joining their individual network backbones to create the global Internet backbone. Within their own networks, the Tier 1 ISPs own the routers, high-speed data links, and other pieces of equipment that join them to other Tier 1 ISP networks. This includes the undersea cables that connect the continents.

Tier 2 ISPs

Tier 2 ISPs are the next tier in terms of backbone access. Tier 2 ISPs can also be very large, even extending across several countries, but very few have networks that span entire continents or between continents. To provide their customers with global Internet access, some Tier 2 ISPs pay Tier 1 ISPs to carry their traffic to other parts of the world. Some Tier 2 ISPs exchange global traffic with other ISPs less expensively through public peering at IXPs. A large IXP may bring together hundreds of ISPs in a central physical location for access to multiple networks over a shared connection.

Tier 3 ISPs

Tier 3 ISPs are the farthest from the backbone. Tier 3 ISPs generally are found in major cities and give customers local access to the Internet. Tier 3 ISPs pay Tier 1 and 2 ISPs for access to the global Internet and Internet services.

Identifying the Structure of the Internet

Network utilities can be used to create a map of the Internet to visualize how ISP networks interconnect. These utilities also illustrate the speed at which each connecting point can be reached. The ping command tests the accessibility of a specific IP address. This command sends an Internet Control Message Protocol (ICMP) echo request packet to the destination address and then waits for an echo reply packet to return from that host, as shown in Figure below. It measures the time that elapses between when the request packet is sent and the response packet is received.

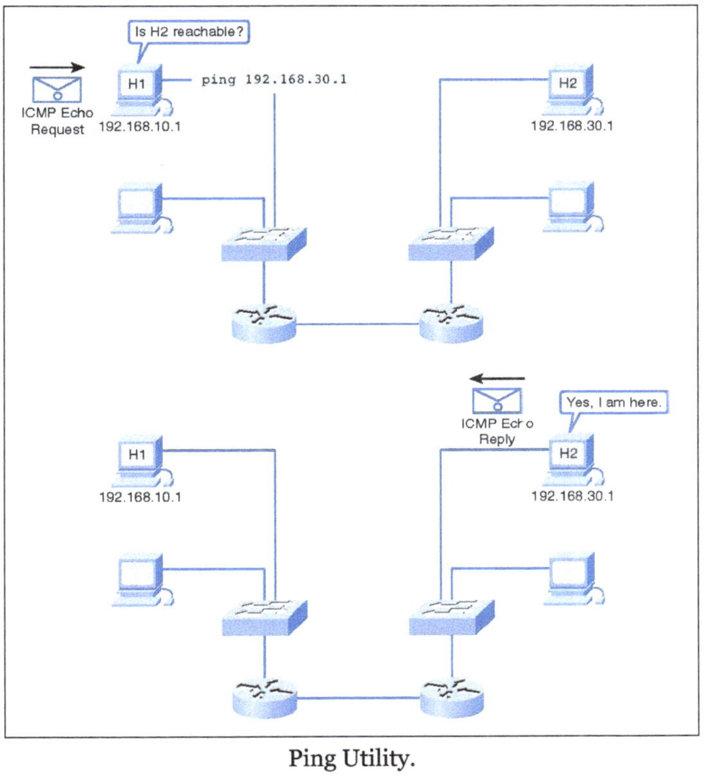

Ping Utility.

The ping command output indicates whether the reply was received successfully and displays the round-trip time for the transmissions. Example 1-1 shows the syntax and result of a successful ping command from a Windows-based host. Note that either the IP address or the domain name may be used. If the Domain Name System (DNS) is not functioning properly, the IP address should be used.

If a packet does not reach the destination, or if delays are encountered along the way, you can use the trace route utility to display information about where the packet encountered problems. The trace route utility displays the path that a packet takes from the source to the destination host. Each router that the packet passes through is called a hop.

The trace route utility displays each hop along the way. It also calculates the time between when the packet is sent and when a reply is received from the router at each hop. If a problem occurs, use the output of the trace route command to help determine where a packet was lost or delayed. The output shows the various ISPs that the packet must pass through during its journey from source to destination. The Windows tracert utility works the same way. Also, a number of visual trace route programs provide a graphical display of the route a packet takes.

ISP Connectivity

ISPs must be able to provide clients with a reliable connection to the Internet. To accomplish this, they require a variety of equipment and controlled power and environmental conditions. In addition, the ISP must be able to provision and install new services for customers as well as support existing services.

ISP Requirements

An ISP requires a variety of devices to accept input from end users and provide services. To participate in a transport network, the ISP must be able to connect to other ISPs. An ISP must also be able to handle large volumes of traffic. Some of the devices required to provide services are shown in Figure:

- Access devices that enable end users to connect to the ISP, such as a DSL access multiplexer (DSLAM) for DSL connections, a cable modem termination system (CMTS) for cable connections, modems for dialup connections, or wireless bridging equipment for wireless access.
- Border gateway routers to enable the ISP to connect and transfer data to other ISPs, IXPs, or large business enterprise customers.
- Servers for such applications as e-mail, network address assignment, web space, FTP hosting, and multimedia hosting.

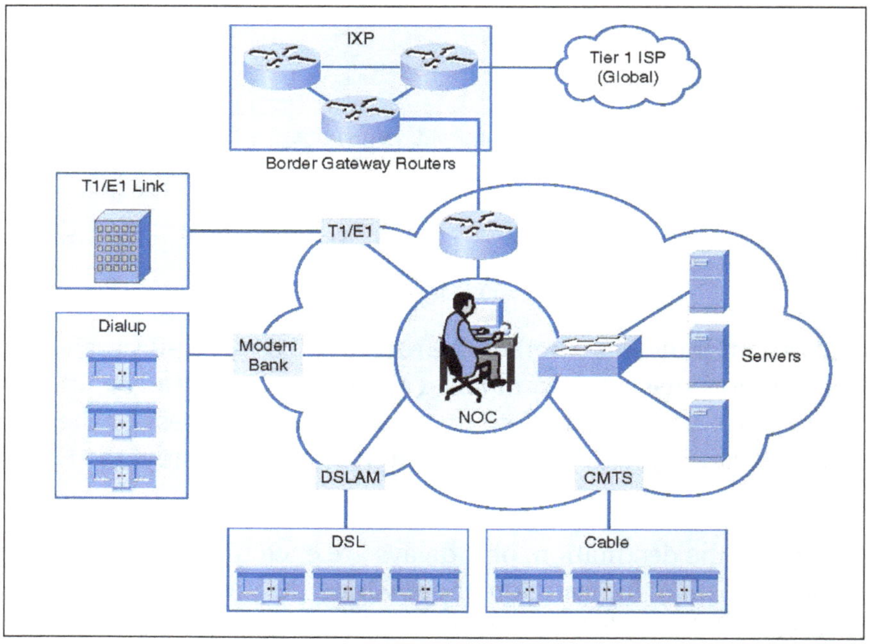

ISP Connection Devices.

In addition, the ISPs must be able to provide uninterrupted power to the devices and also remove the large amount of heat generated by the equipment. To accomplish this, ISPs also require the following:

- Power conditioning equipment with substantial battery backup to maintain continuity if the main power grid fails.
- High-capacity air conditioning units to maintain controlled temperatures.

Like other businesses, ISPs want to expand so that they can increase their income. The ability to expand their business depends on gaining new subscribers and selling more services. However, as the number of subscribers grows, the traffic on the ISP's network also grows.

Eventually, the increased traffic may overload the network, causing router errors, lost packets, and excessive delays. In an overloaded network, subscribers can wait for minutes for a web page to load, or may even lose network connection. These customers may choose to switch to a competing ISP to get better performance. Loss of customers directly translates to loss of income for an ISP. For this reason, it is important that the ISP provide a reliable and scalable network.

Scalability is the ability to allow for future change and growth. A scalable network can expand quickly to support new users and applications without impacting the performance of the service being delivered to existing users. The most scalable devices are those that are modular and provide expansion slots for adding modules. Different modules can have different numbers of ports. In the case of a chassis router, some modules also offer different interface options, allowing for different connection options on the same chassis.

Roles and Responsibilities Within an ISP

ISP organizations consist of many teams and departments. These teams are responsible for ensuring that the network operates smoothly and that the services that the ISP offers are available on a reliable basis. Network support services are involved in all aspects of network management, including planning and provisioning new equipment and circuits, adding new subscribers, network repair and maintenance, and customer service for network connectivity issues. When a new business subscriber orders ISP services, the various network support service teams work together to ensure that the order is processed correctly and that the network is ready to deliver those services as quickly as possible. Each network support service team has its own roles and responsibilities:

- Customer service receives the order from the customer and ensures that the customer's specified requirements are accurately entered into the order-tracking database.
- Planning and provisioning determines whether the new customer has existing network hardware and circuits or whether new circuits need to be installed.
- The onsite installation team is advised of which circuits and equipment to use and then installs them at the customer site.
- The network operation center (NOC) monitors and test the new connection and ensures that it is performing properly.
- The NOC notifies the help desk when the circuit is ready for operation. The help desk contacts the customer to guide the customer through the process of setting up passwords and other necessary account information.

Social Media

Social media is any digital tool that allows users to quickly create and share content with the public. Social media encompasses a wide range of websites and apps. Some, like Twitter, specialize in sharing links and short written messages.

What makes social media unique is that it is both broad and relatively uncensored. While many social media companies impose some limitations—such as taking down images that display violence or nudity—there are much fewer limitations on what someone can share than there with other means of mass communication like newspapers, radio stations, and television channels.

Anyone with internet access can sign up for a social media account. They can use that account to share whatever content they choose to, and the content they share reaches anyone who visits their page or profile. The use of hashtags on social media groups content together by topic, allowing users to connect with strangers who are sharing content related to a topic of interest.

How Social Media Works

Since social media covers so many different kinds of websites and applications, the function of these tools also varies. However, most social media sites start with a user creating a profile, usually by providing a name and an email address.

Once a profile has been created, users can create and share content. For instance, an Instagram user with a new account can take a picture and share it on their profile with a caption. In addition to creating content for their profile, social media users can find other users whose content they want to follow or comment on. Depending on the type of social media, a user may "follow" another user, add them as a "friend," or they may "subscribe" to another user's page.

Social media often uses "feeds" that allow users to scroll through content. Social media companies use algorithms, based on a user's profile data, to determine the content that appears and the order that it appears in. The feed will include content from "followed" users, as well as from entities that pay to promote their content.

Types of Social Media

Social Networks: Facebook, Twitter, LinkedIn

Such types of Social Media are used to associate with individuals (and brands) on the web. They help your business via branding, social awareness, relationship building, customer service, lead generation, and conversion. You can channelize different types of Social Media campaigns on these networks that will help you widen your reach. Some of the benefits of these Social Marketing Networks are:

- They encourage individuals and businesses to interact online and share data and thoughts for ensuring mutually productive relationships.
- In case you are searching for the best ways to optimize current marketing campaigns then you will discover a variety of organic and paid ways to do this on Facebook, Twitter, and LinkedIn sorts of social networks.

Media Sharing Networks: Instagram, Snapchat, YouTube

Media sharing types of Social Media are used to find and share photographs, live video, video and other kinds of media on the web. They are also going to help you in brand building, lead generation, targeting and so on.

They give individuals and brands a place to discover and share media so the target audiences can be targeted and converted into a convincing and result-driven way possible. Social networks nowadays also offer these features, however, for Media Sharing Networks, sharing of media is their basic role.

- Starting with image or video on Instagram, YouTube and Snapchat types of media sharing networks would be more beneficial for you.
- To decide whether you should use these networks for your business or not, you should consider your resources and target audiences. These channels will help you run well-planned campaigns to generate leads and widen your audience base.

Discussion Forums: Reddit, Quora, Digg

Such types of Social Media channels are used for finding, sharing and discussing different kinds of information, opinions, and news. They help businesses by being a top-notch resource for doing immaculate market research. These forums are the oldest ways of running Social Media Marketing campaigns.

Before the entry of popular Social Media players like Facebook, these forums were the places where professionals, experts and enthusiasts used to do different kinds of discussions concerning a variety of fields.

- These discussion forums have a massive number of users and it ensures unprecedented reach for your business. These are the places that provide the answers to different queries of any domain.
- In case your business needs deep customer research then these places would the most befitting one for your business.
- Along with sharing information and knowing answers, these places are very impactful in advertising as well.

Bookmarking and Content Curation Networks: Pinterest, Flipboard

Opting for such types of Social Media will help you find out, share, discuss and save a variety of latest content and media that are trending as well. They are very helpful in channelizing brand awareness for your business, plus, choosing this one to run different types of Social Media Marketing campaigns will help you generate website traffic and customer engagement.

In case you want to run some out of the box highly creative campaigns that can not only inform your audience and but also attract them then this one is the best fit.

- To run a Social Media campaign on Pinterest, you need to have a site that is bookmark-friendly. You should optimize headlines and images for the feeds that Bookmarking and Content Curation Networks use for accessing and sharing your content.

- Flipboard lets you create your own Flipboard magazine by using most engaging content and then you can showcase that to your audiences.

Consumer Review Networks: Yelp, Zomato, TripAdvisor

Using Customer Review networks will help you find out, share and review different information about a variety of products, services or brands. When a business has positive reviews on these networks, their claims turn more credible because reviews on these networks act as Social Proof.

For running a successful Social Media Marketing Campaigns, it is very important for today's businesses to have positive reviews on these sites. In addition, resolving all the issues that your customers are posting on these Review platforms is another thing that is going to be very important for the positive and productive outcomes for your business.

- These networks offer a place to users for reviewing different kinds of products and services that they have used.
- Review content adds great value to any brand because it will influence more and the number of new buyers to attempt your services.
- Yelp and Zomato are the types of social media platforms that offer location-based review services that will help you run location-based social campaigns.

Blogging and Publishing Networks: WordPress, Tumblr, Medium

You should choose these types of Social Media networks for publishing, discovering and commenting on articles, social media blogs and other content on the web. Content marketing is one of the most powerful ways to target, attract, engage and convert a target audience.

It is going to be the base of successful online marketing campaigns that play the most important role in conversion funnels of Digital Marketing campaigns. WordPress and Blogger are the traditional blogging platforms while Tumblr (micro-blogging service) and Medium (Social Publishing Platform) is the latest blogging and publishing networks.

1. These networks are must for the businesses that want to effectively use Content Marketing, plus, you can share this content on a variety of Social Networks like Facebook, Twitter, LinkedIn, etc.

2. Content that you use on these networks will also help you create a niche for your business and audiences who are in search of information concerning that niche will for sure visit your blog or site.

Social Shopping Networks: Polyvore, Etsy, Fancy

Want to find out all the latest trends in the marketing or crave to know the shopping tips then such types of Social Media channels are for you.

In addition, they help you follow different brands, share interesting things and make a purchase on these Social Shopping networks.

Businesses can use such types of Social Media Platforms for creating brand awareness, boosting engagement and selling products on some new and effective platforms. These channels transform e-commerce by making them more engaging via some interesting social elements.

- To use these networks effectively you should create a site that integrates shopping experience with social experience.
- These networks are very result-driven for small businesses and startups as they can sell their products without any land-based office or store.

Interest-Based Networks: Goodreads, Houzz, Last.Fm

You can use such types of Social Media networks for connecting with other people who have the same sorts of hobbies or interests. You can easily find the audiences who are interested in knowing more and more about the kinds of products and services that you offer.

This makes it one of the best networks for engaging with your audience and creating exclusive brand awareness online. Compared to big social networks, using Interest-based networks would help you run a more targeted campaign.

- Choosing these networks will help you focus solely on a single product or service related to any particular subject, for instance, home décor, Digital Marketing Training, Music, Books, etc.
- These networks are the best places to engage with the audiences of a particular niche.

Blog

The word "blog," a contraction of "web log," is an informational web page that consists of discrete units called "posts." The term "log" comes from the history of nautical navigation and originally referred to a record of chronological events kept by a ship's crew. Like a ship's log, blogs on the web tend to maintain an ordered chronology, although they often unfold in reverse order.

Blog posts are often shorter and less formal than other types of writing. Blogs can be personal, artistic, academic, or professional. It is a unique form of online publishing that creates opportunities for producing knowledge, sharing research, building social networks, developing professionally, or documenting personal growth.

Composing a Post

You want your blog to invite readers in and keep them coming back for updates. Great blogs are vibrant and visually interesting, but they are also thoughtful and purposeful. Every post matters for generating and holding attention.

Make a point. While posts do not require a formal thesis or claim, it is important to have an argument, opinion, or purpose in mind when you compose. Consider the following principles when composing.

- Be concise: Use precise language and coherent syntax to make your posts easy to read.
- Post often: Blogs should be updated regularly to hold readers' interest. Actively generate new and interesting content on a daily or weekly schedule.
- Consider inviting guest bloggers to appeal to diverse readers, broaden your blog's scope, or refresh your own perspective on the project.
- Proofread: Careless mistakes and errors can distract readers and make you appear less credible as a writer.
- Create visual interest: Consider which aspects of your content would pair well with visual elements such as photographs, figures, or videos. Break up large chunks of text with visual elements to make your blog more readable.

Using Multimedia

Audio and visual interest helps grab a reader's attention. Blogs give writers the opportunity to use design, images, audio, and video to supplement their writing. Take advantage of these innovative ways to enhance your presentation. Here are some guidelines to have in mind when you choose your blog's multimedia elements:

- Use appropriate content, size, and quality. Make sure your chosen images complement the layout of your text visually. Images should be easy to see without obstructing the text of a post. Choose the highest possible quality image while also making sure it is easy to load. You don't want your readers squinting at blurry pixels, but you won't want them to wait 10 seconds for something to load, either.
- When linking to an online video, consider using a screen shot from that video as your hyperlink. A screen shot can make a reader more likely to click on a link. It can provide a visual preview, as well as demonstrate the clip's relevance to your post.
- Attribute your sources. Like ideas, images and videos are someone else's intellectual property. Whenever possible, provide captions for the reader. Even a simple caption – (Image courtesy of msnbc.com) – will help readers identify the object's origins.

Tips to Maintain a Successful Blog

- Make post titles eye-catching but also reasonably accurate. Example: "Trash Talk" is a post about waste management.
- Consider using the tag function in each post. This will help guide readers through your content thematically instead of chronologically. Keep tags consistent, including punctuation. For example, "African-American" and "African American" would be regarded as two different tags because of the hyphen.
- If your hosting platform allows, link to similar blogs in order to increase your traffic.

- Unlike other writing contexts, you may find it difficult to identify your audience when you are composing blog posts. If your blog is public, you could have a large, diverse, and even global readership. Be aware that you are potentially addressing people with very different knowledge bases and cultural assumptions than yours.
- Handle comments with care. As the blog's creator, the way you handle dissenting or inflammatory voices sets the tone for your readers. Consider adjusting your platform's comment settings if you need to regulate the conversation. For instance, requiring minimum identification to post a comment can address the problem of inappropriate posts by increasing a writer's accountability.

References

- Amplitude-modulation-am, radio: electronics-notes.com, Retrieved 22, March 2020
- High-definition-radio-its-the-new-wave, communications, technologies-21754633: electronicdesign.com, Retrieved 29, January 2020
- Satellite-radio: electronics.howstuffworks.com, Retrieved 11, May 2020
- What-is-internet-radio-ad: which.co.uk, Retrieved 03, July 2020
- Television-312292610: researchgate.net, Retrieved 21, February 2020
- Advantages-and-Disadvantages-of-Television: rfwireless-world.com, Retrieved 14, June 2020
- Mobile-phone-how-it-works: electroschematics.com, Retrieved 17, March 2020
- What-is-social-media-2890301: thebalancesmb.com, Retrieved 05, July 2020
- Blogging-introduction-original: twp.duke.edu, Retrieved 13, February 2020

3

Electronic and Digital Media: Tools and Techniques

Some of the different tools and techniques used in electronic and digital media are computer graphics, morphing, digital content, digital data, digital image, digital audio, digital video and broadcasting. Science and technology have undergone rapid developments in the past decade which has resulted in the discovery of significant tools and techniques in the field of electronic and digital media; which have been extensively detailed in this chapter.

Computer Graphics

The television, the computer, the video games, the cinema screens are mainly emitters of visual images. The social mass media have their reason of being in the diffusion of messages, however, an unprecedented event was the interrelation emerging between the mass media and computer animation, mainly in the cinema and television. As a rule it intervened in the titles or credits of the films, documentaries, series, etc. Letters and animated figures rich in colours and special effects seize the spectators' attention. Then the interaction of the three-dimensionality boosted this event. Now the proof are the continuity designs, chain image, publicity curtains of television, both public and private. These are minutely thought out works, since there the international image of the firm is at stake. The idea they express is constantly repeated during the station's programmes. To this you have to add publicity.

Some creators, designers and programmers of computer animation in the nineties talked about a saturation of 3D inside it, that's why curtains or continuity designs are seen in 2D. This was the main reason why some European channels have subtly returned to bi-dimensionality. In the new millennium 3D prevails over 2D, even in the cases in which there is a combination of both animations by computer. Now the 3D term refers to the infographic synthesis in 3D (Computer Generated Imagery –CGI, and 3D Computer Animation) not to the 3D illusion upon watching the film, the sense recently spread by cinema marketing. The acronym 3D has had a wider diffusion instead of the stereoscopic term. However, the three-dimensionality of the images in origin is more meaningful.

Computer Animation, Mass Media and Creativity: Evolution

In almost five decades, computer animation has progressed and has been internationally spread as a technique and as a means in a fast way. Currently, the computer is an alternative element to the camera that allows the visualization of anything imagined in motion. And computer animations, whatever their genre, are more and more attractive and remarkable. A way of grouping the animations by computer in relation to the mass media or their genre is as follows:

- Development and research with the latest technologies.

- Creative experimentation.
- Short and feature films.
- Visual effects.
- Scientific dissemination.
- Marketing, entertainment and corporative image in TV.

In the two first it can be seen how the origins of computer animation are located starting with the first drawings made by Ivan Sutherland with a computer (Sketchpad) in 1963. In the same year we have the first interactively controlled animation, that is, the first videogame in history: Spacewar 1. Other examples inside the first environment and whose titles in brackets are:

- Application of genetic algorithms to create morphologies of creatures which have to act in a simulated three-dimensional environment (Evolving Virtual Creatures).
- Modelling of natural landscapes and visualization of atmospheric effects (First Flight).
- Demonstration of the creative possibilities of the particles technique: explosions, a water cascade, a snow storm, etc. (Particle Dreams).
- Virtual encounter between two famous actors: Marilyn Monroe and Humphrey Bogart, when the realism of human characters was very hard to accomplish (Rendez-vous a Montreal).
- Recreation of the Parthenon of Athens, starting from the current construction and the remains that are kept at the British Museum.

The creative experience entails the creativity factor. A notion that entails a rhetoric question: What is meant by creativity? Creativity may derive from three different stages: inspiration, experiences (the more one knows, the more creative one is), and luck (the moment in which, through random reasons, one finds that one had been looking for a long time). The two former are contradictory. As long as one reaches something creative that does not respond neither to the first postulate, nor to the second, evidently it is the play of destiny or random. In the experimental environments of the computer animations, in their origins they used to respond to random questions, especially in the artistic context, for instance. Now inside the second group of genres of animations we can mention the following examples:

- One of the first computer animations of free creation made in the USA (Butterflies).
- One of the first experimentations of fractal images accompanied by music. (A volume of Julia Sets).
- One of the representative works by John Whitney, pioneer and driver of audiovisual digital art (Arabesque).
- Coral-like and organic shapes in evolution, whose author is the Englishman William Latham (Biogenesis).

- Numeric models of the image and the sound matching the colours (Limosa).
- Sample of algorithmic art which uses mathematical concepts, musical composition and interactivity (Lormalized).
- A spatial immersion in Pablo Picasso's painting which reveals usually hidden aspects (Picasso's Guernica).

All these works made apparent the artistic potentiality of animated graphic engineering or computer animation where the final errors of the images in the rendering process, for instance, do not have serious consequences as they would have in a scientific or accuracy context, such as is the case of a component for the engine of a car or the pillars that support a building made in the environment of the CAD (Computer Aided Design). This far the production environment of animations which have set a landmark in their international history is the third part of what short length and feature films would mean. In this regard some examples of short films are:

- Short film based on the XIX century science fiction novel by Edwin Abbott about the 2D and 3D of reality (Flatland).
- An articulated lamp plays with its son (Pixar).
- An icon of a pencil, escaped from the interface of an Apple Macintosh II, tries to go back to the screen (Pencil Test).
- The first project of film integrally in 3D (prior to Toy Story) based on the universe of the French cartoonist Moebius (Starwatcher).
- The inconveniences of being the toy of a baby who doesn't respect his/her toys at all (Tin Toy).

Starting from the short length films, the next breakthrough of the computer animations was the big screen, that is, the cinema. From that moment on, the productions in the USA have quickly grown, compared to the rest of the world, thanks to the growing demand for these productions. In principle it was aimed at the kids and teenagers but currently aimed at every age. The short length films have served to create that bridge. In some cinematographic productions real images of actors and actresses are combined with the 2D and 3D. Next some examples of cinema productions:

- Generation of life on a dead planet visualized through fractal techniques (Star Trek II, The Wrath of Khan).
- Submarine adventure with an extraterrestrial presence. A living water-being with the shape of a worm in a character of this film and can only be visualized through a computer (The Abyss).
- Wave effects, froth, fog, etc., of a fisherman in the midst of an impressive storm (The Perfect Storm).
- Successive transformations of some animals. These were the first morphing effects in the cinema (Willow).

- Initial sequence of the film with a zoom from the Earth towards the limits of the universe with the sound background of the human radio broadcasts, theoretically as far as they can be listened to (Contact).

Scientific dissemination through a genre that is based on the contents of the history, geography, astronomical, physics documentaries, such as can be seen in the following group of examples:

- Visualization of the spatial mission to Mars and the actions of the exploring vehicle (Mars Exploration Rover).
- In the television series Cosmos by Carls Sagan: 4 billion years of evolution told in 40 seconds of computer animation (Evolution).
- A sort of cosmic magnifying glass through the 3D map of the most complete universe that exists, starting in the Himalayas and finishing in the Big Bang (The Known Universe).
- A television series that recreates nature and the animal world during the time of the great saurian. (Walking with Dinosaurs).
- 3D models of the body of a man and a woman. The data, of public knowledge, serve to create animated visualizations of human anatomy (The Visible Human Project).
- The researcher James Blinn explaining the principles to achieve realism in the 3D images (The Quest for Realism).

Finally, we have the genre where the computer made images, little by little, have been related to the demographic basis of the population, such as the publicity or institutional spots, channel curtains or transition on television, music videoclips, etc. These are pieces where creativity and originality have converged at the same time:

- The first singer in 3D animation (Doxo).
- Videoclip with the song by the Rolling Stones and some animated innovating characters in On the Wire (Hard Woman).
- Videoclip of the musician Peter Gabriel.
- The publicity heroes of the time set on stage in a world of logotypes and brands (Logorama).
- The Flying Lakes were 3D animations typical of the 80s. This piece treats the topic with humour and imagination (Flying Logos).

However, in some of them one runs the risk of falling into plagiarism, since they are simple reproductions of others, improved from the technical point of view, but that doesn't keep them from being simple imitations. The original creativity of a professional of computer animation must gather a series of variables and components such as imagination, observation, the knowledge of the issue he/she is approaching, among others. In this regard there are definitions about creativity.

- Barron understands as creativity "the disposition towards originality".

- Parker defines it as "the art of seeking, testing and combining, in new ways, knowledge and information. The production of any new thing is essentially subjective, that is, "what is new, is new for the subject".
- On his side, Kneller claims that "creative thought is innovating, explorative, impatient with conventionalisms, dissected towards the unknown, and not determined".
- Lastly, Sillamy tells us that "creativity is the disposition to create that exists potentially in every individual and in all ages, in a narrow dependence of the sociocultural environment".

This natural tendency towards personal realization needs some favourable conditions to be expressed. Without any doubt the graphical software to carry out computer animations has been and remains an ideal pathway for creativity. Some factors that have an influence on creative thought are fluidity or productivity (the approaches opened in the design stage or the animation storyboard boost the production of plentiful alternatives to the original script), the variety (sometimes one only sees one dimension of the problem), the flexibility of perception and the generation of new ideas will give us the measure of the intellectual wealth (you have got to determine the old canons and change them for a wealth of points of view) and originality, which entails the creation of unprecedented answers to specific situations.

The Onion-iceberg Method for the Heuristic Evaluation of the Computer Animation

With the technological and evolution of the graphic software, commercial or not, in many cases it is difficult to differentiate at first sight that which is computer animation from the normal video. This is due to the fact that the final images of the rendering can be additionally retouched, frame by frame, with the self-editing programmes, such as can be Photoshop, for instance. Not for nothing some researcher claim that the image is dead and that we should go back to textual messages.

Within the first step made by the method, we intend to split each one of the layers that make up the generative process of computer animated images, in the search of the isotopic lines which give one sense or another to an audiovisual work, whether it is on the computer screen or in the television or the cinema, to mention just some examples.

In the first place we must consider the genres to which the creations made by the computer belong, establishing the first intersections among them, from a perspective of content such as development and research in the latest technologies, scientific dissemination and creative experimentation. Later on, we may consider from the diachronic point of view the entertainment, marketing and corporative image in television, linked to computer image jump, as in the short film, the feature film, including the visual effects. Simultaneously, it is necessary to consider the kind of images with which we are working, that is, 2D, 3D, combination of 2D and 3D, wire models with rendering, combination of rendering with the wire model.

The colour of the components of the different scenes is essential, since there is a whole range of implicit meanings in their selection and which change from culture to culture. The textures occupy a special section with the different kinds of materials that can be inserted in an object to turn something into wood or into metal. Even in those cases it is important to evaluate the photographs that can be incorporated as textures.

Evidently, photographs that entail a series of techniques and special effects which in rendering can merge with the 2D or 3D computer context of the computer animation and which sometimes go totally unnoticed to the human eye.

Illumination is another of the key elements that make up any of the scenes, with their matching features, such as can be: ambient, semi-directional, indirect, global, skylight, spot/direct, (free or target), etc. In regard to the special effects it is important to consider them from the physical point of view (translation, rotation, forces, deflectors, geometric/deformable, particles and dynamics, etc.), natural (rain, fog, hail, wind, fire, etc.).

Obviously, in animation the camera plays an essential role and its main components are: the camera planes (overall, close-up, American, etc.), its movements (zoom-in, zoom-out, static subjective), the lenses and the field of view (FOV). Then we have the timing and the speed of the animation, that is, if there are pauses, reverse movements, fast advances, etc.

We may find other essential elements such as the typography in the use of the placards, because they also open a range of denotations and connotations, in the plane of meaning, if we stick to a semiotics definition.

The use of the video, cartography and/or maps, drawings, illustration and other kinds of works by artists of international renown, etc., which make up the universe of the static and dynamic images. The figure summarized the main components of the animation or the different onion layers.

At the same time we must take into account that in computer animation we only see the end result. Nevertheless, it is important to know and analyze the iceberg of the stages that make it up to be able to establish the isotopic line, too.

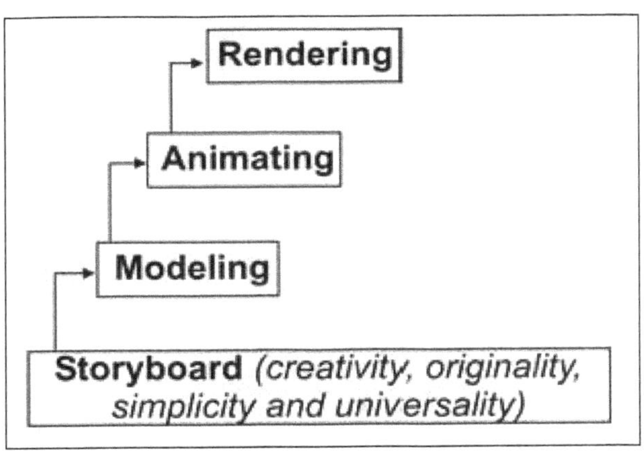

Summary of the main steps that make up a "classical" computer animation.

Computer animation as a cinematographic art starts in paper support with the first sketches of the characters and the storyboard. This history of animation can briefly be divided into several sections or stages: generation of the animation, definition of the characters, scenery (objects, colours, textures, kind of illumination, etc.), character animation (style of movement of the characters in the face of given situations or obstacles to be overcome in movement, facial animation and dialogues, etc.), the insertion of the objects in the scenes, the definition of the different kinds of lighting, the incorporation of the cameras, their lenses, standpoint, their movement, etc. Later on, one proceeds to animation itself, including the special effects. Making of the first tests, and correction of mistakes, until the final animation is rendered with the high quality rendering. Schematically it can be summed up in the following way:

Now in the face of the rhetoric question: Where is the originality of an animation? It is important to consider several aspects which may be visible a priori, but which are related to the combination of techniques and the programming of special modules, aside from the temporal factor. That is, when the user of the commercial applications makes several experiments at the moment of incorporating textures, light reflect effects or transparencies, the development of special solutions where the intersection of solutions is presented to gain time, and time in these cases entails cutting down the production cost and therefore the final cost. For instance, in Maya at the moment of inserting the different lights in the scenes and create an atmosphere in accordance with the storyboard, one can resort in every scene to programming a script in MEL (Maya Embedded Language) so that in an automatic way it places the values of shading, lighting, rendering in the scene at the moment of the files opening.

The temporal factor refers to the solutions presented in the 80s or 90s where in some works they combined 2D and 3D. For instance, real human figures were inserted which appeared as 2D in a 3D animation, as it can be seen in the identification or corporative sign of Telemadrid or the formation of the identification in the second TV channel of the Basque Country, starting from a person who walks until reaching the shape of a number 2.

Telemadrid –Ostra Delta.

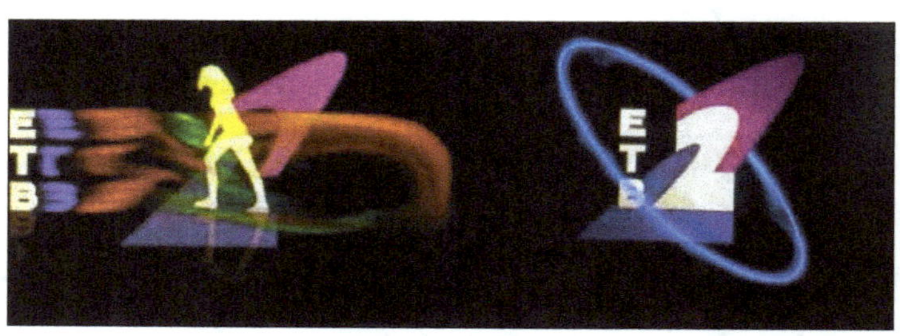

ETB 2 –Ostra Delta.

These are the technical aspects but evidently everything starts from a script that tells a story and it is important that it is simple, universal and with a dose of humour to overcome the linguistic barriers in the international circulation. There is no originality when one makes a simple cut, copy and paste of the video to the computer animations. It is important that the analyst of computer animation has a wide background of technical knowledge of graphic computing and its history, including the cinema, television and literature.

Morphing

The rising popularity of designing media façades using LED, fluorescent lighting and projection technology in contemporary architecture is attributed to the increasing accessibility of such technologies. The BIX façade in the Kunsthaus Graz in Austria is the significant precedent of these approaches. The GreenPix media screen at Beijing designed by Simone Giostra & Partners with Arup is another salient example that involves the use of conventional LED displays for communication and social interaction purposes. However, there are no existing media façades that have been co-utilised as a fenestration device. Permeability properties of an architectural skin that allows moderation between the interior and exterior conditions can be used as a key consideration for designing a media skin. What if a media skin with permeability features can perform similar visual effect to the conventional media screens?

The recently completed Media-ICT building designed by Cloud 9 Architects in Barcelona demonstrates an energy efficient architectural skin that uses soft materials as part of the visual display. The soft façade made of ETFE responds to the user needs. The ETFE skin protects the interior by regulating indoor climate from direct sunlight. When more light is needed, the pneumatic skin deflated to let the daylight in. This pneumatic kinetic shading device sets an early inspiration to conduct this research work; however, further investigation is needed especially in terms of allowing air ventilation and shadow casting of media skins. Another precedent is the project 'ShapeShift' which uses an assembly of kinetic membranes using EAPs (electro active polymers) to prototype robotically fabricated room-dividers. However, this prototype needs extremely high energy for transformation and lack of representation of any media contents.

The term morphing is used in this research to describe the use of form-changing materials to perform kinetic actuations on responsive skins with little use of mechanical components. In contrast to other kinetic or media façade projects, this research investigates new possibilities of attributing softness and elasticity in form-changing material system that applies to an architectural skin. It also responds to environmental stimuli and act as a communicative display. The passive and active form-changing materials such as silicone rubber and shape memory alloy (SMA) are used to test these new possibilities. The simple, thin and lightweight design of the architectural morphing skin (AMS) provides an economical alternative to the conventional digital media surface by adding inherent potential functions to regulate ventilation and sunlight.

Soft Responsive Kinetic System

There are possibilities for implementing the soft responsive kinetic system (SRKS) in physically responsive architectural morphing skin (AMS) in this research. This system provides a platform to shift from hard to soft material system approaches for designing architectural media brise-soliel. It also develops an appropriative method for studying soft responsive morphing skin that improves the quality of our design explorations. Instead of inventing systems or synthetic materials, we shift the approach to exploitation of existing form changing materials that have been applied in other disciplines but are new in the context of this architectural vision. The kinetic actuation of SRKS does not require the use of mechanical components, pistons or motors. Instead the overall system uses form-changing materials for actuation purposes. SRKS served as a proposed system for designing Blind. It is also a novel design method of inquiry which included four elements, Skin, Skeleton, Actuator and Sensor for their individual design strategy and implementation.

Table: Elements, design strategies and implementations of Soft Responsive Kinetic System (SRKS)

Elements	Design Strategies	Implementations
Skin	Elasticity	Flexible
Skeleton	Tensegrity	Transformation
Actuator	Form-changing materials	Actuation
Sensor	Adaptability	Sensing

The design strategy of the Skin element of the SRKS focuses on elasticity to produce flexible architectural skin. Elastic materials deform when force is applied and the deformation is reversed once the force is removed, returning the materials to the original state. The potential energy stored within the material itself can be harnessed to activate the deformation process back to its original state. This offers potential new forms of flexibility, adaptability and deformation using the memory effect in architectural skins. The elastic material used for the design exploration is silicone rubber given its durability, heat resistance and elastic capacity. The heat tolerant material property makes silicone rubber a suitable material to integrate with active form-changing materials (SMAs) to form a morphing skin, addressing elasticity and actuation respectively.

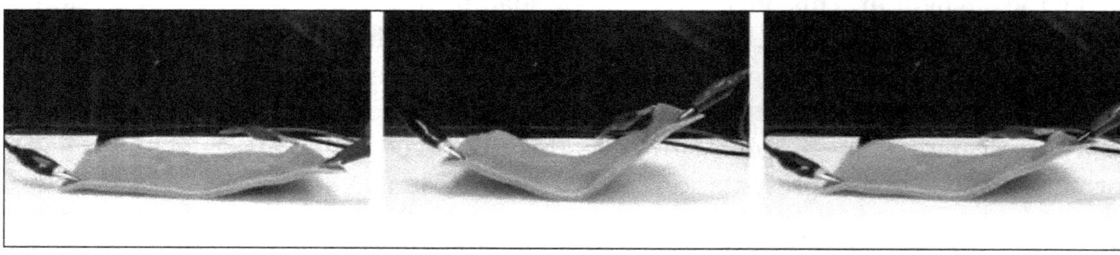

Early experiment for elastic silicone rubber skins set as the elastic component and actuator by electric stimuli.

The skeleton element of SRKS focuses on the tensegrity structural approach that reduces the friction between mechanical joints and achieves a lightweight structure. Due to the interdependent nature of all the elements, a slight change in any of their parameters can result in a significant form transformation. For these reasons the tensegrity skeleton was chosen as part of the SRKS and for its flexibility and lightweight components. The lightweight accessible ABS (Acrylonitrile Butadiene Styrene) used as the primary strong explicit materials to fabricate tetrahedral modular components integrated with stainless steel coated wires. Eventually they form the light weight and flexible tensegrity tetrahedral modular skeleton as the exoskeleton structural system of Blind.

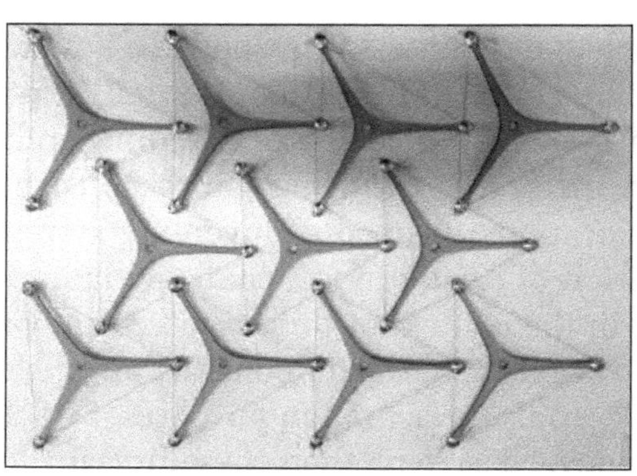

'Simplified' version of tetrahedral modular skeleton.

The actuator element of SRKS addresses the use of active form-changing materials for actuation of the SRKS. We proposed the use of shape memory alloys (SMAs) as the active form-changing materials to investigate the alternative of actuation, since the dynamic deformation, expansion and contraction, of SRKS can be achieved and controlled with electrical stimuli. The deformation of SMAs occurs under electrical stimuli using 5 V for a 1.5 amp current to perform potential actuation.

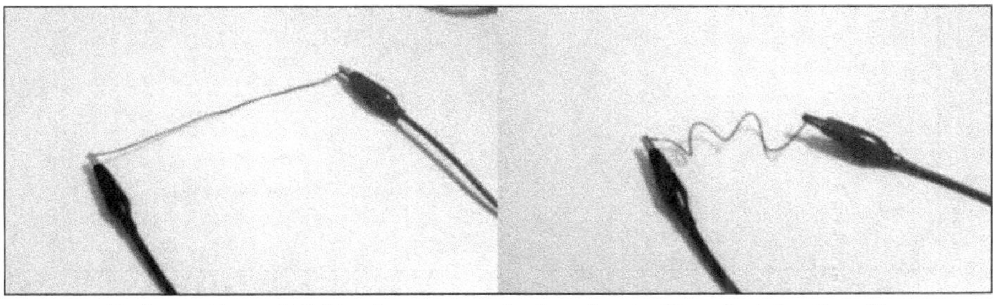

Deformation of SMA wire occurred when heated by electric stimuli.

The sensor element explores the adaptability of SRKS in order to achieve morphing skins that display elastic properties, and respond to digital and physical stimuli. This idea is developed using parametric design tools. The application of Blind is as a prototypical kinetic shading device and media screen with sensing ability that to regulate shading and visual effect. It aims to improve the comfort level as well as visual communication between the exterior and interior of spaces. This application embodies in an experimental process used design tools such as Grasshopper and Firefly parametric software together with Arduino microcontroller and photo resistor. The integration of these open source software and hardware make initial digital simulation and physical experiments possible.

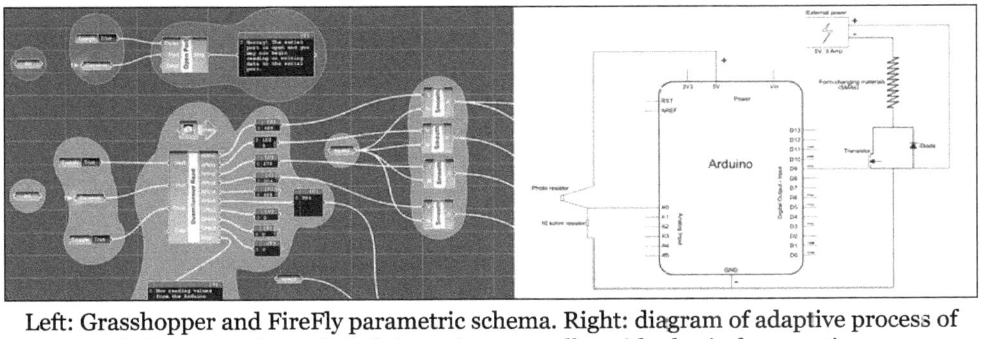

Left: Grasshopper and FireFly parametric schema. Right: diagram of adaptive process of SMA control through Arduino microcontroller with physical computing.

Design Exploration

The design exploration of the responsive architectural morphing skin through soft kinetic system, called Blind. Blind serves as the analogue media brise-soliel to display binary images and motion graphics using the perforation process of the soft surface composed by the 'eye-like' permeable apertures. The 'analogue pixels' of the surface creates a new layer of visual intervention in the form of responsive semi-ellipsoid canopy to allow communication between the ambient environment and the Blind.

Blind is a multilayer architectural morphing skin that composed by two types of triangulated modules. It manipulates sunlight through bending and twisting of its undulating surface. This malleable fenestration through the input of real-time data constantly cast controlled shadows over the surface under its semi-ellipsoid canopy. The shadow casted into the existing surface through this process provides a morphing atmosphere that suggests a continued relationship between exterior and interior space. The conventional digital media screen, in comparison, lacks the consideration of its effect on the interior condition.

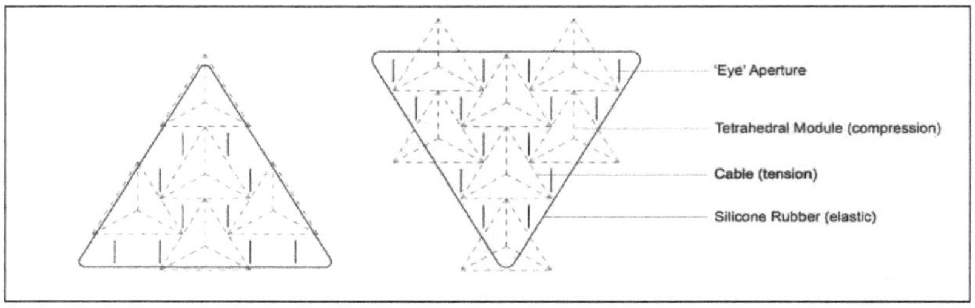

Two typical types of triangulated modular skin embedded with tensegrity tetrahedral components.

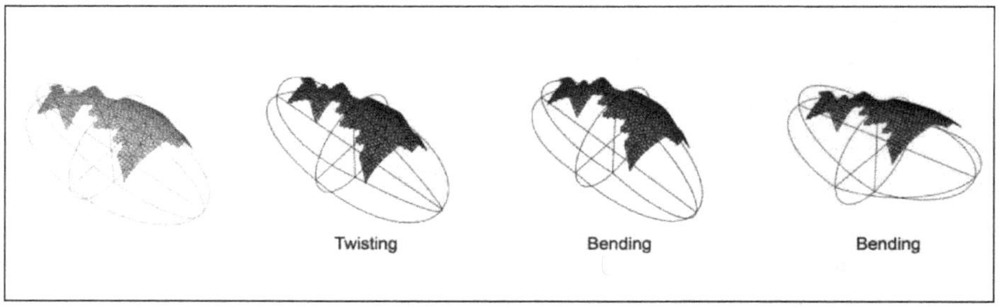

Blind in the form of semi-ellipsoid canopy performed morphological transformation for optimal sunlight manipulation through bending and twisting.

Blind includes two types of transformations that respond enable adaptive visual effects and media communications: Morphological and Patterned. Morphological transformation is a global morphing process of the entire undulating skin structure to control shadows casting and lighting manipulation for various visual effects of space under Blind. Patterned transformation involves local individual openings that are opened and closed to serve simultaneously as 'analogue pixels' and as apertures.

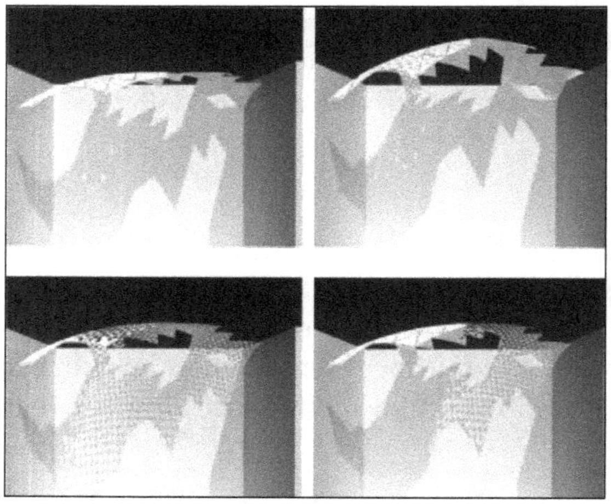

Above: Shadow casting by global morphological transformation. Bottom: Projected domestic morphing shadow and light spot patterns of patterned transformation.

Morphological Transformation

Morphological transformation explores the global surface curvature of Blind to be modifiable while maintains the continuous topology of undulating or flat surface. It responds to various functional drivers to manipulate the lighting effects in global scale. This morphological transformation demonstrates an alternative actuation system using SMA springs integrated with the overall tensegrity structures. The global actuation takes place in between the tetrahedral skeletons and skins and is triggered by the contraction and expansion of the SMA springs through electrical stimuli.

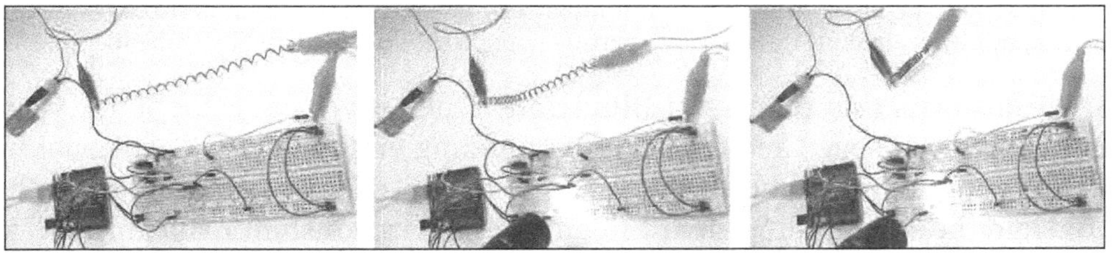

SMA spring responds to direct light through a photo resistor to perform contract and expand actuation.

The adaptability for morphological transformation process of Blind is tested by using a photo resistor as light sensor and the torchlight mimicking the path of sunlight to embody the initial global transformation of physical responsive triangulated modular skin. It responds with various morphological states for optimal visual performance as a direct sunlight modulator that creates multiple lighting effects. This global morphing process constantly redefines the face or image of the existing building environment in order to materialise Blind as a media brise-soliel as well as responsive intervention. This process also allows Blind to serve as a new transformable visual barrier in between interior and exterior spaces that have been overlooked in conventional digital media façades.

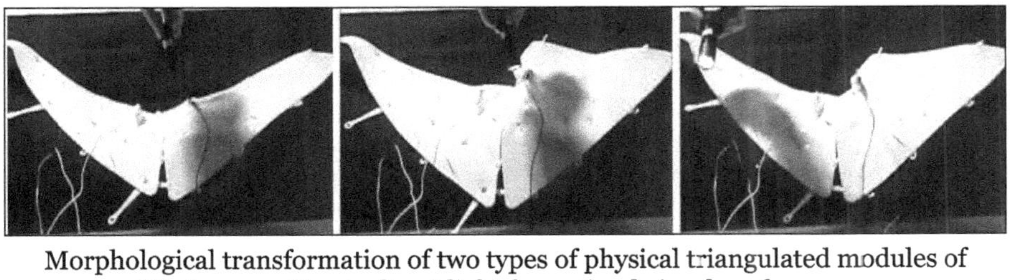

Morphological transformation of two types of physical triangulated modules of Blind responding to direct light for optimal visual performance.

Patterned Transformation

The patterned transformation through permeability of Blind is generated by the individual domestic 'soft' apertures as analogue pixels projecting light spots in response to sunlight penetration. This transformation manipulates the spatial conditions of the interior and exterior spaces through the dynamic patterns of the skin surface. The initial geometry of the membrane aperture is inspired by the performance of the eye. The 'eye-like' apertures in the geometry are determined by their relative curvature on the responsive undulating silicone rubber surfaces and actuated by SMA wires and springs. This analogy of an 'eye-like' permeable aperture functions as a skin muscle mechanism in the eye which allows various changing porous patterns in binary form on the skin. This perforation process created a potential application for the surface of blind as the analogue media brise-soleil, to display binary images or even motion graphics.

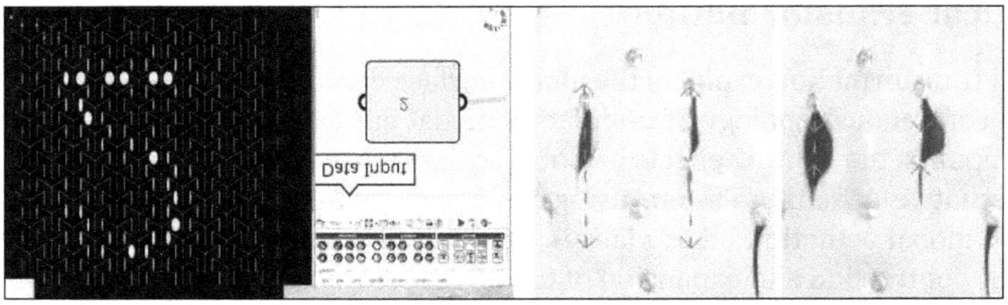

Left: Digital simulation of Light spots fenestration through 'eye' apertures formed numeric texts and textual visual patterns. Right: Physical domestic 'eye-like' apertures open and close actuated by embedded SMA wires.

The patterned transformation process of Blind adds a new layer of aesthetic for visual communication between existing space and external surrounding environment. This visual intervention demonstrated in a digital simulation creates a new media skin for communication between the existing spatial and the surrounding environment through its constant malleable porosity activated by real-time input data. The exterior skin of Blind allows light penetrates the 'eye' apertures to form the numeric texts light spots projected on the surface underneath Blind. Other textual visual patterns also formed by the light spots penetrating through the 'eye' apertures.

The fenestration of patterned transformation also performs the motion graphic representation in an analogue manner. The actuation of the 'eye' apertures of Blind occurs in two states, 'open' and 'close'. This produces an animated 'shadow play', which is an illusion of still and animating images caused by the illumination of the Blind under the sunlight. This real-time 'shadow play' creates, potentially, a 3D volumetric analogue cinematic interior environment that responds to changeable events. The patterned transformation allows Blind to become a projective device by controlling direct sunlight and artificial lights penetration using real-time input data. This process extends the cinematic ability of conventional shadow play but in an architectural context.

Digital Content

Digital content, also known as digital media, is available in many forms, from text, audio and video files to graphics, animations, and images. Digital content usually refers to information available online for download or distribution on electronic media such as an electronic book or iTunes song, but a lot of people in the content industry argue that online content is anything that can be published. Following this line of thinking, it's safe to say that if you're online, you're likely to look at, watch or listen to digital content.

Types of Digital Content

Examples include:

- Video: Types of video content include home videos, music videos, TV shows, and movies. Many of these can be viewed on websites such as YouTube, Hulu, CBS All Access, Disney+, HBO Max, and so on, in which people and companies alike can post content. However, many movies and television shows are not available for free legally, but rather can be purchased from sites such as iTunes and Amazon.

- Audio: Music is the most common form of audio. Spotify has emerged as a popular way for people to listen to music either over the Internet or from their computer desktop. Digital content in the form of music is also available through Pandora and last.fm, both of which allow listeners to listen to music online for no charge.
- Images: Photo and image sharing is another example of digital content. Popular sites used for this type of digital content includes Imgur, where people share self-created pictures, Flickr, where people share their photo albums, and DeviantArt, where people share their artwork. Popular apps that are used for images include Instagram and Snapchat.
- Visual Stories: Stories are a new type of digital content that got introduced by Snapchat. Since then, stories as a format has been introduced in a couple of other platforms such as Facebook and Linkedin. In 2018, Google introduced their AMP Stories, which provides content publishers with a mobile-focused format for delivering news and information as visually rich, tap-through stories. AMP Stories can be easily built without coding with editor platforms, like Ampstor.
- Text: Type of digital content which is available in text or written format. Blog websites which store data in form of textual format.

Paid Digital Content

In order to have access to more premium digital goods, consumers usually have to pay an upfront charge for digital content, or a subscription based fee.

- Video: Many licensed videos, such as movies and television shows, require money in order to be viewed or downloaded. Popular services used by many include streaming giant Netflix and Amazon's streaming service, as well as recent notice put forth by the online video platform YouTube.
- Audio: While songs can be streamed for free, generally in order to download most licensed music, consumers need to purchase songs from web stores, such as the popular iTunes. However, Spotify Premium is emerging as a new model for purchasing digital content on the web: consumers pay a monthly fee to unlimited streaming and downloading from Spotify's music library.

According to a report done by IHS Inc. in 2013, the global consumer spending on digital content grew to over $57 billion in 2013, which was up almost 30% from $44 billion in 2012. In past years, the US has always been a leader in consumer expenditure on digital content, but as of 2013, many countries have emerged with great consumer expenditure. South Korea's overall digital spend per capita is now greater than the US.

Non-Purchasable Digital Content

Not all digital content is purchasable, and is simply anything published digitally. This would include:

- News: In recent years newspapers have attempted to expand their readership by creating access to their newspapers digitally. As of 2012, 39% of readers learned about news from online formats, making news a prevalent form of digital content.

- Advertisements: As media consumers increasingly use digital formats to watch TV, check the weather, and search for content, advertisements have shifted to digital forms to keep up with their viewership. Advertisements are now being made digitally and placed on sites ranging from Facebook to YouTube.
- Question and Answer sites: These sites are a type of Internet forum where people can post questions they want answered, or provide responses to previous inquiries. With millions of questions posted each day, anyone has the ability to create content on these sites, so the information provided may not be 100% reliable or accurate. Popular sites include Yahoo! Answers, WikiAnswers and Quora.
- Web mapping: Sites such as MapQuest and Google Maps provide users with map content. These sites give people the ability to quickly look up the location of a landmark and create routes to a destination. Online maps are a form of free content provided by companies such as Google and AOL, serving as much more efficient alternatives to the traditional Thomas Guide.

Successful Digital Content Creation

Once you've identified your target audience, there are many steps that can help improve the quality and impact of your digital content creation process. Although some steps may not be appropriate for all types of content, they generally apply to most of the content generated by B2B brands. These steps include:

Determine the Purpose

Different types of content have different purposes. For example, case studies show that articles you contribute may be intended to infuse your brand into conversions on news topics, even though your organization's experience and expertise may be targeted towards other areas. By defining the purpose at the beginning of the content creation process, you can improve the likelihood of your content reaching the desired results.

Create Useful and Quality Content

In creating digital content, the rule is that each part of the content you create should be useful and appropriate to the target audience. The more useful the content, the easier it is for the public to place it in the context of their positions and share with others in their circles of influence.

Promote Content on Social Media

Share different content on social media platforms to expand your brand and add a campaign range. The content you share on each site should be unique to give your followers a reason to follow on more than one network. Blog posts and other types of content that have a lot of views, usually have higher search engine rankings.

Utilize Photos and Multimedia

Complete your content with images, graphics, and videos. According to a study by MDG Advertising, content associated with charming images gets 94% of total views on average compared to non-viewers. Millennium Development Goal statistics reveal that 67% of online consumers consider clear, detailed images to be more important than product information or customer ratings.

Implement an SEO Program

Rather than guessing the keywords to use throughout your content in the hope that it will resonate with the public, it is best to apply a formal SEO strategy that implements Google tools and other resources. Powerful SEO helps you discover the most searched and important terms about your site and industry.

Track and Analyze Content

Ideally, the Analytics program should go beyond simple page views to evaluate online behaviors for individuals viewing specific portions of digital content. In addition to that, it's important to stay aware of your ranking in the best search engines and continually aim to improve these rankings.

Digital Data

Digital data is data that shows other forms of data by using specific machine language systems that interprets by a variety of technologies. The binary system is the most fundamental of these systems. Which stores complex audio, video, and also text information in a series of binary characters, traditionally the ones and zeros, or the values "on" and "off."

Businesses are looking to use data in innovative ways to fulfill KPIs. Whether it is the sales vertical or the CRM vertical, data can help take informed decisions. Using what is known as Big Data can go a massive way in helping a business optimizes its performance across multiple levels. It can lead to the creation of a leaner and fitter organization. Using data as a strategy can give businesses a competitive edge over their competition.

The greatest strength of digital data is that all very complex analog inputs can be represented with the binary system. With smaller microprocessors and larger data centers, this information capture model has helped parties such as businesses and government agencies explore new frontiers in data collection and represent more accurate simulations. Impressive via a digital interface.

Features of Digital Data

From early primitive digital data designs to new, highly sophisticated, massive binary data volumes, digital data seeks to capture essentials of the physical world. And also simulate them for technological use. This is done in different ways, but with specific techniques to capture various real events and convert them into digital form.

A simple example is the conversion of a physical scene into a digital image. In this way, the new digital data is somewhat similar to the old data systems that convert a physical view or a scene into a chemical film.

One of the significant differences is that digital data records visual information in a bitmap or rasterized map, which stores a particular color property for each bit on a precise and sophisticated grid. With the use of an essential data transfer system, a digital image was created. It uses similar techniques to record audio streams in digital form.

Digital Data Storage

Digital Data Storage (DDS) is a format for storing and backing up computer data on tape from Digital Audio Tape (DAT) technology. The creation of DAT is for CD-quality audio recording. In 1989, Sony and Hewlett Packard defined the DDS format for storing data using DAT tape cartridges. DAT or DDS tape drives can read DDS compliant tapes. However, DDS tape drives cannot play DAT tapes because they cannot capture sound on the DAT tape. DDS uses a 4mm band. A DDS tape drive uses a helical scan for recording, the same process used by a VCR. There are two reading heads and two writing heads. The read heads check the written data.

If errors are present, the write heads rewrite the data. When restoring a saved file, the recovery software reads the directory of the files at the beginning of the tape, wraps the tape at the location of the file, checks the data, and writes the file to the hard disk. DDS cannot update a saved file to the same location where it was initially saved. In general, DDS requires special software to manage the storage and retrieval of data from DDS tape drives. There are four types of DDS drives:

- DDS-1: On a 120-minute cartridge it stores up to 2 GB of uncompressed data.
- DDS-2: On a 120-minute cartridge Stores up to 8 GB of data in compressed format. DDS-2 is supreme for small network servers.
- DDS-3: On a cartridge of 125-minute, it stores up to 24 GB of data. Also, the DDS-3 drive is ideal for medium-sized servers. It uses PRML (Partial Response Likelihood). PRML eliminates electronic noise for a cleaner data record.

- DDS-4: The new DDS-DDS-4 disk stores up to 40 GB of data on a 125-minute cartridge. Small and medium businesses benefit from the DDS-4 reader.

A DDS cartridge must be removed after 2,000 passes or 100 full backups. And also, you must clean your DDS tape drive every 24 hours with a cleaning cartridge and discard the cleaning cartridge after 30 cleanings. DDS bands have an expected life of at least ten years.

Digital Image

The digital image itself is really a data structure within the computer, containing a number or code for each pixel or picture element in the image. This code determines the color of that pixel. Each pixel can be thought of as a discrete sample of a continuous real image.

It is helpful to think about the common ways that a digital image is created. Some of the main ways are via a digital camera, a page or slide scanner, a 3D rendering program, or a paint or drawing package. The simplest process to understand is the one used by the digital camera.

Figure below shows how a digital image is made with a digital camera. The camera is aimed at a scene in the world, and light from the scene is focused onto the camera's picture plane by the lens. The camera's picture plane contains photosensors arranged in a grid-like array, with one sensor for each pixel in the resulting image. Each sensor emits a voltage proportional to the intensity of the light falling on it, and an analog to digital conversion circuit converts the voltage to a binary code or number suitable for storage in a cell of computer memory. This code is called the pixel's value. The typical storage structure is a 2D array of pixel values, arranged so that the layout of pixel values in memory is organized into a regular grid with row and column numbers corresponding with the row and column numbers of the photosensor reading this pixel's value.

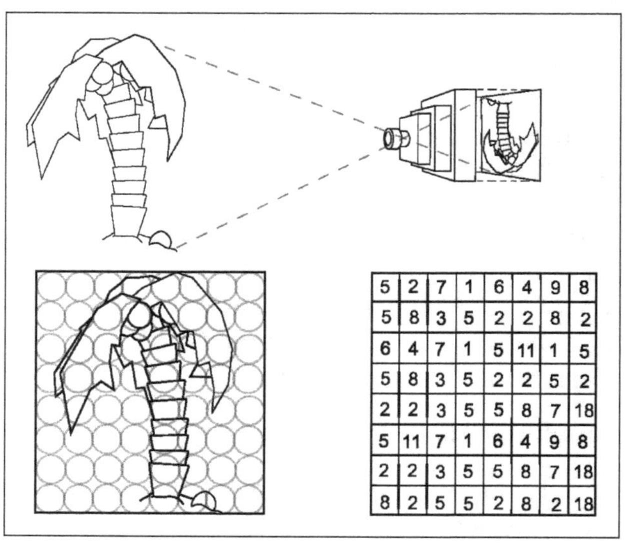

Capturing a 2D Continuous Image of a Scene.

Since each photosensor has a finite area, as indicated by the circles in Figure, the reading that it makes is a weighted average of the intensity of the light falling over its surface. So, although each pixel is conceptually the sample of a single point on the image plane of the camera, in reality it represents a spread of light over a small area centered at the sample point. The weighting function that is used to describe how the weighted average is obtained over the area of the sample is called a point spread function. The exact form of the point spread function is a complex combination of photosensor size and shape, focus of the camera, and photoelectric properties of the photosensor surface. Sampling through a point spread function of a shape that might be encountered in a digital camera is shown in diagram form in Figure below.

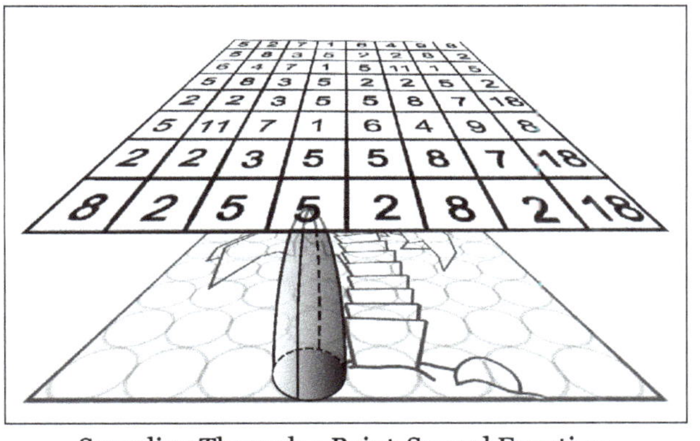

Sampling Through a Point-Spread Function.

A digital image is of little use if it cannot be viewed. To recreate the discretely sampled image from a real continuous scene, there must be as reconstruction process to invert the sampling process. This process must convert the discrete image samples back into a continuous image suitable for output on a device like a CRT or LCD for viewing, or a printer or film recorder for hardcopy. This process can also be understood via the notion of the point spread function. Think of each sample (i.e. pixel) in the digital image being passed back through a point spread function that spreads the pixel value out over a small region.

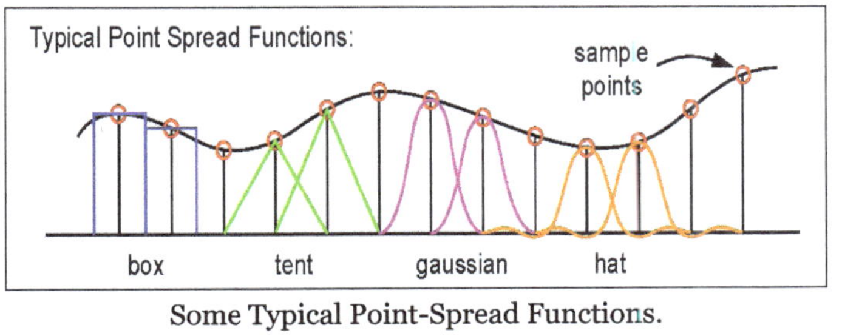

Some Typical Point-Spread Functions.

Bitmaps and Pixmaps

Bitmap: The Simplest Image Storage Mechanism

A bitmap is a simple black and white image, stored as a 2D array of bits (ones and zeros). In this representation, each bit represents one pixel of the image. Typically, a bit set to zero represents black and a bit set to one represents white. The left side of Figure shows a simple block letter U laid out on an 8 × 8 grid. The right side shows the 2-dimensional array of bit values that would correspond to the image, if it were stored as a bitmap. Each row or scanline on the image corresponds to a row of the 2D array, and each element of a row corresponds with a pixel on the scanline.

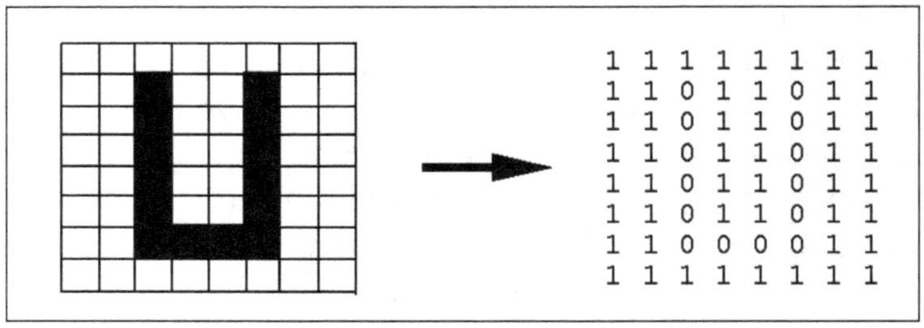

Image of Black Block Letter U and Corresponding Bitmap.

Although our experience with television, the print media, and computers leads us to feel that the natural organization of an image is as a 2D grid of dots or pixels, this notion is simply a product of our experience. In fact, although images are displayed as 2D grids, most image storage media are not organized in this way. For example, the computer's memory is organized into a long linear array of addressable bytes (8 bit groups) of storage. Thus, somewhere in the memory of a typical computer, the block letter U of Figure might be represented as the following string of contiguous bytes:

11111111	11011011	11011011	11011011	11011011	11011011	11000011	11111111

Since the memory is addressable only at the byte level, the color of each pixel (black or white) must be extracted from the byte holding the pixel's value. And, since the memory is addressed as a linear array, rather than as a 2D array, a computation must be made to determine which byte in the representation contains the pixel that we wish to examine, and which bit in that byte corresponds with the pixel.

The procedure `print_bitmap()` in Figure will print the contents of the image stored in the array named `bitmap`. We assume that the image represented by bitmap contains exactly `width` * height pixels, organized into height scanlines, each of length width. In other words, the number of pixels vertically along the image is height, and the number of pixels horizontally across the image is `width. The print_bitmap()` procedure assumes that each scanline in memory is padded out to a multiple of 8 bits (pixels), so that it exactly fits into an integer number of bytes. The variable w gives the width of a scanline in bytes.

```
void print_bitmap(unsigned char *bitmap, int width, int height){

  int w = (width + 7) / 8;  // number of bytes per scanline

  int row;                  // scanline number (row)
  int col;                   // pixel number on scanline (column)
  int byte;                 // byte number within bitmap array
  int bit;                    // bit number within byte
  int value;               // value of bit (0 or 1)

  for(row = 0; row < height; row++){  // loop for each scanline
    for(col = 0; col < width; col++){   // loop for each pixel on line
      byte = row * w + col / 8;
      bit = 7 - col % 8;
      value = bitmap[byte] >> bit & 1;  // isolate bit
      printf("%1d", value);
    }
    printf("\n");
  }
}
```

Procedure to Print the Contents of a Bitmap.

Another issue is that the representation of groups of pixels in terms of lists of ones and zeros is extremely difficult for humans to deal with cognitively. To convince yourself of this, try looking at a group of two or more bytes of information, remembering what you see, and then writing down the numbers from memory. To make the handling of this binary encoded information more manageable, it is convenient to think of each group of 4 bits as encoding a hexadecimal number.

Table: Hexadecimal Notation.

Binary	Hexadecimal	Decimal
0000	0	0
0001	1	1
0010	2	2
0011	3	3
0100	4	4
0101	5	5
0110	6	6
0111	7	7
1000	8	8
1001	9	9
1010	A	10
1011	B	11
1100	C	12
1101	D	13
1110	E	14
1111	F	15

The hexadecimal numbers are the numbers written using a base of 16, as opposed to the usual decimal numbers that use base 10, or the binary numbers of the computer that use base 2. Since 16 is the 4th power of 2, each hexadecimal digit can be represented exactly by a unique pattern of 4 binary digits. With the device of hexadecimal notation, we can now display the internal representation of the block letter U, by representing each 8-bit byte by two hexadecimal digits. This reduces the display to:

FF	DB	DB	DB	DB	DB	C3	FF

Pixmap: Representing Grey Levels or Color

If the pixels of an image can be arbitrary grey tones, rather than simply black or white, we could allocate enough space in memory to store a real number, rather than a single bit, for each pixel. Then arbitrary levels of grey could be represented as a 2D array of real numbers, say between 0 and 1, with pixel color varying smoothly from black at 0.0 through mid-grey at 0.5 to white at 1.0. However, this scheme would be very inefficient, since floating point numbers (the computer equivalent of real numbers) typically take 32 or more bits to store. Thus image size would grow 32 times from that needed to store a simple bitmap. The pixmap is an efficient alternative to the idea of using a full floating point number for each pixel. The main idea is that we can take advantage of the eye's finite ability to discriminate levels of grey.

Bits	# of Combinations	Combinations
1	$2^1 = 2$	0,1
2	$2^2 = 4$	00,01,10,11
3	$2^3 = 8$	000, 001, 010, 011, 100, 101, 110, 111
...	...	...
8	$2^8 = 256$	00000000, 00000001,... , 11111110, 11111111

It is a simple mathematical fact that in a group of n bits, the number of distinct combinations of 1's and 0's is 2n. In other words, n bits of storage will allow us to represent and discriminate among exactly 2n different values or pieces of information. This relationship is shown in tabular form in Table. If, in our image representation, we use 1 byte (8 bits) to represent each pixel, then we can represent up to 256 different grey levels. This turns out to be enough to "fool" the eye of most people. If these 256 different grey levels are drawn as vertical lines across a computer screen, people will think that they are seeing a smoothly varying grey scale.

The structure of a pixmap, then, is a 2D array of pixel values, with each pixel's value stored as a group of 2 or more bits. To conform to byte boundaries, the number of bits used is typically 8, 16, 24 or 32 bits per pixel, although any size is possible. If we think of the bits within a byte as representing a binary number, we can store grey levels between 0 and 255 in 8 bits. We can easily convert the pixel value in each byte to a grey level between 0.0 and 1.0 by dividing the pixel value by the maximum grey value of 255.

Assuming that we have a pixmap storing grey levels in eight bits per pixel, the procedure print_greymap() in Figure below will print the contents of the image stored in the array named greymap. We assume that the image represented by greymap contains exactly width * height pixels, organized into height scanlines, each of length width.

```
void print_greymap(unsigned char *greymap, int width, int height){

  int row;                // scanline number (row)
  int col;                 // pixel number on scanline (column)
  int value;             // value of pixel (0 to 255)

  for(row = 0; row < height; row++){  // loop for each scanline
    for(col = 0; col < width; col++){   // loop for each pixel on line
      value = greymap[row * width + col];  // fetch pixel value
      printf("%5.3f ", value / 255.0);
    }
    printf("\n");
  }
}
```

Procedure to Print the Contents of an 8 bit/pixel Greylevel Pixmap.

The RGB Color Space

If we want to store color images, we need a scheme of color representation that will allow us to represent color in a pattern of bits (just like we represented grey levels as patterns of bits). Fortunately, many such representations exist, and the most common one used for image storage is the RGB or

Red-Green-Blue system. This takes advantage of the fact that we can "fool" the human eye into "seeing" most of the colors that we can recognize perceptually by superimposing 3 lights colored red, green and blue. The level or intensity of each of the three lights determines the color that we perceive.

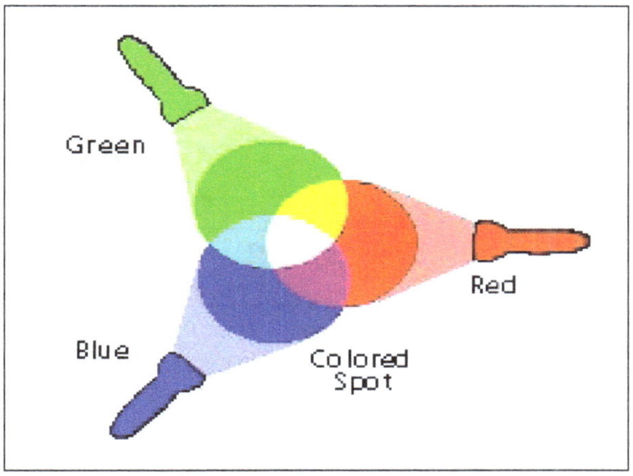

Additive Color Mixing for the Red-Green-Blue System.

If we think of red, green, and blue levels as varying from 0 (off) to 1 (full brightness), then a color can be represented as a red, green, blue triple. Some example color representations using this on/off scheme are shown in Figure. It is interesting and somewhat surprising that yellow is made by combining red and green! Example Colors Encoded as RGB Triples:

(1, 0, 0)=red	(0, 1, 0)=green	(0, 0, 1)=blue
(1, 1, 0)=yellow	(0, 1, 1)=cyan	(1, 0, 1)=magenta
(0, 0, 0)=black	(1, 1, 1)=white	(0.5, 0.5, 0.5)=grey

Now, we can extend this idea by allowing a group of bits to represent one pixel. We can assign some of these bits to the red level, some to green, and some to blue, using a binary encoding scheme like we used to store grey level. For example, if we have only 8 bits per pixel, we might use three for the red level, 3 for green, and 2 for blue (since our eye discriminates blue much more weakly than red or green). A muted green color could be stored using this kind of scheme. The value actually stored is hexadecimal 59, which is then shown in binary broken into red, green and blue binary fields. Each of these binary numbers is divided by the maximum unsigned number possible in the designated number of bits, and finally shown represented as a (RGB) triple of color primary values, each on a scale of 0 – 1.

On a high end graphics computer, it is not unusual to allocate 24 bits per pixel for color representation, allowing 8 bits for each of the red, green and blue components. This is more than enough to allow for perceptually smooth color gradations, and fits nicely into a computer whose memory is organized into 8-bit bytes. If you read specifications for computer displays or use graphics software, you will have noticed that many of these systems use red, green, and blue levels between 0-255. These are obviously systems that use an 8-bit per color primary representation.

$59_{16}=$

010	110	01
R G B		

$= (2/7, 6/7, 1/3) = (0.286, 0.757, 0.333)$

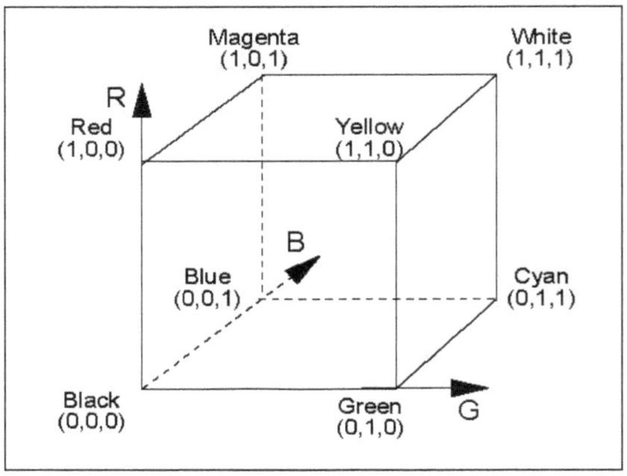

RGB Color Cube.

Since the RGB system organizes color into three primaries, and allows us to scale each primary independently, we can think of all of the colors that are represented by the system as being organized in the shape of a cube, as shown in Figure above. We call this the RGB color cube, or the RGB color space (when we add coordinate axes to measure R, G and B levels). Note that the corners of the RGB color cube represent pure black and pure white, the three primaries red, green and blue, and the 3 secondary colors yellow, cyan and magenta. The diagonal from the black corner to the white corner represents all of the grey levels. Other locations within the cube correspond with all of the other colors that can be displayed.

A pixmap storing RGB levels using eight bits per primary, with an additional eight bits per pixel reserved, is called an RGBA (or Red, Green, Blue, Alpha) pixmap. The procedure print_pixmap() in Figure below will print the contents of the RGBA image stored in the array named pixmap. We assume that the image represented by pixmap contains exactly width * height pixels, organized into height scanlines, each of length width.

```
void print_pixmap(unsigned int *pixmap, int width, int height){

  int row;                        // scanline number (row)
  int col;                         // pixel number on scanline (column)
  unsigned int value;     // pixel as fetched from pixmap
  int r, g, b;                    // RGB values of pixel (0 to 255)

  for(row = 0; row < height; row++){  // loop for each scanline
    for(col = 0; col < width; col++){   // loop for each pixel on line
      value = pixmap[row * width + col];  // fetch pixel value
      r = value >> 24;
      g = (value >> 16) & 0xFF;
      b = (value >> 8) & 0xFF;
      printf("(%5.3f,%5.3f,%5.3f) ",
             r / 255.0, g / 255.0, b / 255.0);
    }
    printf("\n");
  }
}
```

Procedure to Print the RGB Values in a 32 Bit/Pixel RGBA Pixmap.

Other Ways to Organize RGBA Pixmaps

The method of storing red, green, blue and alpha values by packing them into a single `unsigned int` (which is a 32 bit structure), is only one way to organize the storage of RGBA pixels. Another way would be to define a pixel to be an array of four unsigned characters, or a structure whose elements are four unsigned characters. You can do this using a type definition in C. For example:

```
typedef unsigned char RGBApixel[4];
```

defines the type `RGBApixel` to be an array of four `unsigned char`. If you create a variable `RGBApixel pixel`, then `pixel[0]` will store the red value, `pixel[1]` will store the green value, `pixel[2]` will store the blue value, and `pixel[3]` will store the alpha value for the pixel. Alternatively, we could use the form:

```
typedef struct rgbapixel{

      unsigned char r;

      unsigned char g;

      unsigned char b;

      unsigned char a;

} RGBApixel;
```

which defines the type `RGBApixel` to be a `struct` with four elements, each an unsigned char. Using this definition, if you create a variable `RGBApixel pixel`, then `pixel.r` will store the red value, `pixel.g` will store the green value, `pixel.b` will store the blue value, and `pixel.a` will store the alpha value.

In addition, it is a bit cumbersome to have to compute the index `row * width + col` into the pixmap array every time you want to reference an individual pixel at row `row` and column `col`. It would be much easier if we could use a two-dimensional array notation, so that we could index the pixmap array directly using row and `col` as array indices. Unfortunately, it is not possible to do this directly in C if the width of the array (i.e. the number of columns) is not known at compile time. When dealing with digital images this it is usually the case that when you are writing your program you will not know the exact image dimensions. This will usually be determined at run-time. Fortunately we can get around this problem by being clever about how we allocate the data structure to store the pixmap.

The trick that we can use is that C actually implements an array using pointer arithmetic. The name of an array is a pointer to the first cell in the block of memory holding the array. Then, the use of an array index causes the index, times the number of bytes in a cell of the array, to be added to the address of the first cell in the array. So, if we have an array `int array[10];`, then, remembering that an integer takes four bytes in memory, `array[0]` stands for the address of the first cell in the array: `array + 0 * 4`, and array[2] stands for the address of the third cell in the `array`: `array + 2 * 4`.

Here is the construction that we can use. Assuming one of the `typedefs` above for `RGBApixel`, we declare our pixmap variable to be a pointer to a pointer to an RGBApixel. Now, assuming that our pixmap has height rows, and width columns, we allocate an array of height pointers to RGBApixel, then allocate an array of width * height RGBApixel, and finally assign to each element i of the first array a pointer to the beginning of the i'th scanline in the large array. The code for doing this would be:

```
RGBApixel **pixmap;

pixmap = new RGBApixel*[height];

pixmap[0] = new RGBApixel[width * height];

for(int i = 1; i < height; i++)

      pixmap[i] = pixmap[i - 1] + width;
```

The final data structure would look like the diagram shown in Figure below, which shows the layout that would be obtained with height = 5, and width = 6. Once this allocation is done, all references to the pixmap at row row and column col would be in the form pixmap[row][col]. There is no longer any need to do an explicit calculation of the position of the pixel in the array, as pixmap[row] is the address of the cell of the small array corresponding to row, and when we index off of this cell by [col], we get the offset to the specified column in the specified row.

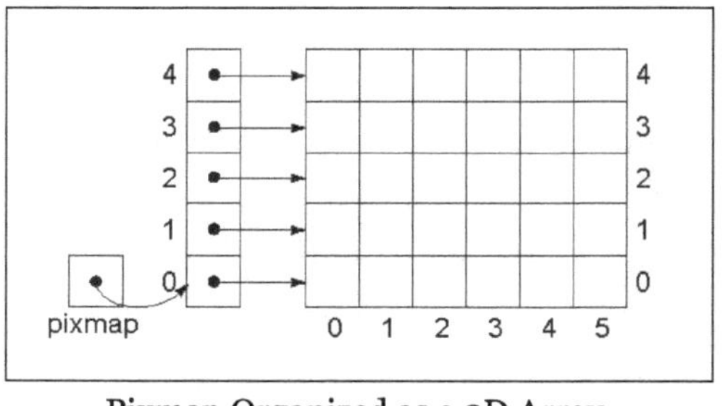

Pixmap Organized as a 2D Array.

Digital Audio

Before the development of high-speed, low-cost digital computers and analog-to-digital conversion circuits, all recording and manipulation of sound was done using analog techniques. These systems functioned by creating an electrical analog of sound waves, converting it to a magnetic representation, storing and processing that analog replica. The analog signal was continuous, meaning that no matter when one looked at the signal, there was a voltage or current value which represented the instantaneous value of the signal. In order to make use of digital representations of the sound, it is necessary to convert the continuous analog representation into a non-continuous stream of numbers. Digital representations of analog signals are not continuous, saving the measured voltages only at the time of each sample. This would appear to throw away the values that exist between samples, which one would expect to severely reduce the accuracy of the new digital representation. As we will see, this is an incorrect assumption as is borne out both by the sampling theorem and by practical implementation.

A/D Conversion

Since no true digital microphones exist, the analog microphone signal must be converted into a digital representation. This process is known as analog-to-digital (A/D) conversion. It is this process and the complimentary conversion back to analog (D/A conversion) that impart many of the potential shortcomings to digital audio. In order to faithfully re-create the original signal, both the sampling rate and measurement (quantization) must be extremely accurate. Quantization is the process by which the amplitude of the signal at a sample time is measured. Digital representations use binary words to encode the measured amplitude. Each word consists of a number of bits that are binary weighted, the more bits used the finer the resolution of the measurement. Early digital audio systems struggled to achieve 16-bit resolution while modern systems use 24 bits at a minimum.

MSB			binary weighting				LSB	
128	64	32	16	8	4	2	1	
0	1	0	1	1	0	1	0	$= 90_{10}$

Binary weighting: Each bit is binary-weighted, with the least significant bit (LSB) coding for 1 and the nth bit for 2^n. The 8-bit word 01011010 encodes the $base_{10}$ value 90.

Since the analog input voltage range of a converter is fixed, the more bits used to quantize the signal, the finer the resolution of the least significant bit. Each additional bit in a word doubles the resolution, since the number of discrete levels a word may distinguish is 2^n, where n is the number of bits. This system is known as fixed point representation, in contrast to a more complicated floating point method of encoding the amplitude that uses exponents to scale the value. Floating point systems have replaced fixed point ones for most digital audio processes since computers natively use floating point math, but most A/D converters are still using fixed-point methods. Modern A/D converters use 24-bit representations, which theoretically exceed the dynamic range possible for electronic circuits at room temperature. This can be misleading, though, since real 24-bit converters only perform linearly to about 20 bits, which is approximately the dynamic range of high-quality analog circuits. Table shows the increasing potential resolution as the number of bits/word is increased.

Table: Word length (n bits) determines the resolution of analog-to-digital conversion. The dynamic range available is approximately equal to $20 \log 2^n$.

n = number of bits/ word	Number of levels = 2^n	Dynamic range ~ $20 \log 2^n$
8	256	48
16	65,536	96
24	16,777,216	144

[The signal-to-error ratio is slightly greater than $20 \log 2^n$ because the signal is more accurately described by the rms statistics that apply to both the signal and the quantization error, which leads to a more precise figure of 6.02n+1.76.]

Quantization

Figure shows how the size of the quantization step, each of which corresponds to the analog value represented by the least significant bit, affects the error of the measurement.

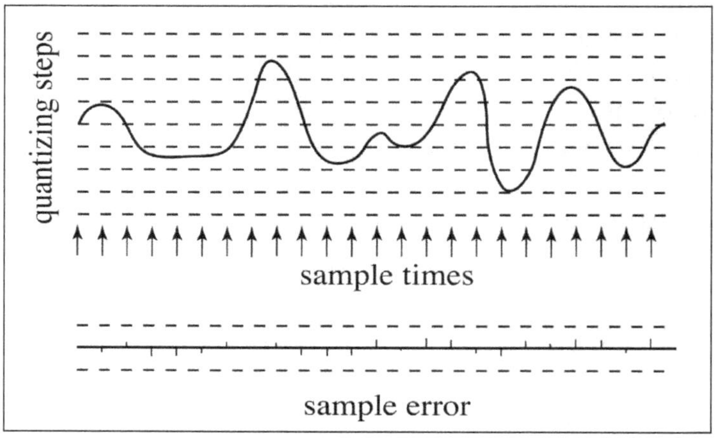

Error in an A/D conversion is at most one half the value encoded by the least significant bit, but is correlated with the signal.

Dither

Since the maximum error of each conversion is 1/2 LSB, increasing the number of bits/word reduces the error of measurement as it reduces the equivalent analog value of the LSB, The error of quantization is correlated with the signal. This sounds quite different from the wide-band noise we encounter in analog circuits because it changes as the signal changes. There is a way to de-correlate the error from the signal - dither: add some random noise! Of course, it seems counter-intuitive to add noise on purpose. However, the noise is quite small, usually a fraction of the LSB rms equivalent voltage. This amount of noise is generally inaudible at normal listening levels but its effects can sometimes be heard on long, slow decays like reverb tails. From a perception perspective, random noise sounds preferable to signal-correlated distortion. Dither should be applied any time the number of bits representing a signal is reduced, as well as during quantization.

While conceptually rather simple, the implementation of dither can become critical when our signals pass through multiple computations, as they do in most recording and mixing software. Each plug-in we use performs mathematical operations on the data, employing extra precision variables that extend the word length for precise computation and returning to the original word length at the output. This requires dither. Many recordings are processed through equalizer and compressor plug-ins multiple times, so proper dither is required to avoid building up audible distortion. The spectral character of the applied dither can be selected to provide the least audible effect on the sound. By shifting the dither spectrum to favor higher frequency noise, the maximally sensitive frequencies of the auditory system can be avoided. Other techniques of shaping the dither spectrum have been tested and most currently used dither algorithms are quite transparent to the listener.

Sample-and-Hold

Another potential issue that appears in the quantization process is caused by the continuous nature of the input signal. It takes finite time to complete a sample measurement and the signal can change while we are trying to sample the signal. The answer is to use a circuit called a sample-and-hold to take an analog sample of the signal at precisely the sample time by holding the analog voltage on a capacitor until it can be measured by the A/D converter. The capacitor is connected to electronic switches that control the input and output connections.

Aliasing

Even if quantization could be made perfectly accurate, there is still a potential problem associated with the conversion process: the signal must not contain any frequencies higher than half the sampling rate. This is a result of the way the audio signal interacts with the sampling frequency. In a way, the process of sampling is equivalent to combining the sampling signal with the audio signal, generating sum and difference frequencies. If the sample rate is low, the difference frequencies are audible and constitute a form of distortion: the so-called "fold-over" distortion or "aliasing".

In order to minimize aliasing, the sample rate should be much higher than the highest frequency present in the signal, at the very least greater than twice the highest frequency present in the signal. This can be accomplished either by increasing the sample rate or by limiting the signal bandwidth. Since increasing the sample rate increases the amount of data which must be stored, it is preferable to keep the sample rate as low as possible. Limiting the bandwidth will decrease the high-frequency content of the signal, also not desirable. We must therefore find a balance between sample rate and signal bandwidth. Of course, as the speed and capacity of digital systems continues to improve, the use of higher sample rates and longer word lengths is relaxing many of the constraints originally adopted to make early digital recording feasible. The mathematics of sampling dictates that we sample at a rate higher than twice the highest frequency present in the signal (the Nyquist Theorem).

If we want the entire audio bandwidth of 20 to 20,000 Hz, we must sample at greater than 40,000 Hz. This means that for 1 second of stereo sound, we will have more than 80,000 numbers. But this assumes that there are no signal components present above 20,000 Hz.

Anti-Aliasing Filters

In order to prevent aliasing, we must remove any frequencies above half the sampling rate from the signal. This is done by filtering the signal. Since we want 20 kHz frequencies to be reproduced, we must filter very sharply above this frequency. Unfortunately, a simple filter cannot remove frequencies near to the 20 kHz cutoff very well without affecting lower frequencies present in the signal. We must use a very sharp, complicated filter to remove the unwanted frequencies while preserving frequencies within the desired audio bandwidth. These filters are known as "brick-wall" filters because they cut off so rapidly above their corner frequency. It was not unusual to find 12 pole filters employed as anti-aliasing filters. As you might imagine, the design of these critical filters is very complicated. It is not possible to filter a signal so heavily without making some changes to the signal which is passed through.

Often, the transient response suffers audibly as the complex filter responds to the driving signal. These filters are responsible for much of the criticism of digital audio, especially for the so-called harshness of early digital recorders. In recent years, the speed of computer chips has increased to the point where sophisticated mathematical processes can be applied to digitized signals which remove the unwanted frequencies from the signal after it is digitized, reducing the need for sharp analog filters. These procedures come under the heading of oversampling, a technique which allows high-speed sampling without increasing the amount of data to be stored. Even in these systems some analog filtering is still required, but simple filters with just a few poles are used, thereby reducing the deleterious effects of brick-wall filters. And as sample rates extend to 96 kHz and even 192 kHz, the requirement for analog filters is further relaxed.

Clocking

The timing accuracy of the clock used to trigger the sampling is another potential problem area for A/D converters. In order to conform to the sampling theorem, perfect sample timing is assumed. In real circuits, this is not as easy as it might sound. Very slight variations in the clocking lead to samples being measured at the wrong time, thereby producing incorrect sample values.

Clock timing variations are known as jitter. Clock pulses are generally created by using a crystal oscillator running at very high frequency and dividing the frequency down to the desired sample rate. When done inside a digital audio device, the circuit pathway used for clock signal distribution can be carefully chosen to avoid capacitance and inductance that would alter the shape of the pulses, leading to inaccurate trigger timing. This is not a simple design issue, but modern digital devices are good at providing an internal clock with low jitter. When digital audio devices are interconnected, they must share the same clocking. Transmitting a clock signal outside the carefully-designed devices introduces more possible issues that can lead to jitter in the receiving device if not properly designed. A circuit known as a phase-locked loop can be used to synchronize an external clock with a receiving device's local clock. Eliminating jitter from A/D conversions is critical, since once the signal is quantized, any jitter present will remain in the recorded signal. Although jitter may not always be obviously audible, it can sometimes be heard to compromise imaging in stereo sound file playback.

D/A Conversion

Once a signal is stored digitally, it must eventually be converted back to analog for us to hear it. This process is essentially the reverse of sampling: the numbers are converted back to analog voltages. But since we have samples at discrete times, what should the output voltage do between the samples? What it should do is what the original signal did, but unfortunately, we no longer know what that was. One solution is to hold the last value until the next value is converted. This results in a staircase-like output which was not present in the original signal. The more bits we use for quantization, the smaller the step size, but we will always have some step-like distortion of the original signal if we use the stored data directly. We must low-pass filter the output to remove the effects of quantization.

D/A converters are conceptually the reverse of the A/D converter. The analog output of the D/A converter is always connected to the outside world, so any momentary glitches that occur would be transmitted as part of the analog signal output. This requires circuitry to hold the output while a conversion is in process, a sample-andhold like that used in the A/D process. The output is then filtered by an anti-imaging filter, similar to the antialiasing filter in the A/D converter. Imaging, like aliasing, is created by combining the sample pulse with the analog signal, but this time it is all the higher frequency sum and difference components that contribute to the problem. Images of the analog signal centered on multiples of the sample rate, sum and difference products at multiples of the sample frequency, appear as the stair-step so often associated with sampled audio signals. The anti-imaging filter removes these components and restores the continuous signal originally captured by the A/D converter.

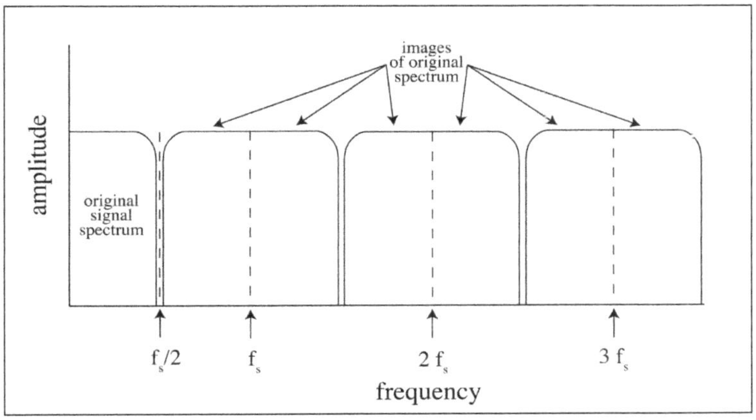

Imaging created by sampling. Frequencies created by combining the sample pulse with an audio signal create new images at multiples of the sample rate f_s.

Figure shows images of the original spectrum centering about the multiples of the sample rate. Removing these images would require sharp filtering, but digital filters may again do the job instead. The technique called oversampling can shift the images to higher effective sample rates, thereby reducing the demands on the anti-aliasing filters. Oversampling uses digital filtering to remove the images around f_s, shifting the first set of images to a higher multiple of the sample rate. This leaves a greater distance between the signal spectrum and the first remaining image, allowing more gentle filtering to eliminate the images from the system output.

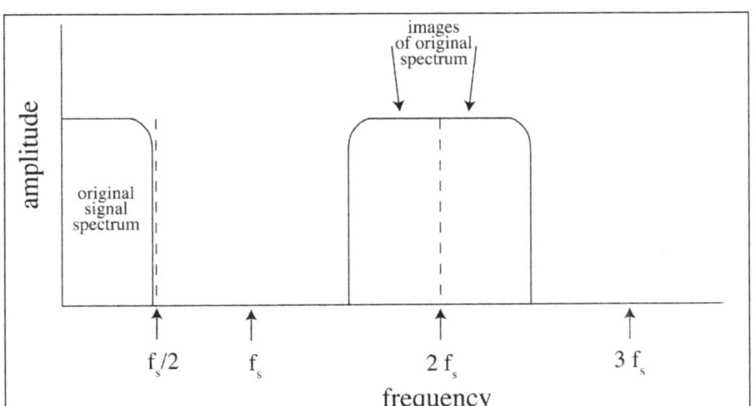

The effect of two times oversampling. Images centered on the sample rate are eliminated.

Figure shows the effect of a two-times oversampling D/A conversion. Practical D/A converters use 8 or 16 times oversampling to place the first set of images far above the audible frequency range. In comparing above figures, it is obvious that the low-pass filter necessary to remove images from oversampled conversions is much gentler.

Time Domain versus Frequency Domain

Figures earlier show amplitude as a function of frequency, a different way of plotting signal data from the more familiar amplitude versus time. In the analog world, signals are time-varying voltages. In the digital domain, the same information can be described in terms of the individual sine waves that compose the complex sound rather than by the voltage variations. This is known as the frequency domain.

The conversion between the two representations is made by the Fourier transform, an algorithm that determines the amplitude and phase of the sine wave components that make up any complex sound signal. Computers can make use of the frequency information to do things that are not easy or even possible in the time domain, like re-synthesizing sounds while eliminating unwanted components like noise, retuning instrument or vocal performances, and creating complex digital filters that would be impossible with analog equipment. Digital signal processing depends extensively on the Fourier transform and the inverse transform to convert back to the analog time domain. Figure below details the difference between time and frequency domain representations of a sinusoidal signal.

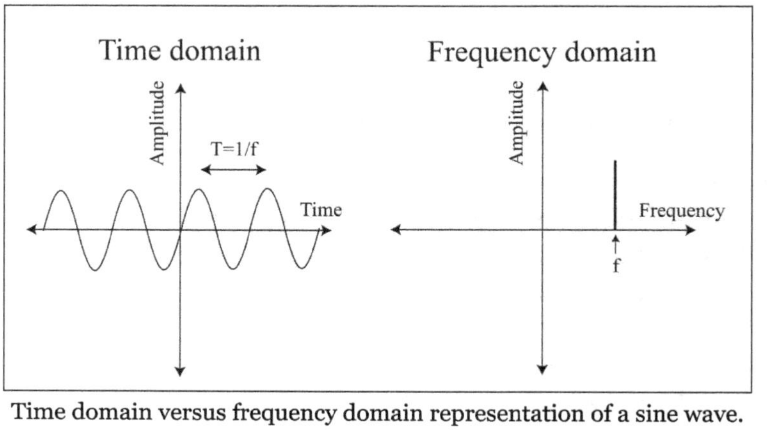

Time domain versus frequency domain representation of a sine wave.

The frequency domain needs a single amplitude and time to represent a sine wave that would take many individual samples to describe. Many of the complex algorithms used in digital audio processing are easier to accomplish in the frequency domain.

Digital Video

Digital video is a type of video recording system that works by using a digital video signal rather than an analog one. Educators and instructional designers are interested in creating effective learning environments. Often this involves the use of various media to implement instructional strategies. The rapid growth of the Internet, and specifically the World Wide Web as a delivery medium has led to an explosion of Web-supported and Web-based courses and instructional materials. In the mid 1990s these Web materials were generally limited to text and static images. But with the increase in network bandwidth, user connection speeds, and hardware processing speed, audio and video have become viable media for instructional environments. These trends have been coupled with growth in the installed base of CDROM (and now DVD-ROM) drives and "multimedia equipped" personal computers.

Technical Overview

Digital video cameras come in two different image capture formats: Interlaced and progressive scan. Interlaced cameras record the image in alternating sets of lines—that is, the odd-numbered lines and even-numbered lines are scanned in alternating fashion. Each set of odd or even lines is referred to as a "field," and a pairing of two consecutive fields of opposite parity is called a "frame."

A progressive scanning digital video camera records each frame as distinct, with both fields being identical. Thus, interlaced video captures twice as many fields per second as progressive video does when both operate at the same number of frames per second. Thus, video has a "hyper-real" look because it draws a different image 60 times per second, whereas film records 24 or 25 progressive frames per second.

Progressive scan camcorders (such as the Panasonic AG-DVX100) are generally more desirable because of the similarities they share with film. They record frames progressively, producing crisper images. They can both shoot at 24 frames per second, which results in motion strobing (blurring of the subject when fast movement occurs). Thus, progressive scanning video cameras tend to be more expensive than their interlaced counterparts. (Although the digital video format allows for only 29.97 interlaced frames per second (or 25 for PAL), 24 frames per second progressive video is possible by displaying identical fields for each frame, and displaying 3 fields of an identical image for certain frames.)

Standard film stocks, such as 16 mm and 35 mm, record at 24 or 25 frames per second. For video, there are two frame rate standards, NTSC and PAL, which shoot at 30/1.001 (about 29.97) frames per second and 25 frames per second, respectively. Digital video can be copied with no degradation in quality. No matter how many generations a digital source is copied, it will be as clear as the original first generation of digital footage.

Digital video can be processed and edited on a non-linear editing (NLE) station, a device built exclusively to edit video and audio. This type of device may import from analog as well as digital sources, but it is not intended to do anything other than edit videos. Digital video can also be edited on a personal computer with the proper hardware and software. Using an NLE station, digital video can be manipulated to follow a sequence of video clips. Avid's software and hardware are almost synonymous with the professional NLE market, but Apple's Final Cut Pro, Adobe Premiere, Sony Vegas, and similar programs are also popular. Digital video is generally edited on a setup with ample disk space. Digital video applied with standard DV/DVCPRO compression takes up about 250 megabytes per minute or 13 gigabytes per hour.

Many types of video compression exist for serving digital video over the internet, and onto DVDs. Although digital technique allows for a wide variety of edit effects, most common is the hard cut and an editable video format like DV-video allows repeated cutting without loss of quality, because any compression across frames is lossless. While DV video is not compressed beyond its own codec while editing, the file sizes that result are not practical for delivery onto optical discs or over the internet, with codecs such as the Windows Media format, MPEG2, MPEG4, Real Media, the more recent H.264, and the Sorenson media codec. Probably the most widely used formats for delivering video over the internet are MPEG4 and Windows Media, while MPEG2 is used almost exclusively for DVDs, providing an exceptional image in minimal size but resulting in a high level of CPU consumption to decompress.

The video manufacturing community defines one standard for resolution after another, although the devices use incompatible resolutions. They insist on their resolution and rescale a video several times from the sensor to the LCD.

As of 2007, the highest resolution demonstrated for digital video generation is 33 megapixels (7680 x 4320) at 60 frames per second ("UHDV"). This resolution, however, has been demonstrated only in special laboratory settings. The highest speed has been attained in industrial and scientific high speed cameras that are capable of filming 1024x1024 video at up to 1 million frames per second for brief recording periods.

Advantages and Applications

Videos can now be edited on readily available, increasingly affordable hardware and software. Even high-budget films, such as Cold Mountain, have been edited entirely on Final Cut Pro, Apple's nonlinear editing software.

Digital video costs significantly less than 35 mm film, as digital tapes can be erased and re-recorded multiple times, viewed on location without processing, and the tape stock itself is far less expensive than 35 mm film. (As of December 2005, a 60-minute MiniDV tape cost about $3 each when bought in bulk. By comparison, 35 mm film stock cost about $1,000 per minute, including processing.)

Digital video is useful outside of movie-making. For example, digital television (including higher quality HDTV) started to spread in most developed countries in the early 2000s. Digital video is also used in modern mobile phones and video conferencing systems. In addition, it is used for the Internet distribution of media, including streaming video and peer-to-peer movie distribution.

Interfaces and Cables

Many interfaces have been designed specifically to handle the requirements of uncompressed digital video (at roughly 400 Mbit/s):

- Serial Digital Interface.
- FireWire.
- High-Definition Multimedia Interface.
- Digital Visual Interface.
- Unified Display Interface.
- DisplayPort.
- USB.

The DVB-ASI interface has been designed for carrying MPEG-Transport compressed video. Compressed video is also carried using UDP-IP over Ethernet. Two approaches exist for this:

- Using RTP as a wrapper for video packets.
- 1-7 MPEG Transport Packets are placed directly in the UDP packet.

Storage Formats

Encoding

Current formats, listed below, are PCM (pulse-code modulation) based. (Pulse-code modulation (PCM) is a digital representation of an analog signal, where the magnitude of the signal is sampled regularly at uniform intervals, then quantized to a series of symbols in a numeric (usually binary) code.)

- CCIR 601 used for broadcast stations.
- MPEG-4 good for online distribution of large videos and video recorded to flash memory.
- MPEG-2 used for DVDs and Super-VCDs.
- MPEG-1 used for video CDs.
- H.261.
- H.263.
- H.264 also known as MPEG-4 Part 10, or AVC.
- Theora standardized but still in development used for video over the Internet.

Tapes

- Betacam, BetacamSP, Betacam SX, Betacam IMX, Digital Betacam, or DigiBeta—Commercial video systems by Sony, based on original Betamax technology.
- HDCAM was introduced by Sony as a high-definition alternative to DigiBeta.
- D1, D2, D3, D5, D9 (also known as Digital-S)—various SMPTE commercial digital video standards.
- DV, MiniDV—used in most of today's videotape-based consumer camcorders; designed for high quality and easy editing; can also record high-definition data (HDV) in MPEG-2 format.
- DVCAM, DVCPRO—used in professional broadcast operations; similar to DV but generally considered more robust; though DV-compatible, these formats have better audio handling.
- DVCPRO50, DVCPROHD support higher bandwidths as compared to Panasonic's DVCPRO.
- Digital8—DV-format data recorded on Hi8-compatible cassettes; largely a consumer format.
- MicroMV—MPEG-2-format data recorded on a very small, matchbook-sized cassette; obsolete.
- D-VHS—MPEG-2 format data recorded on a tape similar to S-VHS.

Disccs

- Video CD (VCD)
- DVD
- HD-DVD
- Blu-ray Disc
- Sony ProDATA

Broadcasting

Broadcasting is the electronic transmission of radio and television signals that are intended for general public reception, as distinguished from private signals that are directed to specific receivers. In its most common form, broadcasting may be described as the systematic dissemination of entertainment, information, educational programming, and other features for simultaneous reception by a scattered audience with appropriate receiving apparatus. Broadcasts may be audible only, as in radio, or visual or a combination of both, as in television. Sound broadcasting in this sense may be said to have started about 1920, while television broadcasting began in the 1930s. With the advent of cable television in the early 1950s and the use of satellites for broadcasting beginning in the early 1960s, television reception improved and the number of programs receivable increased dramatically.

Broadcasting Systems

The Broadcaster and the Government

Most observers recognize that no broadcast organization can be wholly independent of government, for all of them must be licensed in accordance with international agreements. Although broadcasters in democratic countries pride themselves on their freedom with respect to their governments, they are not always free of stockholder or advertiser pressure, nor are producers and editors truly independent if senior executives, under pressure from whatever source, interfere with their editorial functions. Independence, therefore, is a relative term when it is applied to broadcasting.

In a monograph that was written for the European Broadcasting Union, broadcasting systems are classified under four headings: state-operated, those that work under the establishment of a public corporation or authority, those whose systems are a partnership blend of public authorities and private interests, and those under private management. A brief summary of these systems provides an indication of the complex variations that have arisen.

State Operation

Grouped under this heading are broadcasting systems that are operated by a government department or delegated to an administration, perhaps with a legal personality and even possibly independent in financial and administrative matters, but subject to the government and not essentially autonomous. Under this heading came the systems in most communist countries. In the Soviet Union a special committee was set up in 1957 to be in charge of Soviet radio and television under the direct authority of the U.S.S.R. Council of Ministers. Similar arrangements were made in Czechoslovakia and Poland, except that the committees were given a legal personality. Romania had delegated broadcasting to a committee attached to the Council of Ministers. All-India Radio is a department of the Ministry of Information and Broadcasting. Similar arrangements are common in countries that were colonies but have gained their independence since World War II.

Establishment of a Public Corporation or Authority

The BBC has been the prototype of this kind of system. Provided it abides by the charter and terms of the license under which it operates, the BBC has maximum independence as regards the disposal of its funds (although its revenue is subject to governmental decision as to the cost of the license that is required for every television or radio receiver), the production and scheduling of programs, and, above all, editorial control. Certain residual government powers are either hedged around with agreed provisos or never exercised. Its income, save for profits on the sale of programs abroad and the sale of various phonograph records and publications, is exclusively derived from licenses. External broadcasting (i.e., broadcasting to areas outside national boundaries) is separately financed. The chairman and Board of Governors constitute the legal personality of the BBC; they are chosen by the government not as representatives of sectional interests but on the basis of their experience and standing. Political parties in office have been careful to avoid political prejudice in these appointments.

The Canadian Broadcasting Corporation (CBC), or Société Radio-Canada, also has substantial independent powers as determined by the Broadcasting Act of 1958 and its two successors, passed in 1968 and 1991. These later acts responded to technological as well as social changes, such as the specific needs of the regions and the aspirations of French-speaking Canadian citizens. The CBC is dependent on an annual parliamentary grant for its finance, supplemented by an income derived from advertising that amounts to about one-quarter of its annual revenue. Canadian broadcasting as a whole is a mixed system, with private broadcasting companies operating alongside the CBC.

The Japan Broadcasting Corporation, or the Nippon Hōsō Kyōkai (NHK), was charged by a series of acts in 1950 with the task of conducting "its broadcasting service for the public welfare in such a manner that its broadcasts may be received all over Japan." The NHK Board of Governors is appointed by the prime minister with the consent of both houses of the Diet. The system is financed almost exclusively from the sale of licenses for receiving sets. Private broadcasting, allowed since 1950, has led to the creation of 170 private broadcasting companies.

Though German broadcasting is properly included in this category, the situation there is substantially different, for the basic radio and television services are a matter not for the federal government but for the individual states (Länder). The state broadcasting organizations are also grouped together in a national organization, the First German Television network. In each state, though there are some variations, there are a broadcasting council that is appointed by the legislature or nominated by churches, universities, associations of employers or trade unions, political parties, or the press; an administrative council; and a director general. Their revenue comes from receiving-set licenses and sometimes also from advertising.

The broadcasting system in Belgium provides an interesting example of a device that has been used successfully for coping with a two-language country. There are three public authorities: one for French broadcasts, a second for Flemish, and a third that owns the property, owns and operates the technical equipment, and is responsible for the symphony orchestra, record library, and central reference library.

Partnership of Public Authorities and Private Interests

In many cases this partnership is nominal and historical rather than substantial and actual. The outstanding example is Radiotelevisione Italiana (RAI), originally founded in 1924. In 1927 an agreement was made with the government for a 25-year broadcasting concession. The charter was extended to cover television in 1952. Two years later a government agency acquired control, and in 1985 it owned 99 percent of the shares. RAI's administrative council consists of 20 members, 6 of whom are elected by the shareholders' assembly, 10 elected by a parliamentary commission, and 4 selected from a list of candidates representing the regional councils. A parliamentary committee of 40 members is in charge of running the service. The organization must also prepare an outline of programs on a quarterly basis for approval by the Ministry of Posts and Telecommunications, aided by an advisory committee concerned with cultural, artistic, and educational policies. A separate organization runs the broadcast advertising business, which, together with receiving-set licenses, provides the revenue of RAI. State monopoly of broadcasting was terminated in 1976. By the early 1990s there were about 450 private television stations operating in Italy alongside the RAI.

In Sweden the broadcasting monopoly is technically a privately owned corporation in which the state has no financial interest, thus emphasizing the independence of Sveriges Radio from the government. The shares of the corporation must be held by the Swedish press (20 percent), large noncommercial national bodies or movements (60 percent), and commerce and industry (20 percent). The board of governors is made up of a chairman and government nominees and an equal number elected by the shareholders; there also are two employee representatives of Sveriges Radio on the board. The government reserves the right to determine the amount of revenue from receiving-set licenses on an annual basis and thus controls both investment and the amount of broadcasting. The government, however, does not control how that revenue is spent. On balance, Sveriges Radio has a substantial measure of freedom.

In Switzerland too there are elements of partnership between private interests and public authorities, but the federal constitution, the need to broadcast in three languages, and geographical factors have led to a system by which the Swiss Broadcasting Corporation is composed of three regional societies based in Lausanne, Zürich, and Lugano-Besso.

Private Management

Most of the broadcasting organizations under this heading are commercial firms that derive their revenue from advertising, which takes the form of brief announcements scheduled at regular intervals throughout the day. In some cases a program, such as a sports event or concert, may be sponsored by one advertiser or group of advertisers. Methods and degree of government control vary, and no general characteristics may be isolated. Private-enterprise radio predominates in the United States and Latin America.

Subject to similar controls in these countries are many nonprofit educational stations, financed by universities, private subscriptions, and foundations. There is a public-service network, the Public Broadcasting Service, in the United States.

Other methods of distributing sound and vision programs by wire and cable are not strictly broadcasting. In the main, wire-diffusion enterprises concentrate on giving efficient reception of broadcast programs in densely populated areas, large blocks of buildings, and hotels. A tall apartment building, for example, may have one television antenna on its roof to which residents may attach their receivers. Programs such as sports, special events, films, and theatrical performances are also available via direct cable lines to subscribers as "Pay TV." Cable television reached about 56,100,000 homes in the United States in 1991 and has created two industries in broadcasting: one to hook up homes, the other to supply the programs. Cable television has drawn viewers away from the major commercial television networks, whose share of the prime-time audience has fallen and is expected to decline further.

The Broadcaster and the Public

Nature of the Broadcast Audience

The psychology and behaviour of a radio or television audience, which is composed principally of individuals in the privacy of their own homes, differ considerably from those of an audience in a theatre or lecture hall. There is none of the crowd atmosphere that prevails in a public assembly, and listeners are only casually aware that they are actually part of a large audience. This engenders a sense of intimacy that causes the listener to feel a close personal association with the speaker or performer. Furthermore, many people will not accept in their own homes many of the candid forms of expression that they readily condone or support on the stage or in literature.

Because it owes its license to operate to the state, if indeed it is not state-operated, and because of its intimate relationship to its audience, broadcasting functions in a quasi-public domain, open in all its phases to public scrutiny. It is therefore held to be invested with a moral as well as a legal responsibility to serve the public interest and must remain more sensitive to public sentiment and political opinion than most other forms of public expression.

Audience Measurement

For economic reasons, as well as those outlined above, evaluation of audience opinion and response to radio or television programs is important to the broadcaster. Audience measurement presents difficult problems, because there is no box office by which to determine the exact number of listeners. Mail received comes principally from those who have the time and inclination to write and cannot be regarded as wholly representative. Audience-measurement information may also be obtained by telephone-sampling methods, interviews in the home by market-research organizations, or special recording devices attached to individual receiving sets. The latter, installed with the owner's consent, record the amount of time the set is used, when it is turned on and off, and the stations tuned in. These devices are expensive, however, and do not necessarily indicate whether someone is actually watching or listening, and they are therefore limited to small samples of the total audience. Whatever the method of rating, commercial broadcasters are quick to alter or discontinue any program that shows lack of audience appeal, and the listeners are thus influential in determining the nature of the programs that are offered to them. In commercial broadcasting, sponsored programs also are affected by their apparent success or failure in selling the goods advertised.

Educational Broadcasting

It is difficult to give an account of educational broadcasting in countries where broadcasting is largely or wholly a matter of private management and where the larger and more important stations and networks are private commercial enterprises. Nevertheless, considerable numbers of educational transmissions are made in the United States and Latin America by universities and colleges and sometimes by municipal or state-owned stations. The Public Broadcasting Service in the United States has increased the amount of educational and generally more thought-provoking material available on the air, and in Latin America some countries use broadcasts not only to support the work of teachers in schools but also to combat illiteracy and to impart advice to isolated rural populations in matters of public health, agricultural methods, and other social and practical subjects. The Roman Catholic Church has been in the forefront of the latter activity, operating, for example, the Rede Nacional de Emissôras Católicas in Brazil and the Acción Cultural Popular in Colombia. A similar use of broadcasting is made in most of the tropical countries of Africa and Asia.

Japan's NHK has the most ambitious educational-broadcasting output in the world. Each of its two television and AM radio services is devoted wholly to education, while general television services and FM radio also transmit material of this nature. Japan prepares programs for primary, secondary, and higher education, special offerings for the mentally and physically handicapped, and a wide range of transmissions under the general heading of "social education," which includes foreign languages, vocational and technical instruction, advice on agriculture, forestry, fisheries, and business management, plus special programs for children, adolescents, and women. The educational broadcasts of NHK reach more than 90 percent of Japan's primary and secondary schools.

In Europe the French state broadcasting service devotes more than one-half of its radio output to educational and cultural broadcasts in the arts, letters, and sciences; and on television about 14 percent of its first and second networks are devoted to adult education. Primary and secondary instruction is offered, as are refresher courses for teachers and university-level courses.

Although Italian radio devotes less than 1 percent of its output specifically to educational programs for children, nearly 20 percent is given to cultural and allied offerings. Educational television began in Italy in 1958 with courses of a vocational nature, followed by transmissions aimed at secondary schools. In 1966 special programs were initiated for areas where there are no secondary schools. By the early 1980s, 17 percent of Italian television time was devoted to educational and school broadcasts and 4 percent to cultural programs.

Swedish radio offers a comprehensive service of educational and cultural broadcasting, with the output on television higher than that on radio. There is also a substantial output of adult education at the primary, secondary, and university levels, with about 1,400 school broadcasts a year, and Sweden has concentrated on vocational training and refreshment for teachers. German broadcasting, by contrast, has been used much less for formal education. In the Netherlands more than two and a half hours of school and continuing education broadcasting are broadcast weekly on the radio; in addition, nearly eight hours of educational television are transmitted every week.

The BBC pioneered in education; its work, in both radio and television, has steadily expanded. The BBC offers primary and secondary students more than 100 radio series and nearly 40 television series. The BBC also offers a wide range of biweekly programs especially designed for study in degree courses with the Open University, created and financed by the government, with the broadcast teaching supplemented by publications and correspondence work. By the mid-1970s, BBC broadcasts for the Open University averaged 16 hours weekly on radio and more than 18 hours on television. In addition, the Independent Broadcasting Authority in the United Kingdom has required the commercial-program companies to contribute educational material both for schools and for adults; by 1970 this amounted to 10 hours weekly during periods totaling 28 weeks of the year.

In Australia there is a small educational output on the commercial stations, both radio and television, but by far the greater part of educational broadcasting is undertaken by the Australian Broadcasting Corporation. Educational programming accounts for about 4 percent of radio time and 18 percent of television output, the majority of which is broadcast to schools and kindergartens. The Canadian Broadcasting Corporation is required to provide educational programs in both English and French and does so on its AM and FM radio networks, as well as on television.

Broadcasts for External Reception

International broadcasting—the transmission of programs by a country expressly for audiences beyond its own frontiers—dates from the earliest days of broadcasting. The Soviet Union began foreign-language transmissions for propaganda purposes in the 1920s. Fascist Italy and Nazi Germany made such broadcasts at a later date. France, Great Britain, and the Netherlands were next in the field among European countries, though their first use of shortwave broadcasting was aimed at French-, English-, or Dutch-speaking populations overseas. Great Britain began foreign-language broadcasting early in 1938 with a program in Arabic and transmissions in Spanish and Portuguese directed to Latin America. By August 1939, countries broadcasting in foreign languages included Albania, Bulgaria, China, France, Germany, Great Britain, Hungary, Italy, Japan, Romania, the Soviet Union, Spain, the United States, and Vatican City.

During World War II foreign-language broadcasting continued; the programs of the BBC in particular, because of their reliability and credibility, had an important effect in maintaining morale among the countries that were under German occupation. The continuance of international tension after World War II led to remarkable growth of foreign-language services. In 1950, for example, all of the communist countries of eastern Europe except East Germany had launched external services, although these were on a small scale, and even the Soviet Union was transmitting a total of more than 500 hours of broadcasts weekly in all foreign languages. The United Kingdom's output, which had once led the field, had been reduced to slightly more than 600 hours a week and the Voice of America to less than 500 hours per week. By the early 1980s the situation had changed radically. The Soviet Union alone broadcast more than 2,000 hours per week, and the output of all communist countries of eastern Europe (excluding Yugoslavia) totaled about 1,500 hours. The United Kingdom logged 744 hours in 1981; West Germany logged 785 hours; and the United States broadcast over the Voice of America and Radio Free Europe/Radio Liberty 1,925 hours a week. The output of China had risen from 66 hours weekly in 1950 to 1,375 hours by 1981. The increase in Chinese broadcasts reflected in part the rising tension between China and the Soviet Union; significantly, the output of China's ally for much of this period, Albania, rose from 26 to 560 hours weekly during the same period. By the early 1980s Japan was transmitting for 263 hours, while Australia and Canada also sponsored external broadcasts.

Monitoring and Transcriptions

A logical development following from external broadcasting is the monitoring of foreign broadcasts and their analysis for intelligence purposes. The BBC in particular has a highly developed monitoring service; this activity often yields valuable information. The Central Intelligence Agency of the United States is also active in monitoring and analyzing foreign broadcasts. Transcriptions (recordings) of programs produced in either the domestic or the external services of one country can be acceptable for broadcast in others. Radio broadcasts of an educational nature can be used in different countries speaking the same language. Although many radio transcriptions are supplied free, in television the situation is different, and there is a substantial trade in television films.

Pirate and Offshore Stations

In some countries where broadcasting in general or radio alone is a monopoly, radio has had to compete for brief periods with independent commercial stations mounted on ships anchored at sea outside territorial waters. Sweden, Denmark, the Netherlands, and the United Kingdom have been the countries most affected by these stations, which have made use of unauthorized wavelengths, thus endangering other radio communications and operating free of any copyright obligations in respect to any of their broadcast material. Government action gradually has forced closure of such operations: in Sweden a competitive service of popular music proved effective; and in Denmark naval police action (the international legality of which may be questioned), followed by confiscation and heavy penalties, brought an end to the pirate station. The United Kingdom combined legislation penalizing any party who advertised or supplied such ships with the launching by the BBC of Radio 1, substantially a popular music service, to solve the problem. The French have had a particular problem of competition from the so-called postes périphériques, which include Europe No. 1 in the Saar and Radio Andorra in the Pyrenees, not to mention the French-language broadcasts of Monaco, Belgium, Luxembourg, and Switzerland. The strongest competition came from Europe No. 1, in which the French government finally purchased a controlling interest.

Broadcasting as a Medium of Art

The artistic potential of any medium is determined by the unique form it offers and forces on the artist and by its capacity as an effective vehicle of communication in its own right. The form of any art includes the circumstance through which it reaches its public. William Shakespeare's stage was little more than an open platform on which any action he cared to represent could be compassed provided he gave his actors the necessary words to indicate the place, circumstance, and atmosphere of the action. But his plays would have been null as practical drama without the circumscribing enclosure of the Elizabethan circular theatre auditorium—the "wooden O"—which gathered the audience around the platform, sealing them off from the outside world and concentrating their attention on the performance. As active auditors they became an integral part of the drama, and one must be constantly aware of them in the very writing, structure, and timing of the plays. Shakespeare's art was born of the discovery of the potentialities of the actor–audience relationship.

The Art of Radio

In a similar way the art of radio began to be discovered when those engaged in broadcasting became aware of the nature of the medium in which they were working and of their special relationship to their audience. The discovery took time. (The artistic potential of radio was not explored until the 1930s.) Radio was the only medium in which performers were invisible to their audience. Broadcasters tended at first to adopt the manner of the stage or the pulpit: thinking in terms of a mass audience, the inexperienced broadcaster gave his voice and style an artificial inflation totally unsuited to the new medium. His actual audience was composed of small groups and individuals, usually at home or in informal circumstances, often doing other things at the same time. The basic art of radio consisted in adapting manner and style to these new circumstances. Few programs could expect to take their audiences for granted.

News broadcasts were among the exceptions, and news broadcasts in most countries came to be delivered in a fixed, impersonal manner, the newsreader suppressing his personality as far as possible and adopting a "team" voice. Most other spoken radio formats required using the voice in such a way as to hold the attention of the listener, and this in turn meant recognizing the nature of the microphone as a medium. The public's span of attention was found to be limited. The news summary was allotted five or 10 minutes, while a talk might last 15 minutes or in special instances up to 30 minutes. Much consideration was also given to the appropriate styles for various audiences, depending on the classes of listeners to whom broadcasts were addressed.

The art of radio emerged in Britain—and in certain other countries adopting the same "public service" approach—as a medium nominally addressed to everyone but actually resembling a kind of broad-based national journal with special sections addressed to specific interests and tastes, some more demanding on the intelligence than others. The popular radio talk (a form of spoken journalism, or essay, often excellently composed and delivered) was shorter and more informal in style than that of the "serious" or purely educational talk. Broadcasting offered unique opportunities for bringing the nation's highest intelligences into the living rooms of so-called minority audiences (often amounting to millions) who were prepared to listen to concentrated exposition and argument.

From this, particularly in Europe, developed channels specializing in minority interests for part or all of the day. The listeners supported the service by paying an annual license fee. In the United States, on the other hand, privately owned broadcasting companies got their revenues from advertising and tied their programming to the advertiser's desire to reach the widest possible public. In Japan there were both public and commercial broadcasting services, the former being financed, as in Europe, by license fees from owners of receiving sets. In the Soviet Union broadcasting was recognized, in the words of Pravda, as "one of the most powerful weapons of the cultural revolution." Under Stalin virtually all receivers were wired to local exchanges so that the listener could choose only among approved programs. The service had to be regionalized because the U.S.S.R. included populations speaking about 80 principal languages. Aside from news and commentary, the broadcasts were generally cultural rather than directly propagandistic.

The development of radio as an art form was thus dependent on the way it was organized and financed. There were rich new fields to be opened up in drama, light entertainment, and documentary programming, conceived specifically for the medium, while at the same time some traditional art forms (notably stage drama and music) were transmitted with success. Fiction and poetry reading also became a staple part of sound broadcasting.

The Art of Television

In the 1950s and '60s, radio was overtaken by television. At first television as a medium was considered to be little different from film. But, although television was a hungry user of film, it needed film in forms that differed from those required by the theatres.

The difference between film and television as art forms stemmed from the physical and financial conditions governing production, distribution, and exhibition. The relationships between the media and their publics were also different. The initial difference lies in the cameras and their function in production. The film camera supplies a record on celluloid in the form of a two-dimensional image, which, suitably edited, can be subsequently projected onto a screen. The television camera accepts and makes available for immediate transmission a two-dimensional image that remains unrecorded and passes with the event, like the image in a mirror (though this image can, by using additional equipment, be recorded on film or videotape). The film camera is associated with a lengthy effort of photographing, cutting, editing, and dubbing—an elaborate process of selection and assembly that may involve months of work. Although television images may also be stored and edited through videotape, the essential television form is the immediate transmission to the public of events occurring at the moment—political and social events, news summaries, commentary, and discussion.

The basic art of television is the control of this immediate flow of images. They can be preselected insofar as the cameras may be set up at chosen vantage points; after that, however, the director must select among the images they give him. The director-editor uses his skill to secure an immediately effective flow of images from the multiple viewpoints his cameras and their lenses collectively represent. In the film the same end is achieved by the quite different process of fragmenting and recording the action piecemeal, thus creating a succession of images that can be subsequently put together by editing and dubbing.

Those who first struggled with the practical aesthetics of television attempted to see the medium on the one hand as a kind of visual radio and on the other as a form of "diluted cinema," a rather poor cousin of the theatrical film. This was in part because they came either from radio or from filmmaking and saw the medium in relation to their previous occupations. Writers, directors, and performers from radio tended at first to reduce the television image to a "talking head," with the addition of occasional still pictures, film clips, or cut-ins from other broadcasting stations. This was especially the case in countries in which television initially lacked adequate financing (such as France) and directors could not afford costly pictorialization. On the other hand, personnel coming from filmmaking were appalled at the speed with which they were required to prepare and mount their television programs.

Television differs most from film in its relationship to the audience. The film is an event designed for a theatre with an audience specially assembled for the performance. Television, on the other hand, resembles a private performance in the home. The attitude of a person sitting perhaps alone and often for hours on end before a comparatively small picture screened in the familiar surroundings of his living room is quite different from that of a person who has gone out to share the special audience experience of a theatre. The tension is more slack; concentration is constantly threatened by irrelevant interruption. Whereas one is absorbed by a good film in a theatre to the exclusion of all else, one merely "watches" television. The television audience is preoccupied not so much with an individual item as with the free flow of item after item. Television is like a talking picture magazine, going on daily and nightly, asking little, giving out along with its entertainment a quantity of easily assimilated information ranging from formal news coverage to informal, gossipy discussions of the lighter affairs of the day.

Television also differs from film with respect to its visual impact. In the movie theatre a highly magnified image fills the central part of the field of vision in an otherwise darkened hall, exciting curiosity and response to a degree far beyond that obtained by a standard-size television screen in a relatively undarkened, and much smaller, living room. The great, fully loaded images of the big screen, from D.W. Griffith's Intolerance of 1916 to the Russian War and Peace of 1968, have involved the investment of large sums of money in what is called "production value"—the accumulated content of those images with their crowds of people and their elaborate sets. Skilled viewers in the movie theatre perceive and appreciate an astonishing amount of detail. In comparing television, however, one has only to watch a film produced for big-screen theatre to realize the limitations of the small television screen, in which the actors, speakers, or commentators must occupy most of the visual field.

Techniques and Borrowings

It is useful to view all of the media together, ranging from the individual performer appearing in the flesh before his audience to the complex presentations of the electronic and allied media. They may be compared in terms of the relationship of the performer to his audience as shown in Table below.

Relationship of medium to performance		
Medium	Nature of presentation	Type of material
Rostrum	Visible and audible performance by a single person	Oratory, preaching, recital; a speech, sermon, song, reading, monologue, or monodrama.
Live theatre or concert hall	Visible and audible performance by a group or company	A drama, opera, ballet, revue, circus, etc., with or without music; a concert.
Motion picture (silent)	Visible, but not audible, performance presented by means of cinematograph projection	A mimed drama with titles, documentary presentation, news record, or animated film; presented with "live" sound (music, commentator).
Motion picture (sound)	Visible and audible performance presented by means of a cinematograph projection	Original screenplay or material adapted from theatrical, fictional, or other sources; according to degree of adaptation, the sound film supervenes on the form of its source, making something new; also news, factual, and documentary material.
Radio	Audible, but not visible, broadcast performance	The whole range of human activity, from the news bulletin, report, commentary, discussion, talk, or actuality recording to the complete cycle of the audible arts—story and poetry reading, drama and documentary, music and opera, including material specially created for the medium.
Television	Visible and audible broadcast performance	Includes all of the above but seen as well as heard.

The media also vary in the kind of performance on which they can draw, either derivatively or creatively, as shown in Table below.

Relationship of performer to audience		
Performer	Audience	Relationship
Individual speaker, storyteller, or singer.	Assembled group or audience in any place.	Direct; performer to audience.
Company of players, singers, dancers, or musicians.	Assembled audience in a theatre or concert hall.	Direct; in an enclosed area.
Performance by an actor or performer recorded on film; factual film with commentator.	Assembled audience in a motion-picture theatre, hall, classroom, or other formal place.	Remote; through a photographed and projected two-dimensional image on either a large or small screen, with recorded sound.
Radio broadcast by an actor, aural performer, newsreader, or commentator.	Dispersed audience, located mainly in their own homes.	Remote; through a signal broadcast in sound only.
Televised presentation by an actor, singer, dancer, performer, or commentator.	Dispersed audience, located mainly in their own homes.	Remote; through a two-dimensional image on a small screen, accompanied by sound.

The tables make clear the extent to which the various media borrow from each other. Just as the Greek drama drew on ancient myths and legends and the Renaissance drama on classical and contemporary material alike, so the voracious demands of the new 20th-century media have driven producers and scriptwriters to acquire the rights to existent material in other media, particularly the novel and the drama. Radio and television have overlapped increasingly with journalism, many journalists becoming broadcasters and commentators.

But much of the borrowing has been mechanical and technical rather than artistic in nature. Radio broadcasting exploited the phonograph record as a means of preserving sound; in a similar way, television drew upon the film. The invention of magnetic tape for recording both sound and video signals has now linked together all of the mechanized media—phonograph, telephone, radio, sound film, and television—and made available a virtually complete record of the sights, sounds, arts, and culture of modern society.

Preservation by recording is in itself not a creative art but a service to art created elsewhere. A principal function of radio and television broadcasting has been the dissemination of works of art created for other media. This is particularly true of radio; in television these works are more often transformed to meet the requirements of the medium and become different art forms. When an opera is performed in a television studio in a way that meets the potentialities of the electronic cameras, the result is television opera—a different form from stage opera. When an opera is commissioned and composed specifically for television, then television may be considered an artistic medium in its own right.

Dramatic Techniques

Radio began by restoring the ancient art of the storyteller. Writers for radio next learned how to suggest place and time by word of mouth, accompanied by the impressionistic use of sound and music. Thus was born the genre of radio drama. The radio dramatist must address himself to the imagination of listeners who are unable to see what they are experiencing. This limitation carries with it a certain freedom. Just as Shakespeare's independence from stage decor left him free to move his action widely in time and space, so radio has been free to create its own plastic continuities of action and time-space reference. Radio has been highly creative in the fields of drama and documentary and also in quite new forms of imaginative light entertainment.

Television, on the other hand, adapted techniques already established by the sound film of the 1930s and 1940s. In the initial rivalry between film and television, economic and technical factors both played a part. The first television plays were like the simplest kind of film dialogues; they avoided elaborate sets or large casts, because the screen was not large enough and because they cost too much. Television material was highly expendable, like newspapers and journals that are discarded after a single use. Only gradually did the international distribution of selected television programs, particularly within the large Anglo-American market, permit more money to be spent on "production value" in television.

Television drama came into its own during the 1950s with the emergence of writers and directors who shook themselves free from the old models and began to develop their own techniques—an extension of the two-dimensional image with sound into fields that the cinema could not or would not enter. The creativity of television in the purely artistic sense lies in the unique opportunities it offers the maker. These opportunities were beyond the reach of the filmmaker, who had no way of impelling his sponsor to finance him in such ventures. Here art and the nature of sponsorship can be said to overlap, as is so often the case in the history of art.

Film Techniques

The basic principles that the television image shares with the film image are, of course, its freedom to select the compass of each individual shot and its freedom to determine the nature of the movement within it. The form of presentation depends in both cases on a continuity of such shots in order to build up a narrative flow. Film and television narrative are based on the same principles of mobile composition—the selective (or edited) flow of selective shots of the action. Despite the technological differences in their production, they are aesthetically closely linked and will continue to have a close relationship with each other. This relationship naturally extends into the technical field. Television adopted videotape in order to achieve an immediate high-quality record of the electronic image. This seemed at first to be a threat to the use of film in television, but that has not proved to be so; the film camera is indispensable in many branches of television production. On the other hand, filmmakers have found videotape to be useful in cinema production, since it provides the capability of checking the shot before the film is processed.

The development of television as an art form has not excluded its use as a channel for works produced in other media. On the contrary, production in other media increasingly has been financed out of revenues from its subsequent transmission on television. Since the earliest years of its existence, television has depended on the regular screening of a vast backlog of movie films. The high rentals paid on old films have induced television interests themselves to undertake the production of new films to be shown in theatres and subsequently on the television channels they operate. The feature films they produce often have relatively small casts and a higher ratio of in-close shooting, making them suitable for the smaller TV screen, just as most films now shot for wide screens keep the essential action in the centre so that they can later be shown on television.

Broadcasting Operations

Types of Programs and Development of Studios

There are a number of distinguishable types of programs that are broadcast, but they often overlap in technique, subject matter, and style. Radio, for example, broadcasts speech and music, but in an endless number of combinations. Television adds the visual element, greatly increasing the number of possible program forms. Most sizable broadcast organizations, however, have several categories for administrative convenience. But the definitions cannot be too precise, and lines of demarcation are necessarily vague.

Entertainment

Entertainment can include comedy, impossible wholly to differentiate from drama; quizzes, not always easily distinguished from relatively serious programs of information and education; popular music, in which the frontier with jazz and serious music is anything but rigid; and variety, or a series of unrelated acts, nearly always linked by a popular presenter or established performer.

From the early days of radio there was a tendency to make use of a variety format, and, as this approach represented an extension of old music-hall traditions, success was achieved by many programs in this vein. From the music-hall–variety-type program emerged the "gang show," in which a cast of performers remaining the same from week to week would make use of a series of humorous situations or catchphrases, gradually building up a familiar background against which the incongruities of the script could exploit humour to the full. A further development was the "situation comedy," in which a number of characters, such as the members of a family, remain in the same situation week after week but experience comic adventures. Though these laughter programs lost popularity on radio as television gained popular acceptance, they have become the mainstays of television. A contemporary phenomenon has been the comedy program involving substantial amounts of political and social satire. The situation comedy has also been influenced by this trend.

The many types of comedy entertainment programs that are produced around the world all have one common characteristic: not only have the performers needed the stimulus of a studio audience, but also the listeners and viewers are stimulated by the laughter and applause of the audience. This has led to some abuses, such as the superimposition of laughter and applause on prerecorded programs, a practice that is frowned upon but still practiced. It has also meant that large studios are required to accommodate not only the performers, frequently including more than one music combination, but also the audience. In television there must be room for settings that have become increasingly ambitious and for dancers and choruses. Broadcasting organizations have generally been able to build studios of appropriate size, though radiobroadcasters in the early days preferred to purchase or rent small theatres.

In their form and structure, children's entertainment shows resemble those for adults. Animated cartoons, however, represent an exception to this rule; the Hungarians, the Poles, and the French have achieved genuine distinction in this area.

Drama

Radio and television drama is not best produced in a theatre; the nature of the studio is therefore different. Early radio drama was produced in a relatively small studio, often with a single microphone, just as early television plays were produced with a single camera. Radio engineers soon began to employ a control panel with inputs from more than one studio and sound effects ingeniously achieved; their counterparts in television expanded their use of cameras and sets. Mixing in radio from one studio to another and in television from one set to another and employing increasingly sophisticated sound effects and background music have all become accepted techniques in drama production. Inevitably, television drama has borrowed substantially from the techniques of film production.

Feature films, usually originally made for the cinema, continue to form an accepted and important element in television schedules throughout the world. Both radio and television occasionally broadcast live stage plays from theatres, but there is a general feeling that such offerings do not adequately exploit the advantages of either medium. Since the earliest days of radio and television, the studio-produced drama has been an important ingredient in program schedules; in television, as in films, it was not long before shooting on location also became an accepted practice. Offerings have included classical Greek drama, Shakespeare and other Elizabethan dramatists, the Spanish and French theatre, Russian and Scandinavian plays, and modern works.

Serial presentations on television and radio have included adaptations of famous works of literature, such as the novels of Charles Dickens, Honoré de Balzac, and Leo Tolstoy, the Forsyte Saga of John Galsworthy, historical costume dramas based on the lives of such figures as Henry VIII and Elizabeth I of England, and, of course, the romantic melodramas aimed largely at the daytime viewer or listener, known as "soap operas." Radio and television serials of fantasy and adventure are also produced for children.

Three other distinguishable types of drama have achieved almost universal popularity: western adventures; shows involving gangsters, crime, and police; and shows set in hospitals and other medical situations. Violent episodes in some crime and western adventure programs have drawn criticism from those who believe that such violence is harmful to children. In response, many broadcasting organizations have introduced codes of practice to minimize such scenes.

Western adventure programs, largely produced in the United States, have been popular with studios because of their relatively low production costs and ready salability abroad. Dramatic series of this type have been shown all over the world, often with dubbed sound tracks. Although these exported American productions are often much less expensive than home-produced programs, Australia has been able to produce some western-type series, and Canada has exploited its legendary "Mounties." So many American television programs have been exported, however, that broadcasting organizations in some nations, such as Japan and the United Kingdom, have taken steps to ensure that home-produced dramas have priority in terms of percentage of schedule hours and prime time (peak placing).

Spoken Word

Spoken-word programs have included entertainment types, such as "This Is Your Life" and many of the "talk shows," in which a personality interviewer questions celebrities, sometimes with interludes of music or comedy or with serious discussions, documentaries, or lectures. A fear of controversy, the problem of maintaining an overall impartiality, and sometimes the belief that the mass audience would be alienated by programs demanding a conscious effort and concentration combined, in the early days of radio, to limit the time given to serious spoken-word programs. It was not long, however, before many broadcasters developed a sense of pride and responsibility in their function and regarded it as their duty to provide information and opinion. In countries where broadcasting achieved a substantial measure of independence, some broadcasters gradually became concerned not only with the exposition of fact and controversy but also with the task of exposing the ills and abuses of their society.

News continues to be the most important element in spoken-word radio. Since it was inescapable that broadcast news would affect the industry, newspaper proprietors in the early days of radio either made efforts to restrict the sources of news and the times at which it could be broadcast or sought themselves to enter the field. In areas where broadcasting was commercialized, the press was further concerned, because radio competed with it for advertising revenues and because radio could almost always get a story to the public before the newspapers could. Nevertheless, there is no evidence that radio news reduced the circulation of newspapers; some have even maintained that radio whetted the appetite of listeners for news and increased newspaper sales. It would seem, however, that television has adversely affected the daily press and, even more so, weekly or monthly magazines. Long before television outstripped radio, broadcasting organizations were employing reporters and special and foreign correspondents and were supplementing the service received from news agencies. Some broadcast reporters became public personalities in their own right.

Television news presented additional production problems; the announcer at the microphone reading from a script or TelePrompTer was not satisfactory, and it was not long before the greater part of television news was appropriately accompanied by relevant pictures. The need for film shots and the cost and difficulty of obtaining them were, and to some extent remain, serious problems. In spite of substantial expenditure on the supply of such shots, television news is open to the criticism that news values and objectivity are distorted by the availability or nonavailability of pictures.

In general, however, broadcasting organizations have adjusted to the much higher cost of television news. The syndication of film reports, the development of live networks on an international basis, such as Eurovision, and satellite communications have overcome most problems of news reporting on television. On the other hand, it has become apparent that the psychological impact of film shots of war and civil disturbance, as of accidents and disasters, is far greater than that of the radio report.

Television reports of, for example, the Vietnam War did far more to influence public opinion than radio news bulletins could have done. Radio has the advantage, however, of not requiring the same degree of attention; the trend has been toward frequently repeated short bulletins. In the United States there are radio stations that restrict themselves entirely to news, usually in a continuous magazine format, plus, of course, the advertising spots. The newsmagazine, or newsreel, in radio was introduced even earlier on BBC.

A series of brief reports, interviews, and extracts from speeches, making use of many voices and exploiting the technique of frequent renewal of stimulus, proved to be a successful formula. This technique has spread into news bulletins and is increasingly used in the coverage of current affairs, both in radio and television. In all these programs of news and comment, one of the problems has been that of the anchors, or presenters, and the degree to which they may be given freedom to project their personalities or express their views. In the United States there have been fewer inhibitions in this area than in countries where broadcasting is or has been a monopoly and where the need for and tradition of impartiality have been dominant.

In the case of the BBC, newsreaders were long anonymous; but on television the identity of a newsreader, or of the presenter of a magazine of news or comment, cannot be concealed, and these inhibitions have broken down. Nevertheless, in western Europe and Commonwealth countries the impartiality of broadcasting services remains an issue of greater importance than in the United States or Latin America. In Britain, when the Independent Television Authority was created, it was enjoined to see that in the coverage of controversial matters each program was balanced in itself. The BBC, with greater freedom, makes no effort to ensure balance in any one program, provided that an overall balance in respect of any issue is achieved over a reasonable period of time. In all developed countries elaborate programs are prepared to report the results of elections, though it is in the United States and the United Kingdom that these are most ambitious.

In radio straight talk persists in some countries, though less so than in the heyday of the medium. Nevertheless, some successful lectures at much greater length have been scheduled occasionally on television and in some countries on radio. Straight talk of 10 minutes or more does not lend itself to exciting television production, unless it is accompanied by filmed illustrations to the point where it all but becomes a documentary.

Another pattern popular in many countries involves a panel of distinguished figures under a chairman, answering questions of a topical nature from members of a studio audience. In some cases a parabolic microphone is employed so that questions may be asked from any part of the studio or hall in which the program is mounted; others may call for written queries in advance so that questioners can be conveniently seated in the first row. Some radio panel programs also solicit queries from members of the listening audience who call them in on the telephone.

Development of the radio documentary stemmed from drama as writers searched for new material especially appropriate for broadcasting. Not surprisingly, early documentary was in dramatic form, and most of it was based on well-known historical events, of which the programs were in effect dramatic reconstructions. Production of radio documentaries was simplified by the invention of magnetic recording tape that was far easier to edit and use on location than its predecessors, the wax-coated disc and the wire recorder. Ironically, just when these technical advances had made the best form of radio documentary possible, the television documentary on contemporary themes began to supplant its radio counterpart. Documentaries have become more expository of public (current) affairs concerned with international relations, domestic politics, and social problems.

Religion

There have been, in the main, two types of religious program: devotional and information-discussion. The former comprises prayer, religious services, or hymn singing, either mounted in a studio or as outside broadcasts from a church, a chapel, or a hall. A third type is the dramatization of a religious theme, though the tendency has been to devote a good proportion of religious broadcasting time to documentaries, discussions, and interviews. Some sects have produced broadcasts that combine political and religious material. Missionary bodies, mostly under the control of one of the many international or regional religious broadcasting organizations, either buy time on commercial stations or operate stations in many parts of the world, including Latin America, Africa, and Asia.

Outside Broadcasts

Although broadcasts do not constitute a distinct and definable form, they nevertheless have been since the birth of radio the most popular and arresting of all material transmitted on either medium. Sports of every description and ceremonial and political events have exercised an unfailing appeal and, in general, attract the largest audiences. Outside broadcasts have stimulated the imagination and taxed the ingenuity of television-broadcasting engineers to such an extent that they have accustomed the public to feats unimaginable to the pioneers of radio. The improvement of line communications, the development of mobile transmitters, and, above all, the use of satellite communications have given the outside broadcast an elasticity and an almost limitless range.

Music

Radio has had two important effects on the musical life of the world: it has widened the audience for all forms of music, and it has made easier the development of new forms, such as electronic music. Music remains a staple ingredient of radio in its own right, whereas in television, though there are programs of music as such, it is more often an adjunct to something else, as, for example, dancing, or as a small component of a mixed program. In the field of popular music, radio has immensely aided the rapid changes of fashion, which have coincided with technical advances in the making of recordings and their popularity and sales. A recognition by recording companies of the enormous power of radio in popularizing a song or performer has led to some abuses. In the United States record companies gave "payola," or bribes, to prominent radio personalities in return for promotion of their songs.

The development of stereophonic sound techniques has revolutionized the record industry and has played an important role on radio, though earliest in the field of serious music. Frequency modulated (FM) radio broadcasts of serious music, and later of other forms of music, have been popular in many areas; some recordings are broadcast stereophonically but can be received on monophonic radios.

Opera too has profited from broadcasting, and outside broadcasts from opera houses, as well as studio performances on both radio and television, have done much in European and many other countries to bring this form of music to a large public. Music programs have presented more difficulties than most others in the matter of studios, partly because of the size of studio required for a full symphony orchestra and partly because of the delicate balancing of acoustics for proper reproduction of such performances.

Relations with Artists, Speakers, Authors and Unions

In the early days of radio, problems of fees, royalties, performing rights, copyright, and relations with unions rarely were regarded. Entertainers performed largely for publicity purposes. Only gradually did performers appreciate radio's effect, first, as a threat to their theatre earnings and, second, as a highly lucrative substitute. To try to trace how a modus vivendi was reached in these matters in different countries would present a picture of baffling complexity in light of the different prevailing laws and different union structures. Generally speaking, copyright issues have revolved around the rights of record manufacturers and fees for composers. Rates and fees for reproducing recordings often have been the subject of disputes with the unions. Radiobroadcasters soon found that purchasing records or making their own recordings from live musical performances meant substantial economies; these, however, came at the expense of the musicians. Consequently, the musicians unions sometimes attempted to prevent use of phonograph records or recording of live performances. In some countries, such as the Netherlands, the repeat problem has been solved by having the performers receive a fee for each repeat, the fee rising with each successive use of the recording until it ceases to represent an advantage to the broadcaster.

Relations of the broadcasting organizations with their staffs have also been complex. In Canada attempts to exercise a restrictive control have led to revolts and resignations, while in France editors and producers who have been unwilling to conform to government policy have been removed from their jobs, though often under other pretexts. The position of staff is particularly vulnerable in those countries where broadcasting is a state monopoly; an example is Czechoslovakia, where senior broadcasting officials were ousted after the fall in 1968 of Premier Alexander Dubček, who had attempted to liberalize the communist regime.

Internal Organization, Administration and Policy Control

The organization and administration of broadcasting bodies can, in the case of a small independent station, be relatively simple, and the policies can be implemented with ease. Sizable organizations, however, have a complex problem, because it is not possible to determine success or failure purely on the basis of financial returns. Monopoly organizations, though in theory their sole purpose is public service, in practice often must take into account the views of the government. In the case of nonprofit public-service operations dependent upon license fees for revenue but with commercial competition, ratings cannot be completely ignored, and these organizations must compete for mass audiences to some extent in order to justify their existence at the expense of the listening and viewing public.

The broadcasting administration has two essential functions: first, programming—i.e., allocation of funds and setting of schedules—and, second, production, the preparation of programs. The former is in effect a branch of direction, and those in charge of planning program schedules and allocating funds have a power that if not checked can be absolute. On the other hand, these planners are dependent on the goodwill of the production and supply departments.

A main problem arises in the treatment of controversial subjects in the field of current affairs. Where broadcasters are under no obligation to be impartial, as in the Netherlands, or where, as in totalitarian countries, only one point of view may be aired, the problem does not arise. In democratic countries, however, where the broadcaster has independence and where there is a need to achieve an overall impartiality, the problem is very serious. Even though decisions may be reached by discussion and a consensus of opinion, the responsibility usually has to be carried by one person. No broadcasting organization has been able to find a complete solution to the problem that does not involve rigid control and intrusion on the independence of the editorial and production staff.

Administration must also deal with routine matters, such as staff pay and conditions of service, recruitment, finance, accounting, negotiations with unions, procurement of equipment, and provision of office and studio space. In general, it has been found best to subordinate such routine management operations to the needs of those directly concerned with the principal function of broadcasting. Much the same may be said of engineering and technical staff, though their research work and technical advances influence the decisions of direction and development of broadcasting.

4

Broadcasting Techniques

The process of distribution of content to the audience through electronic communications medium is known as broadcasting. A few of the various techniques of broadcasting are radio broadcasting, digital audio broadcasting, commercial broadcasting, public broadcasting, remote broadcasting, microbroadcasting, broadcast syndication, etc. are discussed in this chapter in detail.

Radio Broadcasting

Radio broadcasting is a unidirectional wireless transmission over radio waves intended to reach a wide audience. Stations can be linked in radio networks to broadcast a common radio format, either in broadcast syndication or simulcast or both. Audio broadcasting also can be done via cable radio, local wire television networks, satellite radio, and internet radio via streaming media on the Internet. The signal types can be either analog audio or digital audio.

Long wave radio broadcasting station, Motala, Sweden

Slovak Radio Building, Bratislava, Slovakia (architects: Štefan Svetko, Štefan Ďurkovič and Barnabáš Kissling, 1967-1983)

Broadcasting tower in Trondheim, Norway

History

The earliest radio stations were simply radiotelegraphy systems and did not carry audio. For audio broadcasts to be possible electronic detection and amplification devices had to be incorporated.

The thermionic valve was invented in 1904 by the English physicist John Ambrose Fleming. He developed a device he called an "oscillation valve" (because it passes current in only one direction). The heated filament, or cathode, was capable of thermionic emission of electrons that would flow to the *plate* (or *anode*) when it was at a higher voltage. Electrons, however, could not pass in the reverse direction because the plate was not heated and thus not capable of thermionic emission of electrons. Later known as the Fleming valve, it could be used as a rectifier of alternating current and as a radio wave detector. This greatly improved the crystal set which rectified the radio signal using an early solid-state diode based on a crystal and a so-called cat's whisker. However, what was still required was an amplifier.

The triode (mercury-vapor filled with a control grid) was patented on March 4, 1906 by the Austrian Robert von Lieben independent from that, on October 25, 1906 Lee De Forest patented his three-element Audion. It wasn't put to practical use until 1912, when its amplifying ability became recognized by researchers.

By about 1920, valve technology had matured to the point where radio broadcasting was quickly becoming viable. However, an early audio transmission that could be termed a *broadcast* may have occurred on Christmas Eve in 1906 by Reginald Fessenden, although this is disputed. While many early experimenters attempted to create systems similar to radiotelephone devices by which only two parties were meant to communicate, there were others who intended to transmit to larger audiences. Charles Herrold started broadcasting in California in 1909 and was carrying audio by the next year. (Herrold's station eventually became KCBS).

In The Hague, the Netherlands, PCGG started broadcasting on November 6, 1919, making it, arguably the first commercial broadcasting station. In 1916, Frank Conrad, an electrical engineer employed at the Westinghouse Electric Corporation, began broadcasting from his Wilkinsburg, Pennsylvania garage with the call letters 8XK. Later, the station was moved to the top of the Westinghouse factory building in East Pittsburgh, Pennsylvania. Westinghouse relaunched the station as KDKA on November 2, 1920, as the first commercially licensed radio station in America. The commercial broadcasting designation came from the type of broadcast license; advertisements did not air until years later. The first licensed broadcast in the United States came from KDKA itself: the results of the Harding/Cox Presidential Election. The Montreal station that became CFCF began broadcast programming on May 20, 1920, and the Detroit station that became WWJ began program broadcasts beginning on August 20, 1920, although neither held a license at the time.

In 1920 wireless broadcasts for entertainment began in the UK from the Marconi Research Centre 2MT at Writtle near Chelmsford, England. A famous broadcast from Marconi's New Street Works factory in Chelmsford was made by the famous soprano Dame Nellie Melba on 15 June 1920, where she sang two arias and her famous trill. She was the first artist of international renown to participate in direct radio broadcasts. The 2MT station began to broadcast regular entertainment in 1922. The BBC was amalgamated in 1922 and received a Royal Charter in 1926, making it the first national broadcaster in the world.

Radio Argentina began regularly scheduled transmissions from the Teatro Coliseo in Buenos Aires on August 27, 1920, making its own priority claim. The station got its license on November 19, 1923. The delay was due to the lack of official Argentine licensing procedures before that date. This station continued regular broadcasting of entertainment and cultural fare for several decades.

Radio in education soon followed and colleges across the U.S. began adding radio broadcasting courses to their curricula. Curry College in Milton, Massachusetts introduced one of the first broadcasting majors in 1932 when the college teamed up with WLOE in Boston to have students broadcast programs.

Types

Broadcasting by radio takes several forms. These include AM and FM stations. There are several subtypes, namely commercial broadcasting, non-commercial educational (NCE) public broadcasting and non-profit varieties as well as community radio, student-run campus radio stations and hospital radio stations can be found throughout the world.

Many stations broadcast on shortwave bands using AM technology that can be received over thousands of miles (especially at night). For example, the BBC, VOA, VOR, and Deutsche Welle have transmitted via shortwave to Africa and Asia. These broadcasts are very sensitive to atmospheric conditions and solar activity.

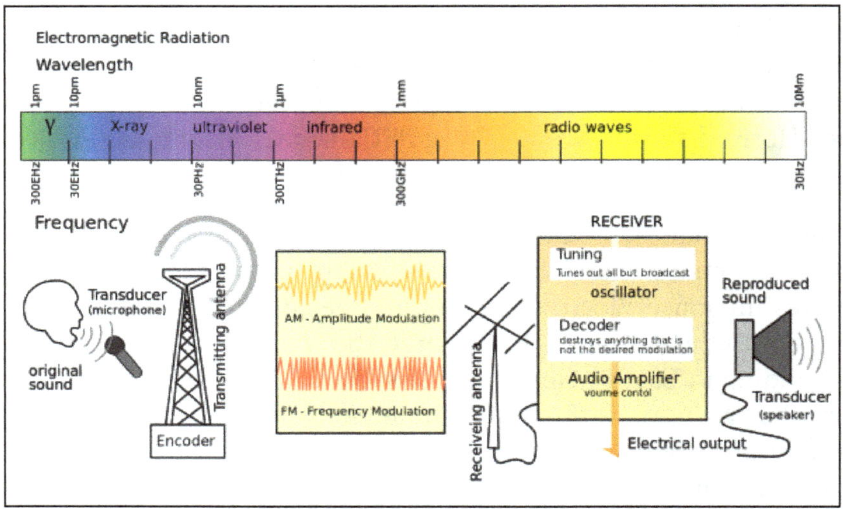

Transmission diagram of sound broadcasting (AM and FM)

Nielsen Audio, formerly known as Arbitron, the United States-based company that reports on radio audiences, defines a "radio station" as a government-licensed AM or FM station; an HD Radio (primary or multicast) station; an internet stream of an existing government-licensed station; one of the satellite radio channels from XM Satellite Radio or Sirius Satellite Radio; or, potentially, a station that is not government licensed.

Shortwave

See shortwave for the differences between shortwave, medium wave and long wave spectra. Shortwave is used largely for national broadcasters, international propaganda, or religious broadcasting organizations.

AM

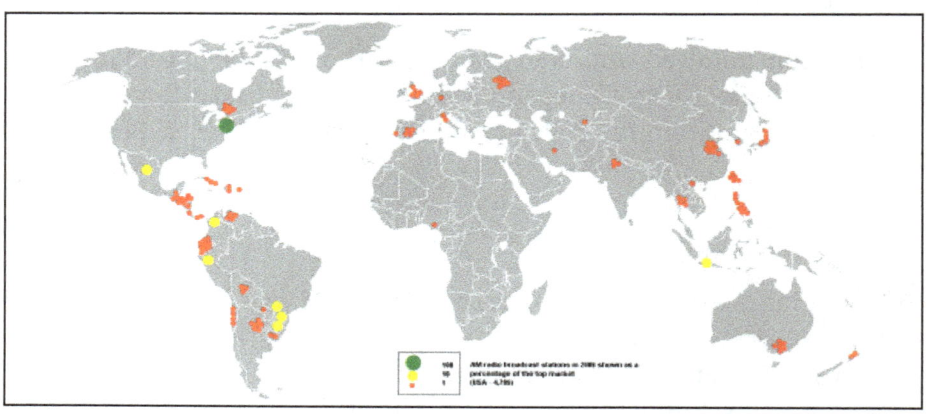

AM broadcasting stations in 2006

AM stations were the earliest broadcasting stations to be developed. AM refers to amplitude modulation, a mode of broadcasting radio waves by varying the amplitude of the carrier signal in response to the amplitude of the signal to be transmitted.

The medium-wave band is used worldwide for AM broadcasting. Europe also uses the long wave band. In response to the growing popularity of FM stereo radio stations in the late 1980s and early 1990s, some North American stations began broadcasting in AM stereo, though this never gained popularity, and very few receivers were ever sold.

One of the advantages of AM is that its signal can be detected (turned into sound) with simple equipment. If a signal is strong enough, not even a power source is needed; building an unpowered crystal radio receiver was a common childhood project in the early decades of AM broadcasting.

AM broadcasts occur on North American airwaves in the medium wave frequency range of 530 to 1700 kHz (known as the "standard broadcast band"). The band was expanded in the 1990s by adding nine channels from 1620 to 1700 kHz. Channels are spaced every 10 kHz in the Americas, and generally every 9 kHz everywhere else.

The signal is subject to interference from electrical storms (lightning) and other electromagnetic interference (EMI).

AM transmissions cannot be ionospherically propagated during the day due to strong absorption in the D-layer of the ionosphere. In a crowded channel environment this means that the power of regional channels which share a frequency must be reduced at night or directionally beamed in order to avoid interference, which reduces the potential nighttime audience. Some stations have frequencies unshared with other stations in North America; these are called clear-channel stations. Many of them can be heard across much of the country at night. During the night, absorption largely disappears and permits signals to travel to much more distant locations via ionospheric reflections. However, fading of the signal can be severe at night.

AM radio transmitters can transmit audio frequencies up to 15 kHz (now limited to 10 kHz in the US due to FCC rules designed to reduce interference), but most receivers are only capable of reproducing frequencies up to 5 kHz or less. At the time that AM broadcasting began in the 1920s, this provided adequate fidelity for existing microphones, 78 rpm recordings, and loudspeakers. The fidelity of sound equipment subsequently improved considerably, but the receivers did not. Reducing the bandwidth of the receivers reduces the cost of manufacturing and makes them less prone to interference. AM stations are never assigned adjacent channels in the same service area. This prevents the sideband power generated by two stations from interfering with each other. Bob Carver created an AM stereo tuner employing notch filtering that demonstrated that an AM broadcast can meet or exceed the 15 kHz baseband bandwidth allotted to FM stations without objectionable interference. After several years, the tuner was discontinued. Bob Carver had left the company and the Carver Corporation later cut the number of models produced before discontinuing production completely.

FM

FM refers to frequency modulation, and occurs on VHF airwaves in the frequency range of 88 to 108 MHz everywhere except Japan and Russia. Russia, like the former Soviet Union, uses 65.9 to

74 MHz frequencies in addition to the world standard. Japan uses the 76 to 90 MHz frequency band.

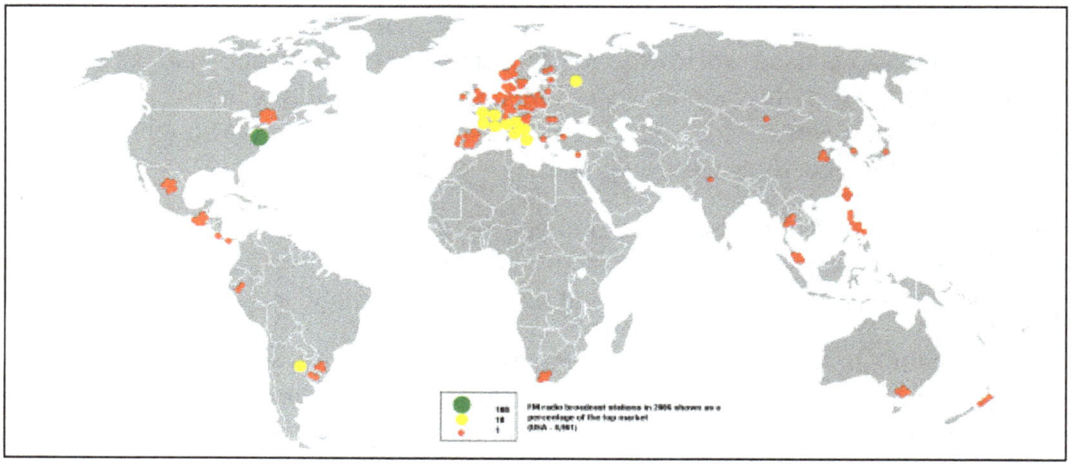

FM radio broadcast stations in 2006

Edwin Howard Armstrong invented FM radio to overcome the problem of radio-frequency interference (RFI), which plagued AM radio reception. At the same time, greater fidelity was made possible by spacing stations further apart in the radio frequency spectrum. Instead of 10 kHz apart, as on the AM band in the US, FM channels are 200 kHz (0.2 MHz) apart. In other countries greater spacing is sometimes mandatory, such as in New Zealand, which uses 700 kHz spacing (previously 800 kHz). The improved fidelity made available was far in advance of the audio equipment of the 1940s, but wide interchannel spacing was chosen to take advantage of the noise-suppressing feature of wideband FM.

Bandwidth of 200 kHz is not needed to accommodate an audio signal — 20 kHz to 30 kHz is all that is necessary for a narrowband FM signal. The 200 kHz bandwidth allowed room for ±75 kHz signal deviation from the assigned frequency, plus guard bands to reduce or eliminate adjacent channel interference. The larger bandwidth allows for broadcasting a 15 kHz bandwidth audio signal plus a 38 kHz stereo "subcarrier"—a piggyback signal that rides on the main signal. Additional unused capacity is used by some broadcasters to transmit utility functions such as background music for public areas, GPS auxiliary signals, or financial market data.

The AM radio problem of interference at night was addressed in a different way. At the time FM was set up, the available frequencies were far higher in the spectrum than those used for AM radio - by a factor of approximately 100. Using these frequencies meant that even at far higher power, the range of a given FM signal was much shorter; thus its market was more local than for AM radio. The reception range at night is the same as in the daytime. All FM broadcast transmissions are line-of-sight, and ionospheric bounce is not viable. The much larger bandwidths, compared to AM and SSB, are more susceptible to phase dispersion. Propagation speeds (celerities) are fastest in the ionosphere at the lowest sideband frequency. The celerity difference between the highest and lowest sidebands is quite apparent to the listener. Such distortion occurs up to frequencies of approximately 50 MHz. Higher frequencies do not reflect from the ionosphere, nor from storm clouds. Moon reflections have been used in some experiments, but require impractical power levels.

The original FM radio service in the U.S. was the Yankee Network, located in New England. Regular FM broadcasting began in 1939, but did not pose a significant threat to the AM broadcasting industry. It required purchase of a special receiver. The frequencies used, 42 to 50 MHz, were not those used today. The change to the current frequencies, 88 to 108 MHz, began after the end of World War II, and was to some extent imposed by AM broadcasters as an attempt to cripple what was by now realized to be a potentially serious threat.

FM radio on the new band had to begin from the ground floor. As a commercial venture it remained a little-used audio enthusiasts' medium until the 1960s. The more prosperous AM stations, or their owners, acquired FM licenses and often broadcast the same programming on the FM station as on the AM station ("simulcasting"). The FCC limited this practice in the 1960s. By the 1980s, since almost all new radios included both AM and FM tuners, FM became the dominant medium, especially in cities. Because of its greater range, AM remained more common in rural environments.

Pirate Radio

Pirate radio is illegal or non-regulated radio transmission. It is most commonly used to describe illegal broadcasting for entertainment or political purposes. Sometimes it is used for illegal two-way radio operation. Its history can be traced back to the unlicensed nature of the transmission, but historically there has been occasional use of sea vessels—fitting the most common perception of a pirate—as broadcasting bases. Rules and regulations vary largely from country to country, but often the term pirate radio generally describes the unlicensed broadcast of FM radio, AM radio, or short wave signals over a wide range. In some places radio stations are legal where the signal is transmitted, but illegal where the signals are received—especially when the signals cross a national boundary. In other cases, a broadcast may be considered "pirate" due to the type of content, its transmission format, or the transmitting power (wattage) of the station, even if the transmission is not technically illegal (such as a web cast or an amateur radio transmission). Pirate radio stations are sometimes referred to as bootleg radio or clandestine stations.

Terrestrial Digital Radio

Digital radio broadcasting has emerged, first in Europe (the UK in 1995 and Germany in 1999), and later in the United States, France, the Netherlands, South Africa and many other countries worldwide. The most simple system is named DAB Digital Radio, for Digital Audio Broadcasting, and uses the public domain EUREKA 147 (Band III) system. DAB is used mainly in the UK and South Africa. Germany and the Netherlands use the DAB and DAB+ systems, and France uses the L-Band system of DAB Digital Radio.

In the United States, digital radio isn't used in the same way as Europe and South Africa. Instead, the IBOC system is named HD Radio and owned by a consortium of private companies that is called iBiquity. An international non-profit consortium Digital Radio Mondiale (DRM), has introduced the public domain DRM system.

Satellite

Satellite radio broadcasters are slowly emerging, but the enormous entry costs of space-based satellite transmitters, and restrictions on available radio spectrum licenses has restricted growth of this market. In the USA and Canada, just two services, XM Satellite Radio and Sirius Satellite Radio exist. Both XM and Sirius are owned by Sirius XM Radio, which was formed by the merger of XM and Sirius on July 29, 2008, whereas in Canada, XM Radio Canada and Sirius Canada remained separate companies until 2010. Worldspace in Africa and Asia, and MobaHO! in Japan and the ROK were two unsuccessful satellite radio operators which have gone out of business.

Program Formats

Radio program formats differ by country, regulation and markets. For instance, the U.S. Federal Communications Commission designates the 88–92 megahertz band in the U.S. for non-profit or educational programming, with advertising prohibited.

In addition, formats change in popularity as time passes and technology improves. Early radio equipment only allowed program material to be broadcast in real time, known as *live* broadcasting. As technology for sound recording improved, an increasing proportion of broadcast programming used pre-recorded material. A current trend is the automation of radio stations. Some stations now operate without direct human intervention by using entirely pre-recorded material sequenced by computer control.

Digital Audio Broadcasting

Digital audio broadcasting (DAB) is a digital radio technology for broadcasting radio stations, used in several countries across Europe and Asia Pacific.

The DAB standard was initiated as a European research project in the 1980s. The Norwegian Broadcasting Corporation (NRK) launched the first DAB channel in the world on 1 June 1995 (NRK Klassisk), and the BBC and Swedish Radio (SR) launched their first DAB digital radio broadcasts in September 1995. DAB receivers have been available in many countries since the end of the 1990s.

DAB may offer more radio programmes over a specific spectrum than analogue FM radio. DAB is more robust with regard to noise and multipath fading for mobile listening, since DAB reception quality first degrades rapidly when the signal strength falls below a critical threshold, whereas FM reception quality degrades slowly with the decreasing signal.

Audio quality varies depending on the bitrate used and audio material. Most stations use a bit rate of 128 kbit/s or less with the MP2 audio codec, which requires 160 kbit/s to achieve perceived FM quality. 128 kbit/s gives better dynamic range or signal-to-noise ratio than FM radio, but a more smeared stereo image, and an upper cut-off frequency of 14 kHz, corresponding to 15 kHz of FM radio. However, "CD sound quality" with MP2 is possible "with 256…192 kbps".

An upgraded version of the system was released in February 2007, which is called DAB+. DAB is not forward compatible with DAB+, which means that DAB-only receivers are not able to receive DAB+ broadcasts. However, broadcasters can mix DAB and DAB+ programs inside the same transmission and so make a progressive transition to DAB+. DAB+ is approximately twice as efficient as DAB due to the adoption of the AAC+ audio codec, and DAB+ can provide high quality audio with bit rates as low as 64 kbit/s. Reception quality is also more robust on DAB+ than on DAB due to the addition of Reed-Solomon error correction coding.

In spectrum management, the bands that are allocated for public DAB services, are abbreviated with T-DAB, where the "T" stands for terrestrial.

More than 30 countries provide DAB transmissions, and several countries, such as Norway, Australia, Italy, Malta, Switzerland, The Netherlands and Germany, are transmitting DAB+ stations.

In many countries it is expected that DAB will gradually replace FM radio. Norway was the first country to announce national FM radio switch-off starting from 2017.

History

DAB has been under development since 1981 at the *Institut für Rundfunktechnik* (IRT). In 1985 the first DAB demonstrations were held at the WARC-ORB in Geneva and in 1988 the first DAB transmissions were made in Germany. Later DAB was developed as a research project for the European Union (EUREKA), which started in 1987 on initiative by a consortium formed in 1986. The MPEG-1 Audio Layer II ("MP2") codec was created as part of the EU147 project. DAB was the first standard based on orthogonal frequency division multiplexing (OFDM) modulation technique, which since then has become one of the most popular transmission schemes for modern wideband digital communication systems.

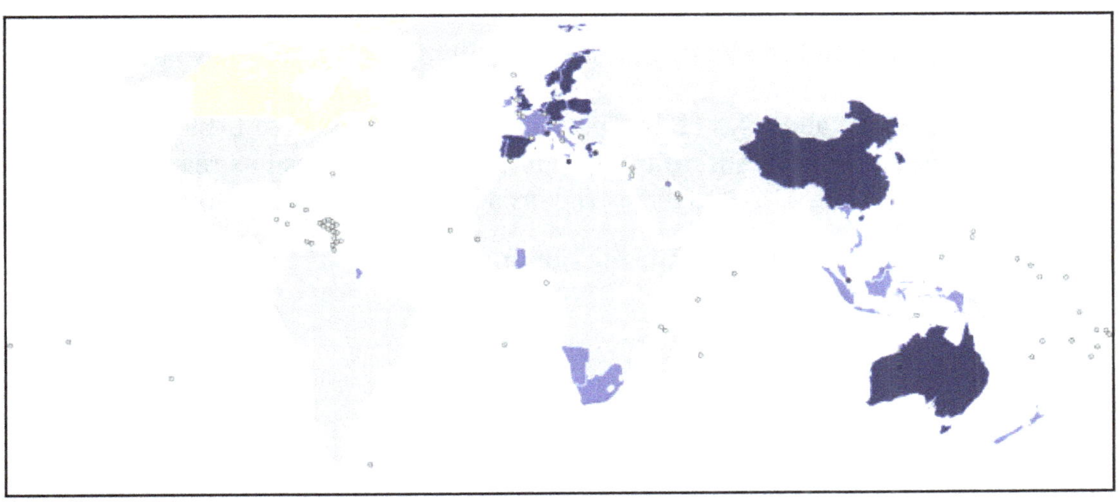

Countries with regular services

Countries with trials / tests

Countries with interest

DAB no longer used

(2012)

A choice of audio codec, modulation and error-correction coding schemes and first trial broadcasts were made in 1990. Public demonstrations were made in 1993 in the United Kingdom. The protocol specification was finalized in 1993 and adopted by the ITU-R standardization body in 1994, the European community in 1995 and by ETSI in 1997. Pilot broadcasts were launched in several countries in 1995.

The UK was the first country to receive a wide range of radio stations via DAB. Commercial DAB receivers began to be sold in 1999 and over 50 commercial and BBC services were available in London by 2001.

The standard was coordinated by the European DAB forum, formed in 1995 and reconstituted to the World DAB Forum in 1997, which represents more than 30 countries. In 2006 the World DAB Forum became the World DMB Forum which now presides over both the DAB and DMB standard.

In October 2005, the World DMB Forum instructed its Technical Committee to carry out the work needed to adopt the AAC+ audio codec and stronger error correction coding. This work led to the launch of the new DAB+ system.

By 2006, 500 million people worldwide were in the coverage area of DAB broadcasts, although by this time sales had only taken off in the United Kingdom and Denmark. In 2006 there were approximately 1,000 DAB stations in operation worldwide.

Technology

Bands and Modes

DAB uses a wide-bandwidth broadcast technology and typically spectra have been allocated for it in Band III (174–240 MHz) and L band (1,452–1,492 MHz), although the scheme allows for operation almost anywhere above 30 MHz. The US military has reserved L-Band in the USA only, blocking its use for other purposes in America, and the United States has reached an agreement with Canada to restrict L-Band DAB to terrestrial broadcast to avoid interference.

DAB has a number of country specific transmission modes (I, II, III and IV). For worldwide operation a receiver must support all 4 modes:

- Mode I for Band III, Earth.
- Mode II for L-Band, Earth and satellite.
- Mode III for frequencies below 3 GHz, Earth and satellite.
- Mode IV for L-Band, Earth and satellite.

Protocol Stack

From an OSI model protocol stack viewpoint, the technologies used on DAB inhabit the following layers: the audio codec inhabits the presentation layer. Below that is the data link layer, in charge of statistical time division multiplexing and frame synchronization. Finally, the physical layer contains the error-correction coding, OFDM modulation, and dealing with the over-the-air transmission and reception of data. Some aspects of these are described below.

Audio Codec

The older version of DAB that is being used in Denmark*, Ireland*, Norway*, Switzerland* and the UK, uses the MPEG-1 Audio Layer 2 audio codec, which is also known as *MP2* due to computer files using those characters for their file extension. Denmark, Ireland, Norway, and Switzerland also use DAB+.

The new DAB+ standard has adopted the HE-AAC version 2 audio codec, commonly known as 'AAC+' or 'aacPlus'. AAC+ is approximately three-times more efficient than MP2, which means that broadcasters using DAB+ will be able to provide far higher audio quality or far more stations than they can on DAB, or, as is most likely, a combination of both higher audio quality and more stations will be provided.

One of the most important decisions regarding the design of a digital radio system is the choice of which audio codec to use, because the efficiency of the audio codec determines how many radio stations can be carried on a multiplex at a given level of audio quality. The capacity of a DAB multiplex is fixed, so the more efficient the audio codec is, the more stations can be carried, and vice versa. Similarly, for a fixed bit-rate level, the more efficient the audio codec is the higher the audio quality will be.

Error-correction Coding

Error-correction coding (ECC) is an important technology for a digital communication system because it determines how robust the reception will be for a given signal strength – stronger ECC will provide more robust reception than a weaker form.

The old version of DAB uses punctured convolutional coding for its ECC. The coding scheme uses unequal error protection (UEP), which means that parts of the audio bit-stream that are more susceptible to errors causing audible disturbances are provided with more protection (i.e. a lower code rate) and vice versa. However, the UEP scheme used on DAB results in there being a grey area in between the user experiencing good reception quality and no reception at all, as opposed to the situation with most other wireless digital communication systems that have a sharp "digital cliff", where the signal rapidly becomes unusable if the signal strength drops below a certain threshold. When DAB listeners receive a signal in this intermediate strength area they experience a "burbling" sound which interrupts the playback of the audio.

The new DAB+ standard has incorporated Reed-Solomon ECC as an "inner layer" of coding that is placed around the byte interleaved audio frame but inside the "outer layer" of convolutional coding used by the older DAB system, although on DAB+ the convolutional coding uses equal error protection (EEP) rather than UEP since each bit is equally important in DAB+. This combination of Reed-Solomon coding as the inner layer of coding, followed by an outer layer of convolutional coding – so-called "concatenated coding" – became a popular ECC scheme in the 1990s, and NASA adopted it for its deep-space missions. One slight difference between the concatenated coding used by the DAB+ system and that used on most other systems is that it uses a rectangular byte interleaver rather than Forney interleaving in order to provide a greater interleaver depth, which increases the distance over which error bursts will be spread out in the bit-stream, which in turn will allow the Reed-Solomon error decoder to correct a higher proportion of errors.

The ECC used on DAB+ is far stronger than is used on DAB, which, with all else being equal (i.e. if the transmission powers remained the same), would translate into people who currently experience reception difficulties on DAB receiving a much more robust signal with DAB+ transmissions. It also has a far steeper "digital cliff", and listening tests have shown that people prefer this when the signal strength is low compared to the shallower digital cliff on DAB.

Modulation

Immunity to fading and inter-symbol interference (caused by multipath propagation) is achieved without equalization by means of the OFDM and DQPSK modulation techniques.

Using values for the most commonly used transmission mode on DAB, Transmission Mode I (TM I), the OFDM modulation consists of 1,536 subcarriers that are transmitted in parallel. The useful part of the OFDM symbol period is 1 millisecond, which results in the OFDM subcarriers each having a bandwidth of 1 kHz due to the inverse relationship between these two parameters, and the overall OFDM channel bandwidth is 1,537 kHz. The OFDM guard interval for TM I is 246 microseconds, which means that the overall OFDM symbol duration is 1.246 milliseconds. The guard interval duration also determines the maximum separation between transmitters that are part of the same single-frequency network (SFN), which is approximately 74 km for TM I.

Single-frequency Networks

OFDM allows the use of single-frequency networks (SFN), which means that a network of transmitters can provide coverage to a large area – up to the size of a country – where all transmitters use the same transmission frequency. Transmitters that are part of an SFN need to be very accurately synchronised with other transmitters in the network, which requires the transmitters to use very accurate clocks.

When a receiver receives a signal that has been transmitted from the different transmitters that are part of an SFN, the signals from the different transmitters will typically have different delays, but to OFDM they will appear to simply be different multipaths of the same signal. Reception difficulties can arise, however, when the relative delay of multipaths exceeds the OFDM guard interval duration, and there are frequent reports of reception difficulties due to this issue when there is a *lift*, such as when there's high pressure, due to signals travelling farther than usual, and thus the signals are likely to arrive with a relative delay that is greater than the OFDM guard interval.

Low power *gap-filler* transmitters can be added to an SFN as and when desired in order to improve reception quality, although the way SFNs have been implemented in the UK up to now they have tended to consist of higher power transmitters being installed at main transmitter sites in order to keep costs down.

Bit Rates

An ensemble has a maximum bit rate that can be carried, but this depends on which error protection level is used. However, all DAB multiplexes can carry a total of 864 "capacity units". The number of capacity units, or CU, that a certain bit-rate level requires depends on the amount of error correction added to the transmission, as described above. In the UK, most services transmit using 'protection level three', which provides an average ECC code rate of approximately ½, equating to a maximum bit rate per multiplex of 1,184 kbit/s.

Services and Ensembles

Various different services are embedded into one ensemble (which is also typically called a multiplex). These services can include:

- Primary services, like main radio stations.
- Secondary services, like additional sports commentaries.
- Data services:
    - Electronic Programme Guide (EPG).
    - Collections of HTML pages and digital images (Known as 'Broadcast Web Sites').
    - Slideshows, which may be synchronised with audio broadcasts. For example, a police appeal could be broadcast with the e-fit of a suspect or CCTV footage.
    - Video.
    - Java Platform Applications.
    - IP tunnelling.
    - Other raw data.

DAB+

The term DAB most commonly refers both to a specific DAB standard using the MP2 audio codec, but can sometimes refer to a whole family of DAB related standards, such as DAB+, DMB and DAB-IP.

DAB+

WorldDAB, the organisation in charge of the DAB standards, announced DAB+, a major upgrade to the DAB standard in 2006, when the HE-AAC v2 audio codec (also known as eAAC+) was adopted. The new standard, which is called DAB+, has also adopted the MPEG Surround audio format and stronger error correction coding in the form of Reed-Solomon coding. DAB+ has been standardised as European Telecommunications Standards Institute (ETSI) TS 102 563.

As DAB is not forward compatible with DAB+, older DAB receivers can not receive DAB+ broadcasts. However, DAB receivers that will be able to receive the new DAB+ standard via a firmware upgrade went on sale in July 2007. If a receiver is DAB+ compatible, there will be a sign on the product packaging.

DAB+ broadcasts have launched in several countries like Australia, Czech Republic, Denmark, Germany, Hong Kong, Italy, Malta, Norway, Poland, Switzerland, the United Kingdom and the Netherlands. Malta was the first country to launch DAB+ in Europe. Several other countries are also expected to launch DAB+ broadcasts over the next few years, such as Austria, Hungary and Asian countries, such as Thailand, Vietnam and Indonesia. South Africa began a DAB+ technical pilot in November 2014 on channel 13F in Band 3. If DAB+ stations launch in established DAB countries, they can transmit alongside existing DAB stations that use the older MPEG-1 Audio Layer II audio format, and most existing DAB stations are expected to continue broadcasting until the vast majority of receivers support DAB+.

Ofcom in the UK has published a consultation with the intention to set up a new multiplex containing a mix of DAB and DAB+ services, with the intention of moving services to this format in the long term. In February 2016 3 DAB+ stations launched in the UK as part of a new national network.

DMB

Digital multimedia broadcasting (DMB) and DAB-IP are suitable for mobile radio and TV both because they support MPEG 4 AVC and WMV9 respectively as video codecs. However, a DMB video subchannel can easily be added to any DAB transmission, as it was designed to be carried on a DAB subchannel. DMB broadcasts in Korea carry conventional MPEG 1 Layer II DAB audio services alongside their DMB video services.

Norway, South Korea and France are countries currently[*when?*] broadcasting DMB.

Countries Using DAB

More than 30 countries provide DAB, DAB+ and/or DMB broadcasts, either as a permanent technology or as test transmissions.

DAB and AM/FM Compared

Traditionally radio programmes were broadcast on different frequencies via AM and FM, and the radio had to be tuned into each frequency, as needed. This used up a comparatively large amount of spectrum for a relatively small number of stations, limiting listening choice. DAB is a digital radio broadcasting system that through the application of multiplexing and compression combines multiple audio streams onto a relatively narrow band centred on a single broadcast frequency called a DAB ensemble.

Within an overall target bit rate for the DAB ensemble, individual stations can be allocated different bit rates. The number of channels within a DAB ensemble can be increased by lowering average bit rates, but at the expense of the quality of streams. Error correction under the DAB standard makes the signal more robust but reduces the total bit rate available for streams.

FM HD Radio Versus DAB

Some countries have implemented Eureka-147 digital audio broadcasting (DAB). DAB broadcasts a single station that is approximately 1,500 kilohertz wide (~1,000 kilobits per second). That station is then subdivided into multiple digital streams of between 9 and 12 programs. In contrast FM HD radio shares its digital broadcast with the traditional 200 kilohertz-wide channels, with capability of 300 kbit/s per station (pure digital mode).

The first generation DAB uses the MPEG-1 Audio Layer II (MP2) audio codec which has less efficient compression than newer codecs. The typical bitrate for DAB programs is only 128 kbit/s and as a result most radio stations on DAB have a lower sound quality than FM, prompting a number of complaints among the audiophile community. As with DAB+ or T-DMB in Europe, FM HD Radio uses a codec based upon the MPEG-4 HE-AAC standard.

HD Radio is a proprietary system from the company Ibiquity. DAB is an open standard deposited at ETSI.

Use of Frequency Spectrum and Transmitter Sites

DAB gives substantially higher spectral efficiency, measured in programmes per MHz and per transmitter site, than analogue communication. This has led to an increase in the number of stations available to listeners, especially outside of the major urban areas.

Numerical example: Analog FM requires 0.2 MHz per programme. The frequency reuse factor in most countries is approximately 15, meaning that only one out of 15 transmitter sites can use the same channel frequency without problems with co-channel interference, i.e. cross-talk. Assuming a total availability of 102 FM channels at a bandwidth of 0.2MHz over the Band II spectrum of 87.5 to 108.0 MHz, an average of 102/15 = 6.8 radio channels are possible on each transmitter site (plus lower-power local transmitters causing less interference). This results in a system spectral efficiency of 1 / 15 / (0.2 MHz) = 0.30 programmes/transmitter/MHz. DAB with 192 kbit/s codec requires 1.536 MHz * 192 kbit/s / 1,136 kbit/s = 0.26 MHz per audio programme. The frequency reuse factor for local programmes and multi-frequency broadcasting networks (MFN) is typically 4 or 5, resulting in 1 / 4 / (0.26 MHz) = 0.96 programmes/transmitter/MHz. This is 3.2 times as efficient as analog FM for local stations. For single frequency network (SFN) transmission, for example of national programmes, the channel re-use factor is 1, resulting in 1/1/0.25 MHz = 3.85 programmes/transmitter/MHz, which is 12.7 times as efficient as FM for national and regional networks.

Note the above capacity improvement may not always be achieved at the L-band frequencies, since these are more sensitive to obstacles than the FM band frequencies, and may cause shadow fading for hilly terrain and for indoor communication. The number of transmitter sites or the transmission power required for full coverage of a country may be rather high at these frequencies, to avoid the system becoming noise limited rather than limited by co-channel interference.

Sound Quality

The original objectives of converting to digital transmission were to enable higher fidelity, more stations and more resistance to noise, co-channel interference and multipath than in analogue FM radio. However, the leading countries in implementing DAB on stereo radio stations use compression to such a degree that it produces lower sound quality than that received from non-mobile FM broadcasts. This is because of the bit rate levels being too low for the MPEG Layer 2 audio codec to provide high fidelity audio quality.

The BBC Research & Development department states that at least 192 kbit/s is necessary for a high fidelity stereo broadcast.

A value of 256 kbit/s has been judged to provide a high quality stereo broadcast signal. However, a small reduction, to 224 kbit/s is often adequate, and in some cases it may be possible to accept a further reduction to 192 kbit/s, especially if redundancy in the stereo signal is exploited by a process of 'joint stereo' encoding (i.e. some sounds appearing at the centre of the stereo image need not be sent twice). At 192 kbit/s, it is relatively easy to hear imperfections in critical audio material.

—BBC R&D White Paper WHP 061 June 2003

When BBC in July 2006 reduced the bit-rate of transmission of Radio 3 from 192 kbit/s to 160 kbit/s, the resulting degradation of audio quality prompted a number of complaints to the Corporation. BBC later announced that following this testing of new equipment, it would resume the previous practice of transmitting Radio 3 at 192 kbit/s whenever there were no other demands on bandwidth.

Despite the above a survey of DAB listeners (including mobile) has shown most find DAB to have equal or better sound quality than FM.

Notwithstanding the above, BBC Radio 4 has extended the periods it broadcasts programmes with a lower bit rate (80 kbit/s) and in mono in 2012, such as the *Today* programme, rather than 128 kbit/s and in stereo. Programmes which had traditionally been broadcast on BBC Radio 4 DAB in stereo (from 1999 to 2011), can now only be heard in the evenings in mono, even though the same programmes still go out in stereo on Radio 4 FM, Digital TV and On-Line. The BBC have issued a statement stating that stereo is still their default for BBC Radio 4 DAB, however after the Olympics, this does not appear to be the case in the evenings, making FM broadcasts (in good reception areas) superior. As very few car radios are currently fitted with DAB if the BBC switch FM off as indicated later in the decade, some listeners may be forced to receive mono broadcasts in the future, a somewhat backward step.

An Audio Quality comparison of PCM, DAB, DAB+, FM and AM is available here

Benefits of DAB

Current AM and FM terrestrial broadcast technology is well established, compatible, and cheap to manufacture. Benefits of DAB over analogue systems are explained below.

Improved Features for Users

DAB radios automatically tune to all the available stations, offering a list for the user to select from.

DAB can carry "radiotext" (in DAB terminology, *Dynamic Label Segment*, or DLS) from the station giving real-time information such as song titles, music type and news or traffic updates. Advance programme guides can also be transmitted. A similar feature also exists on FM in the form of the RDS. (However, not all FM receivers allow radio stations to be stored by name.)

DAB receivers can display time of day as encoded into transmissions, so is automatically corrected when travelling between time zones and when changing to or from Daylight Saving. This is not implemented on all receivers, and some display time only when in "Standby" mode. (Similar Features on RDS: 4A Groups.)

Some radios offer a pause facility on live broadcasts, caching the broadcast stream on local flash memory, although this function is limited.

More Stations

DAB is not more bandwidth efficient than analogue measured in programmes per MHz of a specific transmitter (the so-called link spectral efficiency). It is less susceptible to co-channel interference (cross talk), which makes it possible to reduce the reuse distance, i.e. use the same radio frequency channel more densely. The system spectral efficiency (the average number of radio programmes per MHz and transmitter) is a factor three more efficient than analogue FM for local radio stations, as can be seen in the above numerical example. For national and regional radio networks, the efficiency is improved by more than an order of magnitude due to the use of SFNs. In that case, adjacent transmitters use the same frequency.

In certain areas – particularly rural areas – the introduction of DAB gives radio listeners a greater choice of radio stations. For instance, in South Norway, radio listeners experienced an increase in available stations from 6 to 21 when DAB was introduced in November 2006.

Reception Quality

The DAB standard integrates features to reduce the negative consequences of multipath fading and signal noise, which afflict existing analogue systems.

Also, as DAB transmits digital audio, there is no hiss with a weak signal, which can happen on FM. However, radios in the fringe of a DAB signal, can experience a "bubbling mud" sound interrupting the audio and/or the audio cutting out altogether.

Due to sensitivity to doppler shift in combination with multipath propagation, DAB reception range (but not audio quality) is reduced when travelling speeds of more than 120 to 200 km/h, depending on carrier frequency.

Less Unlicensed ("Pirate") Station Interference

The specialised nature and cost of DAB broadcasting equipment provide barriers to unlicensed ("pirate") stations broadcasting on DAB. In cities such as London with large numbers of undocumented radio stations broadcasting on FM, this means that some stations can be reliably received via DAB in areas where they are regularly difficult or impossible to receive on FM due to undocumented radio interference.

Variable Bandwidth

Mono talk radio, news and weather channels and other non-music programs need significantly less bandwidth than a typical music radio station, which allows DAB to carry these programmes at lower bit rates, leaving more bandwidth to be used for other programs.

However, this had led to the situation where some stations are being broadcast in mono.

Transmission Costs

It is common belief that DAB is more expensive to transmit than FM. It is true that DAB uses higher frequencies than FM and therefore there is a need to compensate with more transmitters, higher radiated powers, or a combination, to achieve the same coverage. However, the last couple of years has seen significant improvement in power efficiency for DAB-transmitters.

This efficiency originates from the ability a DAB network has in broadcasting more channels per network. One network can broadcast 6–10 channels (with MPEG audio codec) or 10–16 channels (with HE AAC codec). Hence, it is thought that the replacement of FM-radios and FM-transmitters with new DAB-radios and DAB-transmitters will not cost any more as opposed to newer FM facilities.

Lower transmission costs are supported by independent network studies from Teracom (Sweden) and SSR/SRG (Switzerland). Among other things they show that DAB is as low as one-sixth of the cost of FM transmission.

Disadvantages of DAB

Reception Quality

The reception quality during the early stage of deployment of DAB was poor even for people who live well within the coverage area. The reason for this is that the old version of DAB uses weak error correction coding, so that when there are a lot of errors with the received data not enough of the errors can be corrected and a "bubbling mud" sound occurs. In some cases a complete loss of signal can happen. This situation has been improved upon in the new DAB standard (DAB+, discussed below) that uses stronger error correction coding and as additional transmitters are built. Like with DBV-T, when the signal is weak or gets interference, it will not work at all.

Audio Quality

Broadcasters have been criticized for 'squeezing in' more stations per ensemble than recommended, by:

- Minimizing the bit-rate, to the lowest level of sound-quality that listeners are willing to tolerate, such as 112 kbit/s for stereo and even 48 kbit/s for mono speech radio such as LBC 1152 and the Voice of Russia.
- Having few digital channels broadcasting in stereo.

Signal Delay

The nature of a Single-frequency network (SFN) is such that the transmitters in a network must broadcast the same signal at the same time. To achieve synchronization, the broadcaster must counter any differences in propagation time incurred by the different methods and distances involved in carrying the signal from the multiplexer to the different transmitters. This is done by applying a delay to the incoming signal at the transmitter based on a timestamp generated at the multiplexer, created taking into account the maximum likely propagation time, with a generous added margin for safety. Delays in the receiver due to digital processing (e.g. deinterleaving) add to the overall delay perceived by the listener. The signal is delayed by 2–4 seconds depending on the decoding circuitry used. This has disadvantages:

- DAB radios are out of step with live events, so the experience of listening to live commentaries on events being watched is impaired;
- Listeners using a combination of analogue (AM or FM) and DAB radios (e.g. in different rooms of a house) will hear a confusing mixture when both receivers are within earshot.

Time signals, on the contrary, are not a problem in a well-defined network with a fixed delay. The DAB multiplexer adds the proper offset to the distributed time information. The time information is also independent from the (possibly varying) audio decoding delay in receivers since the time is not embedded inside the audio frames. This means that built in clocks in receivers will be spot on.

Coverage

As DAB is at a relatively early stage of deployment, DAB coverage is poor in nearly all countries in comparison to the high population coverage provided by FM.

Exceptions include Norway, which will have 99.5% coverage by the end of 2014, and the United Kingdom, where 95% population coverage has been achieved for certain stations.

Compatibility

In 2006 tests began using the much improved HE-AAC codec for DAB+. Virtually none of the receivers made before 2008 support the new codec, however, thus making them partially obsolete once DAB+ broadcasts begin and completely obsolete once the old MPEG-1 Layer 2 stations are switched off. New receivers are both DAB and DAB+ compatible; however, the issue is exacerbated by some manufacturers disabling the DAB+ features on otherwise compatible radios to save on licensing fees when sold in countries without current DAB+ broadcasts.

Power Requirements

As DAB requires digital signal processing techniques to convert from the received digitally encoded signal to the analogue audio content, the complexity of the electronic circuitry required to do this is higher. This translates into needing more power to effect this conversion than compared to an analogue FM to audio conversion, meaning that portable receiving equipment will tend to have a shorter battery life, or require higher power (and hence more bulk). This means that they use more energy than analogue Band II VHF receivers. However, thanks to increased integration (radio-on-chip), DAB receiver is getting closer to FM one. For example, NXP semiconductor is producing both FM only and FM+DAB radio-on-chip, with similar power consumption.

As an indicator of this increased power consumption in the early days of DAB, some radio manufacturers quoted the length of time their receivers can play on a single charge. For a commonly used FM/DAB-receiver from manufacturer PURE, this is stated as: DAB 10 hours, FM 22 hours.. Currently, PURE manufacturer doesn't indicate any more power consumption difference between FM and DAB modes.

FM Radio Switch-off

Norway is the first country that has announced a complete switch-off of national FM radio stations. Switch off will start on 11 January 2017. The switch-off will not affect local and in some way regional radio stations.

Switzerland has announced its plans for a progressive digital switchover between 2020 and 2024.

Other countries like Denmark and Sweden are evaluating a switch-off by 2022.

UK is considering a progressive switch-off in the period 2017–2022.

Commercial Broadcasting

Commercial broadcasting (also called *private broadcasting*) is the broadcasting of television programs and radio programming by privately owned corporate media, as opposed to state sponsorship. It was the United States' first model of radio (and later television) during the 1920s, in contrast with the public television model in Europe during the 1930s, 1940s and 1950s which prevailed worldwide (except in the United States) until the 1980s.

Features

Advertising

Commercial broadcasting is primarily based on the practice of airing radio advertisements and television advertisements for profit. This is in contrast to public broadcasting, which receives government subsidies and tries to avoid paid advertising interrupting the show. During pledge drives they will interrupt shows to ask for donations.

In the United States, non-commercial educational (NCE) television and radio exists in the form of community radio; however, premium cable services such as HBO and Showtime generally operate solely on subscriber fees and do not sell advertising. This is also the case for the portions of the two major satellite radio systems that are produced in-house (mainly music programming).

Radio broadcasting originally began without paid commercials. As time went on, however, advertisements seemed less objectionable to both the public and government regulators and became more common. While commercial broadcasting was unexpected in radio, in television it was planned due to commercial radio's success. Television began with commercial sponsorship and later transformed to paid commercial time. When problems arose over patents and corporate marketing strategies, regulatory decisions were made by the Federal Communications Commission (FCC) to control commercial broadcasting.

Paid Programming

Commercial broadcasting overlaps with paid services such as cable television, radio and satellite television. Such services are generally partially or wholly paid for by local subscribers and is known as leased access. Other programming (particularly on cable television) is produced by companies operating in much the same manner as advertising-funded commercial broadcasters, and they (and often the local cable provider) sell commercial time in a similar manner.

The FCC's interest in program control began with the chain-broadcasting investigation of the late 1930s, culminating in the "Blue Book" of 1946, *Public Service Responsibility For Broadcast Licensees*. The Blue Book differentiated between mass-appeal sponsored programs and unsponsored "sustaining" programs offered by the radio networks. This sustained programming, according to the Blue Book, had five features serving the public interest:

- Sustaining programs balanced the broadcast schedule, supplementing the soap operas and popular-music programs receiving the highest ratings and most commercial sponsors.
- They allowed for the broadcast of programs which, by their controversial or sensitive nature, were unsuitable for sponsorship.
- They supplied cultural programming for smaller audiences.
- They provided limited broadcast access for non-profit and civic organizations.
- They made possible artistic and dramatic experimentation, shielded from the pressures of short-run rating and commercial considerations of a sponsor.

Commercial time has increased 31 seconds per hour for all prime time television shows. For example, ABC has increased from 9 minutes and 26 seconds to 11 minutes and 26 seconds.

Ratings

Programming on commercial stations is more ratings-driven—particularly during periods such as sweeps in the US and some Latin American countries.

Other Factors

Commercial broadcasting (especially free-to-air) is sometimes controversial. One reason is a perceived lack of quality and risk in the programming (to which more conservative elements respond that it is too risqué much of the time), an excessively high ratio of advertising to program time (especially on children's television), and a perceived failure to serve the local interest due to media consolidation. Commercial radio (in particular) is criticized for a perceived homogeneity in programming, covert politically motivated censorship of content, and a desire to cut costs at the expense of a station's identifiable personality. Politics is a major force in media criticism, with an ongoing debate (especially in the United States) as to what moral standards – if any – are to be applied to the airwaves.

Global Commercial Broadcasting

Americas

Commercial broadcasting is the dominant type of broadcasting in the United States and most of Latin America. "The US commercial system resulted from a carefully crafted cooperation endeavor by national corporations and federal regulators."

The best-known commercial broadcasters in the United States today are the ABC, CBS, Fox and NBC television networks and the iHeartMedia radio network, based in the United States. Major cable television in the United States operators include Comcast, Cox Communications and Time Warner Cable. Direct-broadcast satellite (DBS) services include DirecTV and Dish Network.

In an hour of broadcast time on a commercial broadcasting station, 10 to 20 minutes are typically devoted to advertising. Advertisers pay a certain amount of money to air their commercials, usually based upon program ratings or the audience measurement of a station or network. This makes commercial broadcasters more accountable to advertisers than public broadcasting, a disadvantage of commercial radio and television.

Europe

In Europe, commercial broadcasting coexists with public broadcasting (where programming is largely funded by broadcast receiver licences, public donations or government grants).

In the UK, British Sky Broadcasting (BSkyB) is available and WorldSpace Satellite Radio was available.

Asia

One of the best-known commercial services in Asia is the oldest radio station in the region, Radio Ceylon.

Public Broadcasting

Public broadcasting includes radio, television and other electronic media outlets whose primary mission is public service. In much of the world, funding comes from the government, especially via annual fees charged on receivers. In the United States, public broadcasters may receive some funding from both federal and state sources, but generally most financial support comes from underwriting by foundations and businesses ranging from small shops to corporations, along with listener contributions via pledge drives. The great majority are operated as private not-for-profit corporations.

Public broadcasting may be nationally or locally operated, depending on the country and the station. In some countries, public broadcasting is run by a single organization. Other countries have multiple public broadcasting organizations operating regionally or in different languages. Historically, public broadcasting was once the dominant or only form of broadcasting in many countries (with the notable exception of the United States). Commercial broadcasting now also exists in most of these countries; the number of countries with only public broadcasting declined substantially during the latter part of the 20th century.

Defining Public Broadcasting

The primary mission of public broadcasting that of public service, speaking to and engaging as a citizen. The British model has been widely accepted as a universal definition. The model embodies the following principles:

- Universal geographic accessibility.
- Universal appeal.
- Attention to minorities.
- Contribution to national identity and sense of community.
- Distance from vested interests.
- Direct funding and universality of payment.
- Competition in good programming rather than numbers.
- Guidelines that liberate rather than restrict.

While application of certain principles may be straightforward, as in the case of accessibility, some of the principles may be poorly defined or difficult to implement. In the context of a shifting national identity, the role of public broadcasting may be unclear. Likewise, the subjective nature of good programming may raise the question of individual or public taste.

Within public broadcasting there are two different views regarding commercial activity. One is that public broadcasting is incompatible with commercial objectives. The other is that public broadcasting can and should compete in the marketplace with commercial broadcasters. This dichotomy is highlighted by the public service aspects of traditional commercial broadcasters.

Public broadcasters in each jurisdiction may or may not be synonymous with government controlled broadcasters. In some countries like the UK public broadcasters are not sanctioned by government departments and have independent means of funding, and thus enjoy editorial independence.

Economics

Public broadcasters may receive their funding from an obligatory television licence fee, individual contributions, government funding or commercial sources. Public broadcasters do not rely on advertising to the same degree as commercial broadcasters, or at all; this allows public broadcasters to transmit programmes that are not commercially viable to the mass market, such as public affairs shows, radio and television documentaries, and educational programmes.

One of the principles of public broadcasting is to provide coverage of interests for which there are missing or small markets. Public broadcasting attempts to supply topics of social benefit that are otherwise not provided by commercial broadcasters. Typically, such underprovision is argued to exist when the benefits to viewers are relatively high in comparison to the benefits to advertisers from contacting viewers. This frequently is the case in undeveloped countries that normally have low benefits to advertising.

Cultural Policy

Additionally, public broadcasting may facilitate the implementation of a cultural policy (an industrial policy and investment policy for culture). Examples include:

- The Canadian government is committed to official bilingualism (English and French). As a result, the public broadcaster, the CBC employs translators and journalists who speak both official languages and it encourages production of cross-cultural material. Quebec separatists argue that this is also a policy of cultural imperialism and assimilation.

- In the UK, the BBC supports multiculturalism and diversity, in part by using on-screen commentators and hosts of different ethnic origins. There are also Welsh, Irish and Scottish Gaelic language programmes for the home nations, an Asian Network broadcasting in English and five major languages of South Asia, and the BBC World Service broadcasts in 31 international languages, also funded independently of government.

- In New Zealand, the public broadcasting system provides support to Māori broadcasting, with the stated intention of improving their opportunities, maintaining their cultural heritage and promoting their language.

- In Australia, the Australian Broadcasting Corporation is legally required to 'encourage and promote the musical, dramatic and other performing arts in Australia' and 'broadcasting programs that contribute to a sense of national identity' with specific emphasis on regional and rural Australia'. Furthermore, the Special Broadcasting Service (SBS) is intended to reflect the spirit and sense of multicultural richness and the unique international cultural values within Australian society.

Vested Interests

Public broadcasting, unless its independence is vigorously upheld, can become a tool of government. Similarly, private networks can promote the policies of their owners and suppress other viewpoints, alleging it is in the public interest. Conflicts are common; the state alleges that private broadcasters are attacking it in the interests of the owners, and controls them or takes them over.

Implementation of Public Broadcasting Around the World

The model, established in the 1920s, of the British Broadcasting Corporation—an organization widely trusted, even by citizens of the Axis Powers during World War II—was widely emulated throughout Europe, the British Empire, and later the Commonwealth. The public broadcasters in a number of countries are basically an application of the model used in Britain.

Modern public broadcasting is often a mixed commercial model. For example, the CBC has always relied on a subsidy from general revenues of the government, in addition to advertising revenue, to support its television service. This means they must compete with commercial broadcasting. Some argue that this dilutes their mandate as truly public broadcasters, who have no commercial bias to distort their presentation.

Asia

Hong Kong

In Hong Kong, the Radio Television Hong Kong (RTHK) is the sole public service broadcaster.

Although a government department under administrative hierarchy, it enjoys editorial independence. It operates seven radio channels, and produces television programmes and broadcast on commercial television channels, as these channels are required by law to provide time slot for RTHK television programmes. RTHK would be assigned a digital terrestrial television channel within 2013 to 2015, when the new broadcasting building is completed in Tseung Kwan O.

India

In India, Prasar Bharati is India's public broadcaster. However it does have commercial advertising on it. It is an autonomous corporation of the Ministry of Information and Broadcasting (India), Government of India and comprises the Doordarshan television network and All India Radio. Prasar Bharati was established on 23 November 1997, following a demand that the government owned broadcasters in India should be given autonomy like those in many other countries. The Parliament of India passed an Act to grant this autonomy in 1990, but it was not enacted until 15 September 1997.

Japan

In Japan, the main public broadcaster is the NHK (Japan Broadcasting Corporation). The broadcaster was set up in 1926 and was modelled on the British Broadcasting Company, the precursor to the British Broadcasting Corporation created in 1927. Much like the BBC, NHK is funded by a "receiving fee" by every Japanese household, with no commercial advertising and the maintenance of a position of strict political impartiality. However, rampant non-payment by a large amount of households has led the receiving fee to become something of a political issue. NHK runs two national terrestrial TV stations (NHK General and NHK Educational) and two satellite only services (NHK BS1 and NHK BS Premium services). NHK also runs 3 national radio services and a number of international radio and television services, akin to the BBC World Service. NHK has also been an innovator in television, developing the world's first high definition television technology in 1964 and launching high definition services in Japan in 1981.

Macau

In Macau, Teledifusão de Macau TDM is the public service broadcasting company. The firm was established in January 1982 and was modelled on Rádio e Televisão de Portugal RTP. TDM has two independent editorial arms: the Chinese news channel and the Portuguese news channel, each of which may have different information sources, points of view, and priorities of news. TDM runs both television and radio services. In addition, the Chinese national anthem is not played on TDM Portuguese channel, despite the fact that the entire company is a subject of the Macau SAR government.

Malaysia

In Malaysia, the public broadcaster is the state-owned Radio Televisyen Malaysia (RTM). RTM was previously funded publicly through money obtained from television licensing, however it is currently state subsidised as television licences have been abolished.

At present, RTM operates 8 national, 16 state and 7 district radio stations as well as 2 national terrestrial television channels called TV1 and TV2. RTM has also done test transmissions on a new digital television channel called RTMi. Tests involving 2000 residential homes in the Klang Valley began in September 2006 and ended in March 2007.

Nepal

History of public broadcasting in Nepal started from 1951.

Pakistan

In Pakistan, the public broadcasters are the state-owned Pakistan Broadcasting Corporation (PBC), also known as Radio Pakistan and Pakistan Television. In the past Radio Pakistan was partly funded through money obtained from License fees. In 1999, the Nawaz Sharif government abolished license fees for Radio Pakistan and also abolished its tax exempt status protected under PBC Act 1973. The license fees for Pakistan Television continued. The license fees collection for PTV was given to WAPDA during Musharraf government. Currently WAPDA collects Rs. 35 per house hold on electricity bills as PTV license fees. Television Broadcasting started in Pakistan with a small pilot TV Station established at Lahore Radio from where transmission was first beamed in Black & White with effect from 26 November 1964. Television centres were established in Dhaka, Karachi and Rawalpindi/Islamabad in 1967 and in Peshawar and Quetta in 1974. PTV has various channels transmitting throughout the world including PTV National, PTV World, PTV 2, PTV Global, PTV Bolan etc. Radio Pakistan has stations covering all the major cities, it covers 80% of the country serving 95.5 Million listeners. It has world service in eleven languages daily.

Philippines

The Philippines' primary state television broadcaster is People's Television Network (PTV). Created in 1974 as Government Television (GTV), PTV is no longer state subsidised except for a one-time equity funding for capital outlay in 1992. Aside from PTV, the other public broadcaster is the Intercontinental Broadcasting Corporation (IBC), which the government has already put up for sale. The government no longer holds a controlling interest in the former state broadcaster, Radio Philippines Network (RPN).

The Philippine Broadcasting Service (PBS) is the country's sole state radio broadcaster. Established in 1933 as KZFM by the American colonial Insular Government, the radio station was passed to the Philippine government after the country became independent in 1946.

South Korea

South Korea's representative public broadcasting television network is said to be Korean Broadcasting System, or KBS. Originally a government-controlled channel, it is now an independent broadcasting system. KBS began broadcasting radio in 1947 and opened up to television industry in 1961, and officially founded its own identity by 1973. Another public broadcasting channel is the Munhwa Broadcasting Corporation, or MBC. Known to be the second channel of the country, it also shares the roles of being national television with the KBS.

South Korea also has another public broadcasting channel called Educational Broadcasting System, or EBS. Originally considered to be an extension channel of the KBS, it was spun-off as an educational channel but retained its public broadcasting tasks. KBS and EBS mainly are funded by the commercials that they provide in their channels, but due to growing competitions, this is becoming a problem for them as well.

Europe

Inter-European cooperation of public TV

In most countries in Europe, state broadcasters are funded through a mix of advertising and public finance, either through a licence fee or directly from the government.

Albania

Radio Televizioni Shqiptar (RTSH) is the public broadcaster in Albania.

Analogue TV

- Televizioni Shqiptar (TVSH) is the name of the first public channel of Albania. The domestic TV program is distributed analogically throughout the country and digitally in Tirana through RTSH HD.
- TVSH 2 is the second public TV channel dedicated mainly to sports and live events launched in 2003.

Digital TV

- RTSH HD a digital channel launched in 2012 broadcasts TVSH shows in high-definition quality.
- RTSH Sport
- RTSH Muzikë
- RTSH Art

- TVSH Sat, is the international version of the domestic program broadcast to Europe free to air via satellite.

Radio

- Radio Tirana (also, Radio Tirana 1) is the name of Albania's first radio program, concentrating on news, talk, and features.
- Radio Tirana 2 is the name of the second radio program, broadcasting chiefly music and targeted at youth.
- Radio Tirana 3 (Programi i Tretë, Radio Tirana International) is the name of the third program, broadcasting the international service on shortwave in Albanian, English, French, Greek, German, Italian, Serbian, and Turkish.

Regional

- Radio Televizioni Gjirokastra is the local version of RTSH in Gjirokastër
- Radio Televizioni Korça is the local version of RTSH in Korçë.
- Radio Kukësi is the local version of RT in Kukës.
- Radio Shkodra is the local version of RT in Shkodër.

Belgium

Belgium has three networks, one for each linguistic community:

- RTBF, French-language, with 4 TV channels (La Une, La Deux, La Trois and Arte Belgique) and 6 radios.
- VRT, Dutch-language, with 3 TV channels and 10 radios.
- BRF, German-language, with 1 TV channel and 2 radios.

Originally named INR—*Institut national belge de radiodiffusion* (Dutch: *NIR—Belgisch Nationaal Instituut voor de Radio-omroep*)—the state-owned broadcasting organization was established by law on 18 June 1930. Television broadcasting from Brussels began in 1953, with two hours of programming each day. In 1960 the INR was subsumed into RTB (French: *Radio-Télévision Belge*) and BRT (Dutch: *Belgische Radio- en Televisieomroep*).

On 1 October 1945 INR-NIR began to broadcast some programs in German. In 1961 RTB-BRT began a German-language radio channel, broadcasting from Liège.

In 1977, following Belgian federalization and the establishment of separate language communities, the French-language section of RTB-BRT became RTBF (French: *Radio-Télévision Belge de la Communauté française*), German-language section became BRF (German: *Belgischer Rundfunk*) and Dutch-language stays BRT.

BRT was renamed in 1991 to BRTN (Dutch: *Belgische Radio- en Televisieomroep Nederlandstalige Uitzendingen*) and again in 1998 to VRT (Dutch: *Vlaamse Radio- en Televisieomroeporganisatie*).

Croatia

Croatian Radiotelevision (Croatian: *Hrvatska radiotelevizija, HRT*) is a Croatian public broadcasting company. It operates several radio and television channels, over a domestic transmitter network as well as satellite. As of 2002, 70% of HRT's funding comes from broadcast user fees with each house in Croatia required to pay 79 HRK, kuna, per month for a single television (radio device, computer or smartphone), with the remainder being made up from advertising.

Czech Republic

Czech Television and Czech Radio are national public broadcasting companies in the Czech Republic. Czech Television broadcasts from three studios in Prague, Brno and Ostrava and operates six TV channels ČT1, ČT2, ČT24, ČTSport, ČT :D and ČT Art. Czech television is funded through monthly fee 135 CZK which every household has to pay. Since October 2011 advertising on Czech TV was restricted from four to two channels, namely ČT2 and ČTSport. Czech Radio broadcasts four nationwide stations Radiožurnál, Dvojka, Vltava and Plus, several regional and specialised digital stations. Czech Radio 7 – Radio Prague broadcasts abroad in six languages. Czech Radio is funded throung monthly fee 45 CZK. In the Czech Republic, there is also Czech News Agency (ČTK), a public corporation established by law. The state is not responsible for any ČTK obligations and ČTK is not responsible for any state obligations.

Denmark

DR is the national public service broadcaster. The organization was founded in 1925, on principles similar to those of the BBC in the United Kingdom. Danmarks Radio runs six nationwide television channels and a long lists of radio channels. Financing comes from yearly license fees, that everyone who owns either a television set, a radio, a computer with internet access or a mobile phone, that can access the internet, has to pay.

Faroe Islands

Kringvarp Føroya is the organization in Faroe Islands with public service obligations. Formed in 1957 as a radio broadcaster Útvarp Føroya. Merged with Sjónvarp Føroya TV station on 1 January 2007 to form Kringvarp Føroya. Funded by license fees.

Estonia

ERR (Estonian Public Broadcasting) organizes the public radio and television stations of Estonia. ETV (Estonian Television), the public television station, made its first broadcast in 1955, and together with its sister channel ETV2 has ca. 20% audience share.

Finland

The Finnish Broadcasting Company, or Yleisradio (in Finnish) and Rundradion (in Swedish), abbreviated to Yle (pronounced /yle/), is Finland's national public-broadcasting company. Founded in 1926, it is a public limited company majority owned by the Finnish state, employing around 3,200 people.

France

After World War II, the RTF (Radiodiffusion-télévision française – French television and radio broadcasting) was created to operate the only two channels of television in France. The RTF was transformed into ORTF (Office de radiodiffusion-télévision française – French television and radio diffusion office), a more independent structure, in 1964. The ORTF saw the birth of a third channel in 1972, two years before the dissolution of the structure in 1974. From this date to 2000, each channel had its own direction structure. The first channel (TF1) was sold to the private sector in 1987 (in these years, the channel with the most audience was the other public channel Antenne 2). In 1986 a French/German public channel was created, ARTE, originally broadcast on cable and satellite, the fall of the private channel La Cinq freed some frequencies that it had used each day after 19:00. In 1994 a new public channel, La cinquième was created to use the remaining time on the same frequencies. La cinquième and ARTE subsequently shared the same channels with the exception of satellite, cable, and internet channels where both could be broadcast all day long. In 2000 all the public channels were united into one structure, France Télévisions.

Germany

After World War II, when regional broadcasters had been merged into one national network by the Nazis to create a powerful means of propaganda, the Allies insisted on a de-centralised, independent structure for German public broadcasting and created regional public broadcasting agencies that, by and large, still exist today.

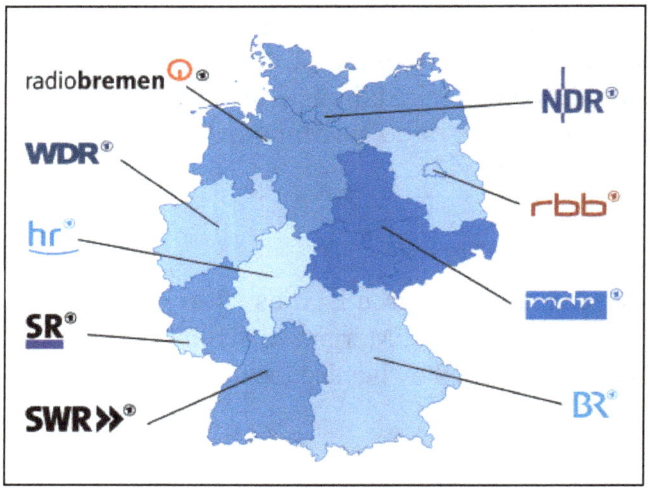

Map of ARD-members

- NDR (Northern Germany), split from former NWDR.
- WDR (North Rhine-Westphalia), split from former NWDR.
- RBB (Berlin and vicinity), merged from SFB and ORB.
- SWR (Germany's south west), merged from SDR and SWF.
- BR (Bavaria).
- MDR (Germany's south east), established in 1991.

- and the smaller hr (Hesse), SR (Saar) and RB (Land Bremen).

In addition to these nine regional radio and TV broadcasters, which cooperate within ARD, a second national television service—actually called Second German Television (German: *Zweites Deutsches Fernsehen*, ZDF)—was later created in 1961 and a national radio service with two networks (Deutschlandradio) emerged from the remains of Cold War propaganda stations in 1994. All services are mainly financed through license fees paid by every household and are governed by councils of representatives of the "societally relevant groups". Public TV and radio stations spend about 60% of the ~10bn € spent altogether for broadcasting in Germany per year, making it the most expensive public broadcasting system in the world.

The Hans-Bredow-Institut, or Hans-Bredow-Institute for Media Research at the University of Hamburg (HBI) is an independent non-profit foundation with the mission on media research on public communication, particularly for radio and television broadcasting (including public service media providers) and other electronic media, in an interdisciplinary fashion.

In Germany also foreign public broadcasters exist. These are AFN for US-military staff in Germany, BFBS for British military staff, Voice of Russia, RFE and Radio Liberty.

Greece

Hellenic Broadcasting Corporation is the state-owned public broadcaster in Greece. It broadcasts four television channels, ERT1, ERT2, ERT3, ERT HD, as well as five national (ERA 1, ERA 2, ERA 3, Kosmos, ERA Sport), and 18 local radio stations. All national television and radio stations are broadcast through ERT digital multiplexes across the country.

Iceland

Ríkisútvarpið (RÚV) ("The Icelandic National Broadcasting Service") is Iceland's national public-service broadcasting organization. RÚV began radio broadcasting in 1930 and its first television transmissions were made in 1966. In both cases coverage quickly reached nearly every household in Iceland. RÚV is funded by a television licence fee collected from every income taxpayer, as well as advertising revenue. RÚV has been a full active member of the European Broadcasting Union since 1956.

RÚV—which by the terms of its charter is obliged to "promote the Icelandic language, Icelandic history, and Iceland's cultural heritage" and "honour basic democratic rules, human rights, and the freedom of speech and opinion"—carries a substantial amount of arts, media, and current affairs programming, in addition to which it also supplies general entertainment in the form of feature films and such internationally popular television drama series as *Lost* and *Desperate Housewives*. RÚV's lineup also includes sports coverage, documentaries, domestically produced entertainment shows, and children's programming.

Ireland

In Ireland there are two state owned public service broadcasters, RTÉ and TG4. RTÉ was established in 1960 with the merger of *Raidió Éireann* (1926) and *Teilifís Éireann* (1960). TG4 was formed as a subsidiary of *RTÉ* in 1996 as *Teilifís na Gealige (TnaG)*, it was re-branded as *TG4* in 1999, and was made independent of *RTÉ* in 2007.

Both Irish public service broadcasters receive part of the licence fee, with RTÉ taking the lion's share of the funding. Advertising makes up 50% of RTÉ's income and just 6% of TG4's income. 7% of the licence fee is provided to the *Broadcasting Authority of Ireland* since 2006. Up to 2006 the licence fee was given entirely to *RTÉ*.

RTÉ offers a range of free to air services on television; RTÉ 1, RTÉ 2, RTÉjr, and RTÉ News Now. On radio; RTÉ Radio 1, RTÉ 2FM, RTÉ Lyric FM, and RTÉ Raidió na Gaeltachta, as well as a number of channels on DAB.

The Sound and Vision Fund is operated by the Broadcasting Authority of Ireland, this fund receives 7% of the licence fee. The fund is used to assist broadcasters to commission public service broadcast programming. It is open to all independent producers provided they get a free to air or community broadcaster's backing, including TV3, Today FM, BBC Northern Ireland, RTÉ, Channel 4, UTV etc. Pay TV broadcaster Setanta Sports have also received funding for programming through the sound and vision fund provided they provide those shows on a free-to-view basis.

TG4 is an independent Irish language public service broadcaster that is funded by the government through subsidy, the licence fee and through advertising revenue.

TV3 is the only independent broadcaster that has public service commitments.

Italy

RAI brand

The Italian national broadcasting company is RAI – Radiotelevisione Italiana, born as URI in 1924. RAI transmits on digital television on fifteen channels: Rai 1, Rai 2, Rai 3, Rai 4, Rai 5, Rai News 24, Rai Movie, Rai Premium, Rai Sport 1, Rai Sport 2, Rai Storia, Rai Gulp, Rai YoYo, Rai Scuola and Rai HD. RAI also broadcasts via satellite and is involved in radio, publishing and cinema. RAI has the largest audience share (45%) of any Italian television network. Proceeds derive from a periodical standing charge (113.5 euros for each household in 2014) and from advertising. The main competitors of RAI are Mediaset, the biggest national private broadcaster, divided in three channels, and La7, owned by Cairo Editore.

Malta

Public Broadcasting Services (PBS) is the national broadcaster of Malta. It operates three television services (TVM, TVM2, and Parliament TV) and three radio services (Radju Malta, Radju Malta 2, and Magic Malta).

Moldova

Teleradio-Moldova (TRM) is the public funded radio-TV broadcaster in Moldova. It owns the TV channels Moldova 1 and TVMI, and the radio channels Radio Moldova and Radio Moldova Internațional.

Montenegro

RTCG (Radio Television of Montenegro) is the public broadcaster in Montenegro.

Netherlands

The Netherlands uses a rather unusual system of public broadcasting. Public-broadcasting associations are allocated money and time to broadcast their programmes on the publicly owned television and radio channels. The time and money is allocated in proportion to their membership numbers. The system is intended to reflect the diversity of all the groups composing the nation.

Poland

The public broadcasters are Telewizja Polska (TVP) television and Polskie Radio. TVP operates three main channels: TVP 1, TVP 2 and TVP Regionalna. It also broadcasts several digital channels (including TVP 1, TVP1 HD, TVP 2, TVP2 HD, TVP Info, TVP Kultura, TVP Historia, TVP HD, TVP Polonia, TVP Sport, TVP Seriale) via satellite and digital terrestrial television system, and 16 regional affiliates (known as TVP Regionalna, regional channels cooperate when creating most of materials). TVP also runs also services with news, a video streaming (video on demand) service as well as live streaming of all its channels. Polskie Radio operates four nationwide radio channels (which are also available via the broadcaster's website). There are also 17 state-owned radio stations broadcasting in particular regions. TVP and Polish Radio are funded from several sources: state funding, advertising, obligatory tax on all TV and radio receivers, and money from authors/copyright associations. The public broadcasters offer a mix of commercial shows and programmes they are, by law, required to broadcast (i.e., non-commercial, niche programmes; programmes for children; programmes promoting different points of view and diversity; programmes for different religious and national groups; live coverage of the parliament's session on its dedicated channel: TVP Parlament; etc.). It has to be politically neutral, although in the past there have been cases of political pressure on TVP and Polskie Radio from the governing party. Recently, a new law has been passed by the ruling Law & Justice party, that in public perception allowed the party to take a much larger control over the media that has been possible before. The party states this law to be the first step to a complete public media overdo. Many worry no such improvements are actually coming and that these recent laws are only another step in taking control over the whole country by the Law & Justice party.

There is an ongoing debate in Poland about the semi-commercial nature of TVP and PR. Many people fear that making them into totally non-commercial broadcasters would result in the licence fee payable by households being increased, and fewer people being interested in programmes they offer; others say that TVP in particular is too profit-driven and should concentrate on programming that benefits the society. Some say that state contributions should be programme-based, rather than channel/broadcaster-based, so as all the broadcasters can get them (in this scenario TVP would be privatised and equal to the private TV channels).

Portugal

RÁDIO E TELEVISÃO DE PORTUGAL

RTP brand

In Portugal, the national public broadcaster is Rádio e Televisão de Portugal (RTP), which started in 1957 the regular emissions of its first channel, now RTP1. In 1968 appeared the second channel, then called "*segundo programa*", now RTP2. In the 1970s, TV arrived to the Portuguese islands of Madeira and the Azores, with the creation of two regional channels: RTP Madeira in 1972 and RTP Açores in 1976.

Until the 1990s, the state owned the monopoly of TV broadcasting, so RTP1 and RTP2 were the only Portuguese channels, both with similar generalist programmes. In 1990, RTP1 was renamed "Canal 1", and in 1992 RTP2 was renamed "TV2". With the creation of the two private channels, SIC in 1992 and Televisão Independente in 1993, the philosophy of the public service changed: in 1995, *TV2* was again renamed RTP2 and became an alternative channel dedicated to culture, science, arts, documentaries, sports (without football), minorities and children. Since then, RTP2 has no advertising. Canal 1, renamed back RTP1 also in 1995, remained the commercial channel of RTP group, focused on entertainment, information and major sport competitions. In 2004, after a great reestructuration period, RTP started its currint branding. That year was also created the two thematic channels of the group—RTPN, 24 hour-news channel which name changed to RTP Informação in 2011; and RTP Memória, dedicated to classic RTP programming. In 2014 the headquarters of RTP2 were transferred from Lisbon to Porto. The group also has two international channels: RTP Internacional, founded in 1992 and dedicated to Europe, Asia and Americas, and RTP África, founded in 1998 focused in Africa, mainly in the CPLP countries of Angola, Cape Verde, Guinea-Bissau, Mozambique and São Tomé and Príncipe.

The RTP group is financed by the advertising revenues from RTP1, RTP Informação, RTP Memória, RTP África, and RTP Internacional, and also by the *taxa de contribuição audiovisual* (broadcasting contribution tax), which is incorporated in electricity bills. Funding from the government budget ceased in 2014, during the Portuguese financial crisis.

Romania

Romanian Television (TVR) is the national public TV broadcaster in Romania. It operates five channels: TVR1, TVR2, TVR3, TVRi, and TVR HD, along with six regional studios in Bucharest, Cluj-Napoca, Ia□i, Timi□oara, Craiova, and Târgu Mure□.

The public radio broadcaster is Romanian Radio Broadcasting Company (Radio Romania). It operates FM and AM, and internet national, regional, and local radio channels. The regional and local stations are branded as Radio România Regional. Broadcasting in 12 languages, Radio Romania International is the company's international radio station.

TVR and Radio Romania are funded through a hybrid financing system, drawing from the state budget, a special tax (incorporated in electricity bills), and advertising too.

Nordic Countries

National public broadcasters in The Nordic countries were modeled after the BBC and established a decade later: Radioordningen (now DR) in Denmark, Kringkastingselskapet (now NRK) in Norway, and Radiotjänst (now Sveriges Radio and Sveriges Television) in Sweden (all in 1925). In 1926 Yleisradio (Swedish: Rundradion) now YLE was founded in Finland. All four are funded from television licence fees costing (in 2007) around €230 (US$300) per household per year.

Serbia

Radio Television of Serbia (RTS) is the national public broadcaster in Serbia. It operates a total of five television channels (RTS1, RTS2, RTS Digital, RTS HD and RTS SAT) and five radio stations (Radio Belgrade 1, Radio Belgrade 2, Radio Belgrade 3, Radio Belgrade 202, and Stereorama). RTS is primarily funded through public television licence fees bundled with electricity bills paid monthly, as well as advertising.

Slovakia

RTVS logo

Radio and Television Slovakia (RTVS) is the national public broadcaster in Slovakia, with headquarters in Bratislava. This organisation was created in 2011 by merger of Slovak Television and

Slovak Radio. RTVS broadcasts two television channels (STV1, STV2), five FM radio stations (Rádio Slovensko, Rádio Devín, Rádio Regina, Rádio_FM and Rádio Patria), one satellite radio channel (Radio Slovakia International) and three digital only radio stations (Rádio Klasika, Rádio Litera and Rádio Junior). RTVS is funded through monthly fee of €4.64, which every household with electricity connection must pay. The director of RTVS is Václav Mika. RTVS is a full member of European broadcasting union.

Spain

In Spain, being a highly decentralised country, two public broadcasting systems coexist: a national broadcasting television, Radio y Televisión Española (RTVE), that can be watched all around Spain, and many autonomic TV channels, only broadcast within their respective Autonomous Community. Televisión Española was founded in 1956, during Franco's dictatorship. It broadcasts two different TV-channels: TVE1 (a.k.a. *La Primera* or *La uno*), that is a wide-range audience general channel; and TVE2, (a.k.a. *La dos*), that tends to offer cultural programation, as well as sport competitions. Till 2008, RTVE was funded both from public sources and private advertising; however, the Spanish government has recently decreed that, starting in September 2009, RTVE's channels shall be funded with taxpayer's money and with private founding raised from the rest of Spain's private TV stations, thus removing advertising from the broadcaster. A TV licence fee has been suggested, but with little popular success.

Moreover, each of the autonomous communities of Spain have their own public broadcaster, all of them members of FORTA, usually consisting in either one or two public channels that tend to reproduce the model set up by Televisión Española: a general channel and a more cultural related one. In the Autonomous Communities that have their own official language besides Spanish, those channels may broadcast not in Spanish, but in the other co-official language. For example, this occurs in Catalonia, where Televisió de Catalunya broadcasts mainly in Catalan. In the Basque Country, Euskal Telebista (ETB) has three channels, two of which broadcast only in basque (ETB 1 and ETB 3), whereas the other (ETB 2) broadcasts in Spanish. In Galicia, the Television de Galicia and the G2. All the autonomic networks are publicly founded, and also admit private advertising.

Sweden

The logo of SVT1

The logo of Sveriges Radio

Sweden has three Public Service broadcasters and those are SVT (Sveriges Television), UR (Utbildningsradion) and SR (Sveriges Radio). SVT is the national public television Broadcaster with

4 channels (SVT 1, SVT 2, SVT Barnkanalen and SVT 24). The aim is to make programs for everybody. For example, Sweden has their original population called the Sami People and SVT make programs in their language for them to watch. There are also Finnish people in Sweden, so SVT sometimed show the news in Suomi, the program is called SVT Uutiset. SR has the same purpose as SVT but SR is the Swedish national radio broadcasting station with the channels, P1, P2, P3, P4, P5 and the Finnish channel SR sisuradio.

United Kingdom

The United Kingdom has a strong tradition of public service broadcasting. In addition to the BBC, established in 1922, there is also Channel 4, a publicly owned, commercially funded public service broadcaster, and S4C, a Welsh-language broadcaster in Wales. Furthermore, the two commercial broadcasters ITV and Channel 5 also have significant public service obligations imposed as part of their licence to broadcast.

In the UK there are also small community broadcasters. There are now 228 stations with FM broadcast licences (licensed by Ofcom). Community radio stations typically cover a small geographical area with a coverage radius of up to 5 km and run on a nonprofit basis. They can cater for whole communities or for different areas of interest—such as a particular ethnic group, age group or interest group. Community radio stations reflect a diverse mix of cultures and interests. For example, you can listen to stations catering to urban or experimental music, while others are aimed at younger people, religious communities or the armed forces and their families.

North America

Canada

In Canada, the main public broadcaster is the national Canadian Broadcasting Corporation (CBC; French: *Société Radio-Canada*) which operates two national television networks (CBC Television and Ici Radio-Canada Télé), four radio networks (CBC Radio One, CBC Radio 2, Ici Radio-Canada Première and Ici Musique) and several cable television channels including two 24-hour news channels (CBC News Network and Ici RDI) in both of Canada's official languages and the French-language science channel Ici Explora. CBC's national television operations and some radio operations are funded partly by advertisements, in addition to the subsidy provided by the federal government. The cable channels are commercial entities owned and operated by the CBC and do not receive any direct public funds, however, they do benefit from synergies with resources from the other CBC operations. The CBC has been frequently dealt with budget cuts and labour disputes, often resulting in a debate about whether the service has the resources necessary to properly fulfill its mandate.

In recent years, the CBC has also expanded into new media ventures including the online radio service CBC Radio 3, music streaming service CBC Music, and the launch of online news services, such as CBC Hamilton, in some markets which are not directly served by their own CBC television or radio stations.

In addition, several provinces operate public broadcasters; these are not CBC subentities, but distinct networks in their own right. These include the English-language TVOntario (TVO) and the

French-language TFO in Ontario, Télé-Québec in Quebec, and Knowledge Network in British Columbia. TVO and Télé-Québec operate through conventional transmitters and cable, while TFO and Knowledge Network are cable-only channels.

Amherst Island public radio

Canada is also home to a number of former public broadcasting entities that have gone private. CTV Two Alberta, which is licensed as an educational television station in Alberta, was once owned by the Alberta government as the public broadcaster Access, until the channel was sold to CHUM Limited in 1995. To fulfill its license conditions as an educational station, it broadcasts educational and children's programming during daytime hours while airing entertainment programming favoured by advertisers and viewers in primetime. Public radio station CKUA in Alberta was also formerly operated by Access, before being sold to the non-profit CKUA Radio Foundation which continues to operate it as a community-funded radio network. CJRT-FM in Toronto also operated as a public government-owned radio station for many years; while no longer funded by the provincial government, it still solicits most of its budget from listener and corporate donations and is permitted to air only a very small amount of commercial advertising. One television station, CFTU in Montreal, operates as an educational station owned by a private not-for-profit consortium of educational institutions in the province of Quebec called CANAL. City Saskatchewan was once the Saskatchewan Communications Network, a cable-only educational and cultural public broadcaster owned by the government of Saskatchewan, until it was sold to Bluepoint Investment Corporation in 2010 and later to Rogers Media in 2012. Live CTV Two Alberta it airs educational and children's programming during the day as a condition of license.

Some local community stations also operate non-commercially with funding from corporate and individual donors. In addition, cable companies are required to produce a local community channel in each licensed market. Such channels have traditionally aired community talk shows, city council meetings and other locally oriented programming, although it is becoming increasingly common for them to adopt the format and branding of a local news channel.

Canada also has a large number of campus radio and community radio stations.

United States

Early public stations were operated by state colleges and universities, and were often run as part of the schools' cooperative extension services. Stations in this era were internally funded, and did not rely on listener contributions to operate; some accepted advertising. Networks such as Iowa, South Dakota, and Wisconsin Public Radio began in this way.

The Gregory Hall on the campus of University of Illinois at Urbana-Champaign hosted an important meeting of the National Association of Educational Broadcasters in the 1940s, that spawned both PBS and NPR

The concept of a "non-commercial, educational" station *per se* does not show up in U.S. law until the 1940s, when the FM band was moved to its present location; the part of the band between 88.1 and 91.9 MHz is reserved for such stations, though they are not limited to those frequencies. For example, WFIU-Bloomington, Ind. has its FM frequency at 103.7 MHz. Houston's KUHT was the nation's first public television station, and signed on the air on 25 May 1953 from the campus of the University of Houston. This phenomenon continued in other big cities in the 1950s; in rural areas, it was not uncommon for colleges to operate commercial stations instead (e.g., the University of Missouri's KOMU-TV, an NBC affiliate in Columbia).

In the United States, other than a few direct services, public broadcasting is almost entirely decentralized and is not government operated, but does receive some government support. Some of the funding comes from community support to hundreds of public radio and public television stations, each of which is an individual entity licensed to one of several different non-profit organizations, municipal or state governments, or universities. Sources of funding also include on-air and online pledge drives and the sale of underwriting "spots" (typically 15–30 seconds) to sponsors. Public radio and television stations often produce their own programs as well as purchase additional programming from national producers and program distributors such as National Public Radio (NPR), Public Broadcasting Service (PBS), Public Radio International (PRI), American Public Television (APT), American Public Media (APM), and Public Radio Exchange (PRX). U.S. federal government support for public radio and television is filtered through a separate organization, the Corporation for Public Broadcasting (CPB).

Public broadcasting is sometimes also referred to as *public media*, in an effort to capture the expansion of public broadcasting content from radio and television into digital technologies, in particular the web and mobile platforms. While some consider public media to be analogous to public broadcasting, others use the term more broadly to include all noncommercial media.

Individual stations and programs rely on highly varied proportions of funding. Program-by-program funding creates the potential for conflict-of-interest situations, which must be weighed program by program under standards such as the guidelines established by PBS. Donations are widely dispersed to stations and producers, giving the system a resilience and broad base of support but diffusing authority and impeding decisive change and priority-setting.

Television

In the United States, the Public Broadcasting Service (PBS) (formerly National Educational Television) and American Public Television (formerly Eastern Educational Television Network) distribute television programs to a nationwide system of independently owned and operated television stations (some having the term "PBS" in their name) supported largely by state and federal governments as well as viewer support, with commercial underwriters donating to specific programs and receiving a short thanks for their contributions. Such underwriting may only issue declarative statements (including slogans) and may not include "calls to action" (i.e., the station cannot give out prices, comparative statements, or anything that would persuade the listener to patronize the sponsor). Most communities also have Public-access television channels on local cable television systems, which are generally paid for by Cable television franchise fees and sometimes supported in part through citizens donations.

The U.S. government produces one channel for domestic citizen consumption: NASA TV, a suite of channels covering the country's space program and a collection of science education programs. Formerly, there was the DoD News Channel, which distributed news regarding the country's military operations. NASA TV is and the DoD News channel was distributed solely by satellite and Internet and thus do not have the extensive reach of other countries' national broadcasters.

U.S. public broadcasting for television has, from the late 1960s onward, dealt with severe criticism from conservative politicians and think-tanks, which allege that its programming has a leftist bias.

Radio

A public radio network, National Public Radio (NPR), was created in 1970, following the passage of the Public Broadcasting Act of 1967, which established the Corporation for Public Broadcasting. This network is colloquially though inaccurately conflated with *public radio* as a whole, when in fact "public radio" includes many organizations. Some independent local public radio stations buy their programming from distributors such as NPR; Public Radio International (PRI); American Public Media (APM); Public Radio Exchange (PRX); and Pacifica Radio, most often distributed through the Public Radio Satellite System (PRSS). Around these distributed programs, stations fill in varying amounts of local and other programming. A number of public stations are completely independent of these programming services, producing all or most of their content themselves. Public radio stations in the United States tend to broadcast a mixture of news and talk programs along with music and arts/cultural programming. Some of the larger operations split off these formats into separate stations or networks. Music stations are probably best known for playing classical music, although other formats are offered, including the time-honored "eclectic" music format that is rather freeform in nature common among college radio stations. Jazz is another traditional, but declining, public radio programming staple. Cultural Native American and Mexican American music and programming are also featured regionally.

The U.S. government operates some limited direct broadcasting services, but all are either highly specialized (and, since the dawn of the millennium, automated) information services (WWV/WWVH time service, NOAA Weather Radio) or targeted at foreign audiences like Voice of America. From 1948 to 2013, foreign-targeted broadcasts, many of which were intended as propaganda, were barred from U.S. audiences because of the Smith–Mundt Act, a restriction that has since been lifted. While NOAA Weather Radio has individual terrestrial repeaters across the United States (albeit on a special band reserved for such broadcasts), WWV, VOA and others operate from single shortwave facilities; none of these services can be heard on the AM or FM bands most common on U.S. radio.

Local stations derive some of the funding for their operations through regular pledge drives seeking individual and corporate donations, and corporate underwriting. Some stations also derive a portion of their funding from federal, state and local governments and government-funded colleges and universities (in addition to receiving free use of the public radio spectrum). The local stations then contract with program distributors and also provide some programming themselves. NPR produces its own programming. PBS, by contrast, does not create its own content. NPR also receives some direct funding from private donors, foundations, and from the Corporation for Public Broadcasting.

Although most "public" radio stations are noncommercial, not all noncommercial stations are public. Community radio stations may have some independently produced programs in common with their public counterparts but, because they do not rely on government subsidy of any sort, cannot be considered public, even in the American sense of the term.

Oceania

Australia

In Australia, the Australian Broadcasting Corporation (ABC) is owned by the Australian Government and is 100% taxpayer funded. The multicultural Special Broadcasting Service (SBS), another public broadcaster, now accepts limited sponsorship and advertising.

In addition, there is a large Australian community radio sector, funded in part by federal grants via the Community Broadcasting Foundation, but largely sustained via subscriptions, donations and business sponsorship. As of June 2005, there were 442 fully licensed community radio stations (including remote Indigenous services) and a number of community television stations (most operating as Channel 31 despite being unrelated across different states). They are organised similarly to PBS and NPR stations in the United States, and take on the role that public access television stations have in the US.

New Zealand

In New Zealand all broadcasters are given a small slice of public broadcasting responsibility, because of the state-funded agency NZ On Air. This is because of NZ On Air's requirement for public-service programmes across all channels and stations, instead of being put into one single network. The former public broadcaster BCNZ (formerly NZBC – New Zealand Broadcasting Corporation) was broken up into separate state-owned corporations, Television New Zealand (TVNZ) and Radio New Zealand (RNZ). While RNZ remains commercial-free, about 90% of funding for TVNZ comes from selling advertising during programmes on their two stations. TVNZ continues to be a public broadcaster; however like CBC Television in Canada it is essentially a fully commercial network in continuous ratings battles with other stations, which continues to be a controversial issue within New Zealand. With the shutdown of TVNZ 7, the only fully non-commercial public-service network in New Zealand is Radio New Zealand.

Aside from television, New Zealand has a rich public radio culture, Radio New Zealand being the main provider, with a varied network (Radio New Zealand National) and a classical musical network (Radio New Zealand Concert). RNZ also provides the Pacific with its Radio New Zealand International. Aside from RNZ almost all of New Zealand's 16 regions has an "access radio" network. All these networks are commercial-free.

South America

Argentina

State presence in television had a strong history, not in the way of European style public service radio or television. The private sector has taken an active role in the development of television in Buenos Aires. In opposition, state broadcasters tend to be federal and technical innovative, such as the Argentinian Televisión Publica, the first 60 years old national TV station.

Brazil

In Brazil, the two main public broadcasters are the EBC (Empresa Brasil de Comunicação) and the Fundação Padre Anchieta. The EBC was created in 2007 to manage the Brazilian federal government's radio and television stations. EBC owns broadcast networks such as TV Brasil (launched in 2007, being the merger of Rio de Janeiro's TV Educativa (1975-2007) and Brasília's TV Nacional (1960-2007)), the Nacional and MEC radios. The Padre Anchieta Foundation was created by the government of the state of São Paulo in 1967 and includes a television station (TV Cultura, launched in 1969 in São Paulo), and a radio station (Rádio Cultura). The Padre Anchieta Foundation is a privately held company which maintains autonomy.

Chile

Unlike most of Latin America, Chilean television was founded in an attempt to bring public television. Thus, the first TV stations were not commercial, but were part of some of the biggest universities in Chile: the University of Chile (owner of the former Channels 9 and 11 until 1993), the Catholic University of Chile on channels 2 and 13 until 2010, and the Pontifical Catholic University of Valparaíso on channels 8 and 4. Channel 8, in Valparaíso, is the first and oldest station on Chile, transmitting since October 5, 1957. Anyway, as the Universities found themselves in a quite bad economic situation, as soon as 1961 they began transmitting advertisements between their programming, being the first of them the channel 9, showing a Motorola TV set. This kind of disguised advertising took the name of "Payola". This situation, added to the fact that TV was only reaching Santiago and Valparaíso, led to the creation of a state network that should serve all the country.

This network, created in 1964 and in operation since October 24, 1969, is known as "Televisión Nacional de Chile". After the military government of Augusto Pinochet, the television was deregulated. Thus, two new commercial channels were born: Megavisión (Channel 9, on October 23, 1990) and La Red (Channel 4, on May 12, 1991). The University of Chile's channel 11 also was privatized on October 1, 1993. This network is known today as "Chilevisión".

The closest model to the British BBC is that of Chile's Televisión Nacional, an open channel serving the entire country (including Easter Island and Antarctica bases). Televisión Nacional, popularly known as channel 7 because of its Santiago frequency, is governed by a seven-member board appointed by both the President and the Senate. It is meant to be independent of political pressures, although accusations of bias have been made, especially during election campaigns.

Ecuador

Ecuador TV is the public service channel of Ecuador established in October 2007. The channel was established at the same time as the installation of the Ecuadorian Constituent Assembly so that the sessions could be transmitted live to all the country.

Venezuela

Recently, under the initiative of the Venezuelan government of president Hugo Chávez, and with the sponsorship of the governments of Argentina, Bolivia, Cuba, Ecuador and Nicaragua, the news and documentary network teleSUR was created with the intended to be an instrument toward the "concretizing of the Bolivarian idea" through the integration of America, and as a counterweight to what the governments that funds it consider a "distorted view of Latin American reality by privately run networks that broadcast to the region". There is an ongoing debate on whether teleSUR will be able become a neutral and fair news channel able to counter the huge influence of global media outlets, or whether it will end up as a propaganda tool of the Venezuelan government, which owns a 51 percent share of said channel.

List of Public Broadcasters

Africa

- SABC–South Africa
- Television:
  - SABC 1
  - SABC 2
  - SABC 3
- Radio (Each official language has a station):
  - SAfm (English)
  - RSG (Afrikaans)
  - Ukhozi FM (Zulu)

- Umhlobo Wenene FM (Xhosa)
- Thobela FM (Pedi)
- Lesedi FM (Sotho)
- Motsweding FM (Tswana)
- Phalaphala FM (Venda)
- Munghana Lonene FM (Tsonga)
- Ligwalagwala FM (Swazi)
- Ikwekwezi FM (Ndebele)
- X-K FM (!Xu and Khwe)—These are not official languages but significant communities exist in the Northern Cape Province

- Botswana TV—Botswana
- GBC—Ghana
- Televisão Pública de Angola—Angola
- Televisão de Moçambique—Mozambique
- SNRT—Morocco
- Établissement public de télévision—Algeria:
  - Programme National
  - Canal Algérie
  - A3
  - Chaîne 4
  - Coran TV
- ERTU—Egypt
- LJBC—Libya
- LBS—Liberia
- NTA—Nigeria
- FRCN—Nigeria
- NBC—Namibia
- TBC—Tanzania

Asia

Asian Legends

- Pakistan Television Corporation—Pakistan

- Educational Broadcasting System—South Korea
- Korean Broadcasting System—South Korea
- Munhwa Broadcasting Corporation—South Korea; semi-public, semi-private
- NHK—Japan
- Prasar Bharati—India:
  - All India Radio
  - Doordarshan
- Israel Broadcasting Authority—Israel
- IRIB—Iran
- JRTV—Jordan
- Télé-Liban—Lebanon
- Nepal Television (NTV)—Nepal:
  - NTV Metro 2
  - Radio Nepal
- Vietnam Television—Vietnam
- People's Television Network—Philippines
- Radio Televisyen Malaysia—Malaysia
- Syrian Television—Syria
- Televisi Republik Indonesia—Indonesia
- Thai Public Broadcasting Service—Thailand
- Abu Dhabi TV—United Arab Emirates
- Al Jazeera—Qatar

Brunei Darussalam

- Radio Televisyen Brunei(RTB)

China

- China Central Television
- Radio Television Hong Kong （香港電台|RTHK） — Hong Kong
- Teledifusão de Macau （澳門廣播電視股份有限公司 “澳廣視” |TDM） -Macau

Indonesia

- Televisi Republik Indonesia (TVRI)

- Radio Republik Indonesia (RRI)

Malaysia

- Radio Televisyen Malaysia (RTM)

North Korea

- Korean Central Television (KCTV)

Singapore

- Media Corporation of Singapore (MediaCorp)

South Korea

- Korean Broadcasting System (KBS)
- Educational Broadcasting System (EBS)

Taiwan

- Taiwan Broadcasting System （台灣公共廣播電視集團|TBS）
- Radio Taiwan International （中央廣播電台|RTI）
- National Education Radio （國立教育廣播電臺|NER）
- Police Radio Station （警察廣播電台|PRS）
- Taipei Broadcasting Station （台北廣播電台|TBS）
- Kaohsiung Broadcasting Station （高雄廣播電台|KBS）

Europe

- 3sat-Germany/Austria/Switzerland
- ARD—working partnership of German public-service broadcasters:
    - Westdeutscher Rundfunk, WDR—Cologne
    - Norddeutscher Rundfunk—Hamburg
    - Mitteldeutscher Rundfunk—Leipzig
    - Bayerischer Rundfunk—Munich
    - Südwestrundfunk—Stuttgart
    - Rundfunk Berlin-Brandenburg—Berlin
    - Hessischer Rundfunk—Frankfurt
    - Saarländischer Rundfunk—Saarbrücken
    - Radio Bremen—Bremen
    - German radio and TV from ARD: each broadcaster has several radio programs, like

the biggest one (WDR) more than five "full" radio stations ("1 Live", WDR 2 (pop and info radio), WDR 3 (classical music) ... WDR 5) plus regional radio. WDR produces one TV-programme for its state and contributes to "Das Erste"–TV of ARD and to more TV-channels.

- Arte— France/Germany
- BBC—United Kingdom:
    - BBC Alba
    - BBC One
    - BBC Two
    - BBC Four
    - BBC News
    - BBC Parliament
    - BBC HD
    - CBBC
    - CBeebies
    - BBC Radio 1
    - BBC Radio 2
    - BBC Radio 3
    - BBC Radio 4
    - BBC Radio 5 Live
    - BBC Radio 1Xtra
    - BBC Radio 4 Extra
    - BBC Radio 5 Live Sports Extra
    - BBC Radio 6 Music
    - BBC Asian Network
    - BBC World Service
    - BBC Radio Scotland
    - BBC Radio nan Gàidheal
    - BBC Radio Shetland
    - BBC Radio Orkney
    - BBC Radio Wales

  - BBC Radio Cymru
  - BBC Radio Ulster
  - BBC Radio Foyle
  - BBC Local Radio—40 stations
- BBC Worldwide:
  - BBC World News
  - BBC Lifestyle
  - BBC Knowledge
  - BBC HD
  - BBC World Service
  - BBC Entertainment
  - BBC America
  - BBC Canada
  - BBC UKTV
- BNT—Bulgaria
- BRF—German-speaking Community of Belgium
- BVN—Flanders and Netherlands television
- Česká televize—Czech Republic
- Channel 4—United Kingdom
- Danmarks Radio—Denmark
- Duna TV—Hungary
- EITB–Basque Country
- EAT (Greek Public Television)—Greece (formerly)
- ERT—Greece (1938 – 11 June 2013; 11 June 2015–present)
- ETV—Estonia
- LRT–Lithuania
- France Télévisions—France:
  - France 2
  - France 3
  - France 4

  - France 5
- GBC—Gibraltar
- KNR—Greenland
- HRT—Croatia
- LRT—Lithuania
- LTV—Latvia
- Magyar Televízió—Hungary
- MRT—Macedonia
- NERIT—Greece (formerly; 4 May 2014 – 11 June 2015)
- Netherlands Public Broadcasting—Netherlands:
  - AVRO
  - BNN
  - EO
  - KRO
  - LLiNK
  - MAX
  - NCRV
  - TROS
  - VARA
  - VPRO
- NRK—Norway
- NTKU-Ukraine
- ORF—Austria
- OTR (*Общественное Телевидение России*, Obshchestvennoe Televidenie Rossii)—Public Television of Russia
- Polish Radio-Poland
- PBS—Malta
- Radio France—France:
  - France Inter
  - France Info

    - France Culture
    - France Musique
    - France Bleu
    - FIP
    - Le Mouv'
- Radio France Internationale—France
- Ràdio i Televisió d'Andorra—Andorra
- Radio România
- RAI—Italy
- RAS—Italy
- RTBF—Wallonia, Belgium
- RTCG—Montenegro
- RTÉ—Ireland:
    - RTÉ 1
    - RTÉ 2
    - RTÉjr
    - RTÉ News Now
    - RTÉ Radio 1
    - RTÉ 2FM
    - RTÉ Lyric FM
    - RTÉ Raidió na Gaeltachta
- RTP—Portugal:
    - RTP1
    - RTP2
    - RTP Informação
    - RTP Memória
    - RTP África
    - RTP Internacional
    - RTP Açores
    - RTP Madeira

  - RDP Antena 1
  - RDP Antena 2
  - RDP Antena 3
  - RDP Internacional
  - RDP África
  - RDP Açores
  - RDP Madeira
- RTS—Serbia
- RTSH—Albania
- RTK–Kosovo
- RTV Slovenija—Slovenia
- RTVE—Spain:
  - TVE1
  - TVE-2
  - Clan TVE
  - Canal 24 Horas
  - Teledeporte
  - TVE Internacional
- RÚV—Iceland
- S4C—Wales, United Kingdom
- Kringvarp Føroya—Faroe Islands:
  - Sjónvarp Føroya
  - Útvarp Føroya
- SRG SSR—Switzerland:
  - SRF 1
  - SRF zwei
  - SRF info
  - RTS Un
  - RTS Deux
  - RSI La 1

    - RSI La 2
    - Televisiun Rumantscha
- SMtv—San Marino
- SVT – Sveriges Television—Sweden
- SR – Sveriges Radio—Sweden
- UR—Sweden
- TG4 — Ireland
- TVP—Poland:
    - TVP 1
    - TVP 2
    - TVP Info
    - TVP Regionalna
    - TVP Kultura
    - TVP Historia
    - TVP Seriale
    - TVP HD
    - TVP Sport
    - TVP Rozrywka
    - TVP ABC
    - Biełsat TV
- Televisió de Catalunya—Spain
- TVR—Romania
- TRT—Turkey
- VRT—Flanders, Belgium
- YLE – Yleisradio—Finland
- ZDF—Germany

North America

Barbados

- Caribbean Broadcasting Corporation—Saint Michael, Barbados

Costa Rica

- Canal 13 (SINART)—Costa Rica
- Canal 15 (Universidad de Costa Rica)—Costa Rica

Cuba

- Cubavisión—Cuba

Canada

- Canadian Broadcasting Corporation—national:
    - CBC Television
    - CBC News Network
    - CBC North
    - Documentary
    - Ici Radio-Canada Télé
    - Réseau de l'information
    - ARTV
    - Explora
    - TV5 Québec Canada
    - CBC Radio One
    - CBC Radio 2
    - CBC Radio 3 (no terrestrial broadcasting)
    - Ici Radio-Canada Première
    - Espace musique
    - Radio Canada International (no terrestrial broadcasting; international broadcasting only)
    - CBC Parliamentary Television Network (former)
    - Bande à part (former)
    - Newsworld International (former; international broadcasting only)
    - Trio (former; international broadcasting only)
    - CBC-2 (proposed)
    - Télé-2 (proposed)
- BBC Worldwide—national

    - BBC Canada
    - BBC Kids
- Knowledge—British Columbia
- TVOntario—Ontario
- Télé-Québec—Quebec
- TFO—Ontario
- CFTU-TV—Montreal, Quebec (non-profit)
- CKUA Radio Network—Alberta (non-profit)
- CJRT-FM—Toronto, Ontario (non-profit)
- Access—Alberta (former)
- Saskatchewan Communications Network—Saskatchewan (former)

United States

- Public Broadcasting Service (October 1970)
- National Public Radio (February 1970)
- New York Public Radio (July 1924)
- Chicago Public Radio (April 1943)
- Pacifica Radio (April 1949)
- Boston Public Radio (October 1951)
- American Public Television (1961)
- American Public Media (January 1967)
- MHz Networks (March 1972)
- Public Radio International (1983)
- World (TV channel) (December 2005)
- Create (TV network) (January 2006)

Oceania

Australia

- Australian Broadcasting Corporation:
    - ABC TV
    - ABC2
    - ABC3

- ABC News 24
- ABC Local Radio—*54 stations*
- ABC Radio National
- ABC NewsRadio
- ABC Classic FM
- ABC Triple J
- ABC Radio Australia
- ABC Radio Grandstand

- Special Broadcasting Service—*Also available in New Zealand in selected regions*:
    - SBS One
    - SBS Two
    - SBS Radio—*Includes SBS Radio One, Two, Pop Asia, and CHILL*

East Timor

- Radio-Televisão Timor Leste

New Zealand

- RNZ
    - RNZ National
    - RNZ Concert
    - RNZ Parliament
- Māori Television
- TVNZ—*six channels, commercial television and public television*
- Triangle TV—*Auckland Region broadcaster*

NZ Local Networks (Can be Included)

- CUETV
- TVHB
- 45 South TV
- Channel North Television
- Access Taranaki 104.4FM
- Access Manawatu 999AM
- Access Wellington 783AM

- Mainland TV Nelson

Oceania International Services

- Australia Network
- RNZ INTERNATIONAL

Pacific Islands

- FBC Fiji
- SBC Samoa
- TBC Tonga
- PBS American Samoa

South America

Argentina

- Canal 7 Argentina—Argentina (nationwide)
- Canal 10 – Tucumán—Tucumán, Argentina
- Canal 10 – Rio Negro—Rio Negro, Argentina
- Canal 10 – Córdoba—Córdoba, Argentina

Brazil

- Empresa Brasil de Comunicação:
    - TV Brasil — Rio de Janeiro, Brasília, São Paulo, São Luís and broadcast affiliates
    - TV Brasil Internacional—Available in Africa, Americas, Portugal and Japan by cable and satellite
    - Rádio Nacional—Rio de Janeiro, Brasília and Amazon region
    - Rádio MEC—Rio de Janeiro and Brasília
- Fundação Padre Anchieta
    - TV Cultura—São Paulo and broadcast affiliates.
    - MultiCultura—São Paulo
    - Univesp TV—São Paulo
    - TV Rá-Tim-Bum—Nationwide by cable and satellite.
    - Rádio Cultura—São Paulo

Chile

- Televisión Nacional de Chile—Chile (nationwide)

Colombia

National

- Radio Televisión Nacional de Colombia:
    - Señal Colombia
    - Señal Institucional

Regional

- Canal 13
- Teleantioquia
- Telecafé
- Teleislas
- Televisión Regional del Oriente
- Telecaribe
- Telepacífico

Local

- Canal Capital
- Telemedellín

Ecuador

- Ecuador TV—Ecuador http://www.ecuadortv.ec

Guyana

- National Communications Network (NCN)

Uruguay

- TNU – Televisión Nacional de Uruguay
- S.O.D.R.E—Servicio Official Radioletrico (en desuso)
- Radio Clasica
- Radio Uruguay
- Radio Nacional

Venezuela

- Venezolana de Televisión—Venezuela (nationwide)
- Televisión Educativa—Venezuela
- Visión Venezuela—Venezuela

Transnational

- teleSUR—Reaches the entire continent, Europe and Northern Africa. Owned by La Nueva Televisora del Sur, a public company sponsored by several American countries.

Remote Broadcasting

In broadcast engineering, a remote broadcast (usually just called a remote or a live remote, or in news parlance, a live shot) is broadcasting done from a location away from a formal television studio and is considered an electronic field production (EFP). A remote pickup unit (RPU) is usually used to transmit the audio and/or video back to the television station, where it joins the normal airchain. Other methods include satellite trucks, production trucks and even regular telephone lines if necessary.

History

The first airing of a remote broadcast came in 1924, when Loew's Theater publicist and WHN (New York City) station manager Nils Granlund leased telegraph lines from Western Union to provide the first link in what became called cabaret broadcasting." By early 1925, Granlund had established remote lines between WHN and more than thirty New York City jazz nightclubs, including the Silver Slipper, The Parody Club, the Cotton Club, the Strand Roof, and Club Moritz. These big band remotes would become a staple of the old-time radio era, lasting well into the 1950s.

Nils T. Granlund cited the 1925 WHN airing of Senator James J. Walker's announcement of his New York City mayoral candidacy through a remote broadcast from the New York Press Club as the first such remote link for a political forum.

In Latin America, on October 27, 1920 Dr Sussini made the first remote transmission in Argentina from the theatre El Coliseo in Buenos Aires. In Mexico on September 27, 1921, Adolfo Gomez Fernandez made a transmission from the Teatro Ideal, Mexico DF.

The very first live remote broadcast to the nation was by the Canadian Broadcasting Corporation in 1938 when Frank Willis reported on the Moose River Gold Mine disaster in Nova Scotia http://archives.cbc.ca/economy_business/natural_resources/clips/3860/

On June 11, 1955, NBC, The National Broadcasting Company, provided the 1st live remote broadcast to the nation from Niagara Falls, New York.

Radio

In radio, remotes are often used for special events, such as concerts or sporting events, where either the entire event or advertisements for the event are broadcast on location. The cost of personnel and equipment is usually paid for by the host at each performance. However, if the event is recurring, such as a weekly broadcast from a nightclub, then dedicated lines are usually installed by the local telephone company in order to save on costs. With low range radio stations, and at events with no telephone lines, several radio stations call into the studio request line with a cell phone and microphone setup. From there, another dj in the studio will put them on-location dj live on the air via the studio request line. Some stations use this method when doing live broadcasts in areas where signal is weak.

Originally, analog audio broadcasts were sent through telephone hybrids, which, although low quality, were found to be acceptable for voice broadcasts. Later, frequency extenders were developed that used additional lines, shifting higher treble audio frequencies down on one end and back up on the other, providing a reasonable reproduction of the original sound. Currently, digital lines, such as ISDN or DSL, are used to send compressed digital audio back to the studio. In addition, modern remote pickup units have become extremely portable and can transmit single-channel monophonic FM-quality audio over regular telephone lines using built-in modems and advanced compression algorithms (MPEG-4, etc.).

Television

In TV, live television remotes are an almost daily part of television news broadcasts in the U.S. As a part of electronic news gathering (ENG), remotes are meant to bring the audience to the scene of the action, although often nothing directly related to the story is happening there anymore. In some cases live remotes have even taken ridicule, particularly for reporters who stand out in the middle of a hurricane's winds, risking their lives while telling viewers not to do the same.

To get to the scene quickly, a live remote may be done from a helicopter.

Live television remotes may often be used in a manner similar to radio remotes (and vice versa) as well.

Microbroadcasting

Microbroadcasting is the process of broadcasting a message to a relatively small audience.

Microbroadcasting, in radio terms, is the use of low-power transmitters (often Title 47 CFR Part 15 in the United States, or its equivalent elsewhere) to broadcast a radio signal over the space of a neighborhood or small town. Similar to pirate radio broadcasting, microbroadcasters generally operate without a license from the local regulation body, but sacrifice range in favor of using legal power limits (for example, 100 mW for medium wave broadcasts in the United States). Higher power levels can be achieved using carrier current techniques, which are widely used in colleges and universities. Both AM and FM bands are used, although AM tends to have better propagation characteristics at low power.

Microbroadcasting is also used by schools and businesses to serve just the immediate campus of the operation; well-known uses include audio tour guide systems, airport information services, and drive-in theaters, which often provide movie audio over the driver's car audio system. It has also been adopted as an advertising technique, particularly by car dealers and real estate agents.

Broadcast Syndication

In broadcasting, syndication is the licensing of the right to broadcast television and radio programs by multiple television and radio stations, without going through a broadcast network. It is common in countries where broadcast programming is scheduled by television networks with local independent affiliates, particularly in the United States. Syndication is less common in the rest of the world, as most countries have centralized networks or television stations without local affiliates and syndication, although shows can also be syndicated internationally. The three main types of syndication are "first-run syndication", which is programming that is broadcast for the first time as a syndicated show and is made specifically to sell directly into syndication; "off-network syndication", which is the licensing of a program that was originally run on network TV or in some cases first-run syndication (colloquially called a "rerun"); and public broadcasting syndication.

Types

- First-run syndication refers to programming that is broadcast for the first time as a syndicated show and is made specifically to sell directly into syndication (not any one particular network), or at least first so offered in a given country (programs originally created and broadcast outside the US, first presented on a network in their country of origin, have often been syndicated in the US and in some other countries);
- Off-network syndication involves the licensing of a program that was originally run on network television or in some cases first-run syndication: a rerun; these are usually found on stations affiliated with smaller networks like Fox or The CW, especially since these networks broadcast one less hour of prime time network programming than the Big Three television networks. This usually occurs when a show has built up about four seasons worth or a minimum of 88–100 episodes. Successful shows in syndication can cover production costs and make a profit, even if the first run of the show was not profitable.
- Public broadcasting syndication has arisen in the US as a parallel service to member stations of the Public Broadcasting Service (PBS) and the handful of independent public broadcasting stations. This form of syndication more closely resembles the news agency model, where nominally competing networks share resources and rebroadcast each other's programs. For example, National Public Radio (NPR) stations commonly air the Public Radio Exchange's *This American Life*, which may contain stories produced by NPR journalists.

When syndicating a show, the production company, or a distribution company called a syndicator, attempts to license the show to one station in each media market or area, or to a commonly owned station group, within the country and internationally. If successful, this can be lucrative, but the syndicator may only be able to license the show in a small percentage of the markets. Syndication differs from licensing the show to a television network. Once a network picks up a show, it is usually guaranteed to run on most or all the network's affiliates on the same day of the week and at the same time (in a given time zone, in countries where this is a concern). Some production companies create their shows and license them to networks at a loss, at least at first, hoping that the series will succeed and that eventual off-network syndication will turn a profit for the show. A syndicated program is licensed to stations for "cash" (the stations purchase the rights to insert some or all of the advertisements at their level); given to stations for access to airtime (wherein the syndicators get the advertising revenue); or the combination of both. The trade of program for airtime is called "barter".

In the US (as a result of continued relaxation of station ownership regulations since the 1970s), syndicated programs are usually licensed to stations on a group level, with multiple stations owned and/or operated by the same broadcasting group carrying the program in different markets (except in areas where another station holds the market rights to the program) – making it increasingly more efficient for syndicators to gain widespread national clearances for their programs. Many syndicated programs are traditionally sold first to one of five "key" station groups (ABC Owned Television Stations, NBC Owned Television Stations, CBS Television Stations, Fox Television Stations and Tribune Broadcasting), allowing their programs to gain clearances in the largest US TV markets (such as New York City, Los Angeles, Chicago and Philadelphia, where all five aforementioned groups each own stations), before striking deals with other major and smaller station owners. Shows airing in first-run syndication that are carried primarily by an owned-and-operated station group of a network may sometimes be incorrectly referenced as a network program, regardless to its distribution to stations of varying network affiliations and despite the fact it is not part of an individual network's base schedule.

Since the early 2000s, some programs being proposed for national distribution in first-run syndication have been test marketed on a selected number of or on all stations owned by certain major station groups, allowing the distributor to determine whether a national rollout is feasible based on the ratings accrued in the selected markets where the program is being aired.

While market penetration can vary widely and revenues can be unreliable, the producers often enjoy more content freedom in the absence of network standards and practices departments; frequently, some innovative ideas are explored by first-run syndicated programming which the networks are leery of giving airtime to. Meanwhile, top-rated syndicated shows in the United States usually have a domestic market reach as high as 98%. Very often, series that are aired in syndication have reduced running times. For example, a standard American sitcom runs 22 minutes, but in syndication it may be reduced to 20 minutes to make room for more commercials.

Syndication can take the form of either weekly or daily syndication. Game shows, some "tabloid" and entertainment news shows, and stripped talk shows are broadcast daily on weekdays, while most other first-run syndicated shows are broadcast on a weekly basis and are usually aired on weekends only. There was a big discussion sometime in the 1990s and 2000s about whether a show could be syndicated while it was still on the air. There had been much opposition to this idea and it was generally viewed as leading to a death of the show. However, licensing a program for syndication actually resulted in the increased popularity for shows that were still in production. A prime example is *Law & Order*.

First-run Syndication in the U.S.

As with radio in the U.S., television networks, particularly in their early years, did not offer a full day's worth of programming for their affiliates, even in the evening or "prime time" hours. Some stations were not affiliated with any network, operating as independent stations. Both groups sought to supplement their locally produced programming and whatever network feeds there were with content that could be flexibly scheduled. The development of videotape and, much later, enhanced satellite downlink access furthered these options. While most past first-run syndicated shows were shown only in syndication, some canceled network shows continued to be produced for first-run syndication or were revived for syndication several years after their original cancellation. Until about 1980, most syndicated series were distributed to stations either on 16mm film prints (off-network reruns, feature films, and cartoons) or videotape (topical series such as the talk shows of Mike Douglas and Merv Griffin, and variety and quiz shows.)

Ziv Television Programs, Inc., after establishing itself as a major radio syndicator, was the first major first-run television syndicator, creating several long-lived series in the 1950s and selling them directly to regional sponsors, who in turn sold the shows to local stations. Ziv's first major TV hit was *The Cisco Kid*. Ziv had the foresight to film the Cisco Kid series in color, even though color TV was yet to be a reality. Among the most famous and widely watched Ziv offerings were *Sea Hunt*, *I Led Three Lives* and *Highway Patrol*. Some first-run syndicated series were picked up by networks in the 1950s and early 1960s, notably *The Adventures of Superman* and *Mr. Ed*. The networks started syndicating their reruns in the late 1950s, and first-run syndication shrank sharply, for a decade. Some stalwart series continued, notably *Death Valley Days*; other ambitious projects were also to flourish, however briefly, such as *The Play of the Week* (1959–1961), produced by David Susskind (of the syndicated talk show *Open End* and also producer of such network fare as *NYPD*).

Other popular syndicated series of the 1950s included MCA's *The Abbott and Costello Show* (vaudeville-style comedy) and Guild Films' *Liberace* (musical variety) and *Life With Elizabeth*, a domestic situation comedy that introduced Betty White to a national audience. In addition to *The Adventures of Superman*, many other series were based on comic strips and aimed at the juvenile audience, including *Flash Gordon*, *Dick Tracy*, *Sheena, Queen of the Jungle*, and *Joe Palooka*. Original juvenile adventure series included *Captain Gallant of the Foreign Legion*, *Cowboy G-Men*, and *Ramar of the Jungle*. Series based on literary properties included *Sherlock Holmes*, *Long John Silver* (based on *Treasure Island*), *The Invisible man*, and *The Three Musketeers*. Several of these were co-productions between US and European (usually British) companies. *Crusader Rabbit* pioneered in the area of first-run animated series; followed by *Bucky and Pepito*, *Spunky and Tadpole*, *Q.T. Hush*, and others. (All of these were five-minute shorts designed to be placed within locally hosted kiddie shows.) Syndicated sports programming included *Championship Bowling* and *All-Star Golf*, both produced by Chicago-based Walter Schwimmer, Inc.

In addition to regular series, syndicators also offered packages of feature films, cartoons, and short subjects originally made for movie theatres. Until late in the 1950s, however, much of the theatrical product available consisted of low-budget secondary features (mainly Westerns) with relatively few notable stars. One syndication company, National Telefilm Associates, attempted to create a "film network" of stations showing its lineup of first-run series, which included syndicated programs such as *Police Call* (1955), *How to Marry a Millionaire* (1957-1959), *The Passerby*, *Man Without a Gun* (1957-1959), and *This is Alice* (1958). The venture lasted several years, but was ultimately unsuccessful.

However, FCC rulings in the late 1960s curtailed the U.S. networks' ability to schedule programming in what has become known as the "early fringe", notably the 7–8 p.m. (Eastern and Pacific

Time) hour of "prime time", with the stated hope that this might encourage more local programming of social and cultural relevance to communities (off-network syndicated repeats were also banned); some projects of this sort came to fruition, though usually relatively commercial and slick ones such as Group W's *Evening Magazine/PM Magazine* franchise, and such pre-existing national projects as the brief commercial-television run of William F. Buckley, Jr.'s interview/debate series *Firing Line*. The more obvious result was an increase in Canadian-produced syndicated dramatic series, such as *Dusty's Trail* and the Colgate-sponsored *Dr. Simon Locke*. Game shows, often evening editions of network afternoon series, flourished, and a few odd items such as *Wild Kingdom*, canceled by NBC in 1971, had a continuing life as syndicated programming tailor-made for the early fringe.

1970s and 1980s

In 1971, the U.S. Federal Communications Commission passed the Prime Time Access Rule and Financial Interest and Syndication Rules, which prevented networks from programming one particular hour of prime time programming on its television stations each night and required the networks to spin off their syndication arms as independent companies. Although the intent of the rule was to encourage local stations to produce their own programs for this time slot, budgetary limits instead prompted stations to buy syndicated programs to fill the slot. This, coupled with an increase in UHF independent stations, caused a boom in the syndication market. In the 1970s, first-run syndication continued to be an odd mix: cheaply produced, but not always poor quality, "filler" programming. These included the dance-music show *Soul Train*, and 20th Century Fox's *That's Hollywood*, a television variation on the popular *That's Entertainment!* theatrically released collections of film clips from the Metro-Goldwyn-Mayer library.

There were also many imported programs distributed this way. These include the documentary series *Wild, Wild World of Animals* (repackaged by Time-Life with narration by William Conrad) and Thames Television's sober and necessarily grim *The World at War*. *The Starlost* (1973) was a Canadian series, apparently modified from the vision of science fiction writers Harlan Ellison and Ben Bova. Britain's ITC Entertainment, headed by Lew Grade, made *UFO* (1970) and *Space: 1999* (1975). These two series were created by Gerry Anderson (and his associates), who was previously best known for supermarionation (a combination of puppetry and animation) series such as *Thunderbirds*. The most successful syndicated show in the United States in the 1970s was probably *The Muppet Show*, also from Lew Grade's company. Animated series from the 1980s *Dogtanian and the Three Muskehounds* and *Around the World with Willy Fog* came from Spanish animation production company BRB Internacional and their Japanese co-producers Nippon Animation.

Game shows thrived in syndication during the decade. Nightly versions of *What's My Line?*, *Truth or Consequences*, *Beat the Clock* and *To Tell the Truth* premiered in the late 1960s and found loyal audiences for many years. Several daytime network games began producing once-a-week nighttime versions for broadcast in the early evening hours, usually with bigger prizes and often featuring different hosts (emcees were limited to appearing on one network and one syndicated game simultaneously) and modified titles (*Match Game PM*, *The $100,000 Name That Tune* or *The $25,000 Pyramid*, for example). A few independent game shows, such as *Sports Challenge* and *Celebrity Bowling*, also entered the syndication market around this time. Of these shows, *Let's Make a Deal* and *Hollywood Squares* were the first to jump to twice-a-week syndicated versions around 1973. Another popular daytime show to have a weekly syndicated version was *The Price Is Right*, which began concurrently in weekly syndication and on CBS; the syndicated "nighttime" version was hosted by Dennis James for its first five years, after which daytime host Bob Barker took over for another three years of weekly episodes (even though, by this point, the daytime and nighttime shows had diverged noticeably). The nighttime version of *Family Feud* (1977) quickly jumped from once-weekly to twice, and finally to five-day-a-week airings, and its massive popularity, along with that of new five-day-a-week entries like Jack Barry's *The Joker's Wild* (1977) and *Tic-Tac-Dough* (1978) and Chuck Barris's increasingly raunchy remakes of his 1960s hits *The Newlywed Game* and *The Dating Game*, brought an end (with rare exceptions) to the era of once-a-week games. Also popular in first-run syndication and daytime was *The Gong Show*, hosted by Barris throughout most of its run (Gary Owens hosted the first syndicated season).

A number of half-hour musical-variety shows were also offered in the early 1970s, generally built around personable middle-of-the-road singers like Bobby Vinton, Bobby Goldsboro, Dolly Parton, and Andy Williams, or groups like Sha Na Na, The Johnny Mann Singers, and The Golddiggers. *Wait Till Your Father Gets Home* (1972) was a Hanna-Barbera cartoon series attempting to ape the *All in the Family*-style sitcoms; *Skippy the Bush Kangaroo* (1969) was an Australian children's series in the manner of *Flipper* or *Gentle Ben* (a decade later, the decidedly not-for-children Australian *Prisoner: Cell Block H* would have a brief U.S. syndicated run); and a Canadian sketch-comedy series began appearing on U.S. television stations in 1977 – *Second City Television*, which would eventually find a home, for two seasons, on NBC, as *SCTV Network 90* (and on premium cable channel Cinemax by 1983).

The Universal/Paramount-produced package of original programming, *Operation Prime Time*, began appearing on *ad hoc* quasi-networks of (almost by necessity) non-network stations in the U.S. in 1978, with a mini-series adaptation of John Jakes's *The Bastard*. From the later 1960s into the late 1970s, Westinghouse also found considerable success with *The Mike Douglas Show*, a variety/talk show hosted by a singer with an easygoing interview style, which aired in the afternoons in most markets; similar programs soon followed featuring Merv Griffin, who had been the host of CBS' most sustained late-night answer to *The Tonight Show Starring Johnny Carson* previously, and another network veteran, Dinah Shore. Also notable was the growing success of audience-participation talk shows, particularly that of the innovator of the format, Phil Donahue.

First-run syndication in the 1970s also made it possible for some shows that were no longer wanted by television networks to remain on the air. In 1971, ABC canceled *The Lawrence Welk Show*, which went on to produce new episodes in syndication for another 11 years, and currently continues to much success in weekend reruns (with new segments featuring Welk cast members inserted within the episodes) distributed to PBS stations by the Oklahoma Educational Television Authority. Also in 1971, CBS dropped *Lassie* and *Hee Haw*, the latter show's run ending as part of the network's cancellation of all of its rural-oriented shows (known then as "rural purge", which also resulted in the cancellations of *The Beverly Hillbillies* and *Green Acres*). *Lassie* entered first-run syndication for two years, while *Hee Haw* continued to produce new episodes until 1992.

First-run Syndicated Comedy

Throughout the mid-to-late 1980s into the early 1990s, sitcoms continued to enter first-run syndication after being canceled by the networks, the most successful of which were *Mama's Family* and *Charles In Charge*. Other sitcoms during this time to enter first-run syndication after network cancellation included *Silver Spoons, Punky Brewster, Webster, It's a Living, Too Close for Comfort, 9 to 5, What's Happening!!*, and *WKRP in Cincinnati*. Many of these sitcoms produced new shows in syndication mainly to have enough episodes for a profitable run in reruns. Other sitcoms, such as *Small Wonder, Out of This World, The Munsters Today*, and *Harry and the Hendersons* (as well as more action-adventure oriented series like *Superboy* and *My Secret Identity*) enjoyed success in syndication throughout their entire run.

Dramatic First-run Syndicated Programs

The broadcast networks aired many action-adventure programs from the 1950s to the 1980s. By the late 1980s, however, increasing production costs made them less attractive to the networks. Studios found that reruns of one-hour dramas did not sell as well as sitcoms, so they were unable to fully recoup the shows' costs using the traditional deficit financing model. Such shows instead moved to syndication, starting with *Star Trek: The Next Generation*, which debuted in 1987 and became one of the most watched syndicated shows throughout its seven-year run. Its great success caused many others to debut; by 1994, there were more than 20 one-hour syndicated shows.

When NBC canceled the television series adaptation of *Fame* after only two seasons, the producers made special arrangements with LBS Communications, which resulted in MGM reviving the series for first-run syndication in the fall of 1983, where it continued for four more seasons, with the last first-run episode airing in the U.S. on May 18, 1987. *Friday the 13th: The Series* (a horror series which shared its title with the successful movie franchise) also debuted in 1987. The next syndicated shows that debuted in 1988 were *War of the Worlds* and *Freddy's Nightmares*.

Baywatch, which debuted in 1989 on NBC and was canceled after one season also became one of the most watched syndicated shows throughout its ten-year-run, garnering a worldwide audience. Another series to be one of the few shows to nearly match *Baywatch* would be the television series *Renegade*. *Star Trek: Deep Space Nine* was also syndicated. *Hercules: The Legendary Journeys* and its spin-off series *Xena: Warrior Princess* helped build the audiences for such shows; *Babylon 5* and *Forever Knight* drew devoted "cult" audiences; *Psi Factor* and *Poltergeist: The Legacy* attempted to draw on the audience for the Fox series *The X-Files* (as did, even less probably, the short-lived spinoff *Baywatch Nights*).

Among the other series were *Relic Hunter, VIP, High Tide, She Spies* and *Once a Thief*. In 1997, *Earth: Final Conflict*, based on ideas from Gene Roddenberry, premiered in syndication. Three years later, a second Gene Roddenberry series, *Andromeda* also premiered in syndication. After that series' ended in 2004, there would not be a first-run syndicated drama (or a first-run scripted series in syndication) until 2008, when Disney-ABC Domestic Television and ABC Studios teamed up with Sam Raimi to launch a new first-run syndicated series *Legend of the Seeker*, based on Terry Goodkind's *Sword of Truth* novel series. Another gap in first-run scripted series in syndication followed four years after *Legend of the Seeker* was canceled in 2009, until Trifecta Entertainment & Media (a company that mainly distributes programs for off-network syndication) began producing *SAF3* in 2013.

Animated Series

During the late 1970s and 1980s, independent stations signed on in mid-sized and many small markets. The market for made-for-television cartoons grew as a result to include a branch for such stations. It usually had a greater artistic freedom, and looser standards (not mandated by a network). The older Bugs Bunny and Popeye cartoons made way for first-run syndicated cartoons such as *He-Man and the Masters of the Universe*, *Rambo: The Force of Freedom*, *ThunderCats*, *Dennis the Menace*, *My Little Pony*, *The Transformers*, *G.I. Joe*, *Voltron*, *M.A.S.K.*, *The Centurions*, *Teenage Mutant Ninja Turtles*, and reruns of *Scooby-Doo*, *Garfield and Friends*, and *The Pink Panther*, among many others.

In 1987, The Walt Disney Company tried its luck at syndication; *DuckTales* premiered that September and would eventually last for 100 episodes. The success of *DuckTales* paved the way for a second series two years later, *Chip 'n Dale Rescue Rangers*. The following year, the two shows aired together under the umbrella block *The Disney Afternoon*. In fall of 1990, Disney added another hour to *The Disney Afternoon*; the block continued in syndication, running additional first-run animated series until 1999.

These cartoons initially competed with the ones that were nationally televised on the broadcast networks. In the 1980s, national broadcast networks only aired cartoons on Saturday mornings, not competing with the weekday and Sunday syndication blocks aired by local independent stations; however, by the 1990s, Fox and then The WB launched their own weekday afternoon children's program blocks. By the end of the 1990s, both syndication distributors and broadcast networks ended up losing most of its children's market to the rise of cable television channels aimed at that audience such as Nickelodeon and Cartoon Network, which provided appealing children's entertainment throughout the week at nearly all hours.

Syndication remains a method of choice for distributing children's programming, although this has gradually shifted to only produce programs to satisfy the federally mandated "educational-informational" (E/I) rule imposed in the late 1990s as part of an amendment to the Children's Television Act of 1990 that requires stations to air three hours of educational children's programs every week, regardless of the station's format. Syndication is generally a less expensive option for a local station than to attempt to produce its own locally originated E/I programming; not all networks provide their own E/I programs, so stations that are affiliated with networks that do not carry children's program blocks acquire E/I programs off the syndication market to fulfill the requirements.

News Programming and Late-night Talk Shows

Also in the 1980s, news programming of various sorts began to be offered widely to stations. *Independent Network News*, which was produced by WPIX in New York City, was a half-hour nightly program that ran from 1980 to 1990 on independent stations (in some markets, *INN* was paired with a locally produced primetime newscast); CNN would offer a simulcast of programming from its sister network Headline News (now HLN) to broadcast stations later, though it was used mainly to fill overnight time periods and was effectively discontinued in syndication with the 2006 launch of that network's "Headline Prime" talk show block. *Entertainment Tonight* began its long and continuing run as a "soft" news daily strip, with a number of imitations following (among which have included such entertainment news shows as *TMZ on TV*, *Extra* and *ET*'s own spin-off *The Insider*); and "tabloid" television, in the wake of ABC's *20/20* and, more immediately, 20th Television's *A Current Affair*, would become a syndication staple with such series as *Hard Copy* and *Real TV*.

Another area where network dominance was challenged by syndicated programming in the 1980s was with late-night talk shows; *The Arsenio Hall Show* was the only very successful one (it would be canceled after five years in 1994 due to ratings declines spurred by many CBS affiliates pushing the show to later timeslots following the debut of the *Late Show with David Letterman*, and was later revived in 2013), but similar programs were attempted such as Alan Thicke's earlier short-lived *Thicke of the Night*, Lauren Hutton's innovatively shot *Lauren Hutton and...*, and talk shows hosted by Dennis Miller, Whoopi Goldberg, David Brenner and Keenen Ivory Wayans; Magic Johnson's *The Magic Hour* was seen as a massive flop, similar to *Thicke of the Night*. The popularity of syndicated talk shows fell dramatically in the mid-1990s as network and cable offerings expanded in the wake of Johnny Carson's retirement.

Reality and Live-action Children's Shows

Long before their popularity on network television from the 2000s onward, reality competition shows in one form or another, such as *Star Search* and *American Gladiators*, enjoyed popularity in syndication as early as the mid-1980s. Since the now-defunct networks UPN and The WB began offering their affiliates additional nights of prime time programming in the late 1990s, there have been fewer first-run scripted series in syndication, at least, in the U.S.; much as with the closing of windows that provided opportunity for Ziv in the 1950s and various producers in the early 1970s. The more expensive dramatic projects are less attractive to syndicators (particularly when they might be sold, with somewhat less risk, to cable channels); "reality" series such as *Cheaters* and *Maximum Exposure* and several dating series began to be more common in the early 2000s. Some of the more low-key programs in this category were designed to appeal to children, such as *Beakman's World*, *Animal Rescue* and *Jack Hanna's Animal Adventures*. They were able to get significant clearance because of stricter Federal Communications Commission (FCC) enforcement of rules on children's television programming.

Game Shows

Several game shows are currently syndicated; historically, the most popular had been *Wheel of Fortune* and the current version of *Jeopardy!*, both created by television personality Merv Griffin, respectively premiering in 1983 and 1984. The shows have been #1 and #2 or #1 to #3 in the syndication ratings consistently since at least the late 1980s. In fact, according to the *Guinness Book of World Records*, *Wheel* is the most popular syndicated television program both within and outside the United States. *Family Feud* ended its first syndication run in 1985. Three years later, a revival of the program became a moderate hit and continued for seven seasons. A third revival hit the airwaves in 1999 and has gone through four hosts. The first three hosts (Louie Anderson, Richard Karn and John O'Hurley) struggled in their respective runs and only lasted three to four years. The current run of the program, hosted by Steve Harvey, has been a major ratings success; on the week of June 12, 2015, for the first time ever, *Family Feud* was the highest-rated syndicated program in terms of average household ratings. A *Hollywood Squares* revival also thrived beginning in 1998, running six seasons until its 2004 cancellation. By far the most successful entry into the market in the 2000s has been the daily version of *Who Wants to Be a Millionaire*, which premiered in 2002.

Because game shows are very inexpensive to produce, with many episodes completed each day of production, successful ones are very profitable; for example, in 1988 *Jeopardy!* cost an estimated

$5 million to produce but earned almost $50 million in revenue. New game show concepts (that is, not based on an existing or pre-existing format) are rarely tried and usually unsuccessful in syndication; somewhat of an exception to this was *Street Smarts*, which lasted from 2001 to 2006 (despite the series airing in late night slots in many markets). Between 2003 and 2007, no new game shows debuted in syndication, marking four consecutive seasons where no new shows with that genre debuted, a syndication first. That streak ended with the fall 2007 debuts of *Temptation* and *Merv Griffin's Crosswords*, bringing the daytime tally to six game shows; both ended production after one year, though *Crosswords* aired in reruns in some cities during the 2008–09 season before those reruns moved exclusively to cable.

More new shows were added for the 2008–09 fall season, including a daytime run of *Deal or No Deal* (which featured certain elements that differed from the show's franchised format, most notably with prospective players instead of models holding briefcases that held the monetary amounts) and an adaptation of the popular board game *Trivial Pursuit*. While *Deal* caught on and was renewed for the 2009–2010 season, *Trivial Pursuit: America Plays* suffered low ratings throughout its run and was canceled.

For the 2009–2010 season, the Fox game show *Are You Smarter than a 5th Grader?* moved to syndication with a new, less expensive format. *Don't Forget the Lyrics!* followed for the 2010–2011 season. *Deal*, suffering from falling ratings, was canceled in February 2010, with the final episodes airing in late May of that same year. *5th Grader* and *Don't Forget the Lyrics* were canceled the following year for the same reason (although reruns of *5th Grader* remain on cable). Reruns of the popular Discovery Channel show *Cash Cab* began airing in syndication in January 2011. Reruns of the GSN dating game show *Baggage* first aired in syndication as a test run in early 2011 on stations owned by the Sinclair Broadcast Group, which preceded its full launch into other markets in fall 2012; although it was removed from syndication after one season.

The 2014-15 season saw the introduction of *Celebrity Name Game*, hosted by former *The Late Late Show* host Craig Ferguson; the series was renewed for a second season in January 2015, while Ferguson would also win a Daytime Emmy Award for Outstanding Game Show Host for his work on the program. In January 2016, Fox owned-and-operated stations began a test run of *South of Wilshire*—a game show produced by TMZ.

Stripped Talk Shows

The dominant form of first-run syndication in the U.S. for the last three decades has been the "stripped" (or "strip") talk show, such as *Donahue*, *Oprah Winfrey*, *The Tyra Banks Show*, and *The Jerry Springer Show*. Strip programming is a technique used for scheduling television and radio programming to ensure consistency and coherency. Strip programming is used to deliver consistent content to targeted audiences. Broadcasters know or predict the times at which certain demographics will be listening to or watching their programs and play them at that time. As with game shows, talk shows are inexpensive to produce and very profitable if successful. In many markets, a stripped show will be seen twice daily, usually with different episodes (one being a more recent episode and the other being an episode from a previous season). Sometimes, station groups with more than one station in a market, or a "duopoly", will run one episode of a strip on one of their stations in the morning, and the other available episode on another of their stations that night.

Meanwhile, the popularity of some of the audience-participation talk shows continues to encourage new participants, some of whom, such as Morton Downey, Jr. and Rosie O'Donnell, have brief periods of impressive ratings and influence; others, such as Oprah Winfrey and Maury Povich, have a sustained run. A notable scheduling decision was made by KRON-TV in San Francisco: a 2000 dispute with NBC led to that station's disaffiliation from that network after 52 years, and since all the other larger networks were already represented in San Francisco, KRON decided to become one of the largest commercial independent stations by market size on the VHF band in the U.S., and soon tried running *Dr. Phil*, a popular new stripped series hosted by Winfrey-associate Phil McGraw, in primetime, with impressive ratings results.

2000s

First-run syndicated shows in the US include talk shows (e.g., *The Dr. Oz Show*, *Dr. Phil* and *The Ellen DeGeneres Show*); tabloid/newsmagazine shows (e.g., *TMZ Live*); crime/law enforcement shows (e.g., *Crime Watch Daily*); game shows (e.g., *Family Feud*, *Jeopardy!* and *Wheel of Fortune*); reality court shows (e.g., *Judge Judy*); and sitcoms (e.g., *The First Family*).

Influence on Television Schedules

In earlier times, independent stations thrived on syndicated programming, including some venerable and quite profitable stations such as KMSP-TV in the Minneapolis-St. Paul market. With the loosening of FCC regulations and the creation of new additional broadcast networks (such as Fox, The CW, MyNetworkTV and Ion Television), most of these independents have joined one or another of these or smaller (religious or low-budget) networks.

In another case, like those of KCAL-TV in Los Angeles, KMCI-TV in Lawrence-Kansas City and WMLW-TV in Racine-Milwaukee, those independent stations are used to complement their network-affiliated sister station (respectively in the mentioned cases, KCBS-TV, KSHB-TV and WDJT-TV) by allowing a duopoly control of more syndicated programming than would be possible on one station (and to spread it throughout the schedule of the two stations, often several times a day), or to air news programming in times unavailable on the larger network station, along with fulfilling network and syndicated programming commitments, which allows popular or network programming to be moved to the independent stations due to breaking news or sports commitments without the traditional inconvenience of a late night or weekend airing of the pre-empted show. A duopoly of a network-affiliated and independent station also allows a network station to move a low-rated syndicated program to their sister independent station to stem revenue losses.

Off-network Syndication

Off-network syndication occurs when a network television show is syndicated in packages containing some or all episodes, and sold to as many television stations and markets as possible to be used in local programming timeslots. In this manner, sitcoms are preferred and more successful because they are less serialized, and can be run non-sequentially, which is more beneficial and less costly for the station. In the United States, local stations now rarely broadcast reruns of primetime dramas (or simply air them primarily on weekends); instead, they usually air on basic cable channels, which may air each episode 30 to 60 times.

Syndication rights typically last for six consecutive showings of a series within three to five years; if a program continues to perform well enough in broadcast or cable syndication during the initial cycle, television stations or cable networks can opt to renew an off-network program for an additional cycle.

Syndication has been known to spur the popularity of a series that only experienced moderate success during its original network run. The most notable example of this is *Star Trek*, which ran for three seasons on NBC from 1966 to 1969, garnering only modest ratings, but became a worldwide cult phenomenon after it entered off-network syndication. Its success in syndication led to the *Star Trek* film series, *Star Trek: The Next Generation*, and several other series.

It is common for long-running series to have early seasons syndicated while the series itself is still in first-run network production. In order to differentiate between new and rebroadcast content, up until the 1980s it was not uncommon for series to be syndicated under a different title than that used in their original broadcast run. Examples include *Bonanza* (which was syndicated as *Ponderosa*), *Gunsmoke* (as *Marshall Dillon*), *Emergency!* (as *Emergency One*), *Ironside* (as *The Raymond Burr Show*), *Hawaii Five-O* (as *McGarrett*), *M*A*S*H* (as *M*A*S*H 4077th*), *Marcus Welby, M.D.* (as *Robert Young, Family Doctor*), *CHiPs* (as *CHiPs Patrol*), and *Happy Days* (as *Happy Days Again*).

Syndication of older episodes can also increase exposure for a television show that is still airing first-run network episodes. In the case of the CBS sitcom *The Big Bang Theory*, its syndication, particularly on TBS, is one of the reasons attributed for a rise in first-run ratings for its sixth season. The sixth season episode "The Bakersfield Expedition", for example, was the first episode of that series to attract 20 million viewers.

Strip/Daily Syndication

Off-network syndication can take several forms. The most common form is known as strip syndication or daily syndication, when episodes of a television series are shown daily five times a week in the same time slot. In the 1960s and 1970s, independent stations with no news departments began viewing strip syndication as a necessary means of obtaining effective counterprogramming to the local news programs airing on network affiliates. Typically, this means that enough episodes must exist (88 episodes, or four seasons, is the usual minimum, though many syndicators prefer a fully rounded 100 episodes) to allow for continual strip syndication to take place over the course of several months, without episodes being repeated. However, there are exceptions, such as the 65-episode block (common in children's programming), which allows for a 13-week cycle of daily showings, so there will only be four repeats in a year.

In some cases, more than one episode is shown daily. Half-hour sitcoms are sometimes syndicated in groups of two or four episodes, taking up one or two hours of broadcast time. If a series is not strip syndicated, it may be aired once a week, instead of five times a week. This allows shows with fewer episodes to last long in syndication, but it also may mean viewers will tire of waiting a week for the next episode of a show they have already seen and stop watching. More often, hour-long dramas in their first several runs in syndication are offered weekly; sitcoms are more likely to get stripped. In recent years, there has been something of a trend toward showing two consecutive episodes of a program on Saturday and Sunday nights after prime time (generally following the local news). This pattern has been particularly prominent for shows which are still in production but have run long enough to have many previous episodes available.

As with commercial stations, not all the airtime nor all the perceived audience are met by the productions offered U.S. public-broadcasting stations by PBS; additionally, there are some independent public television stations in the U.S. which take no programming from that (somewhat) decentralized network. As a result, there are several syndicators of programming for the non-profit stations, several of which are descendants of the regional station groups which combined some, not all, of their functions into the creation of PBS in 1969. American Public Television (APT) is the largest of these, nearly matched by the National Educational Telecommunications Association (NETA); similarly, the recently defunct Continental Program Marketing was another of the syndicator-descendants (of the Northeastern, Southeastern, and Rocky Mountain educational networks, respectively) of the pre-PBS era. Among the other notable organizations in the U.S. are Westlink Satellite Operations (based at Albuquerque's KNME), BBC Worldwide Americas (which often works with other distributors and individual stations, since it has no satellite access of its own in the U.S.), Deutsche Welle, Executive Program Services, the Program Resource Group and PBS's Long Island, New York member station WLIW, which is (with the arguable exception of KNME) the most prolific contributor of any individual station of syndicated programming, most obviously the *BBC World News*, *Doctor Who* and *Monty Python's Flying Circus* in the U.S.

Monetary Rates

In 1993, Universal Studios became one of the first studios to cash in on the cable trend, first selling repeats of *Major Dad* to USA Network in 1993 for $600,000 per episode, the first time a network program was exclusively sold to a cable network for its first run rights. Later it sold reruns of *Law & Order* to A&E for about $155,000 an episode; in 1996, the studio got $275,000 from USA Network for repeats of *New York Undercover*, a far less successful show. *Law & Order* drew A&E's highest daytime ratings – one million viewers per episode.

Universal sold reruns of *Xena: Warrior Princess* and *Hercules: The Legendary Journeys* to USA for $300,000 each. And even long-forgotten shows can find new life: The Nashville Network bought *The Dukes of Hazzard* from Warner Bros. in 1997 for well over $10 million. USA Network paid $750,000 for the rights to *Walker, Texas Ranger*; while USA's reruns of the show drew an average of 2.3 million viewers – outstanding by cable standards – Perth says the show will need *an enormous number of airings to have any sort of profitability."*

Year sold	Show	Studio	Cable network	Price*
1986	*Falcon Crest*	Lorimar-Telepictures	Turner Broadcasting	$10,000
	Knots Landing	Lorimar-Telepictures	Turner Broadcasting	$12,000
1988	*Murder, She Wrote*	Universal Television	USA Network	$525,000
1991	*Unsolved Mysteries*	Buena Vista Television	Lifetime	$180,000
1993	*The Commish*	ABC Productions	Lifetime	$195,000
1994	*Law & Order*	Universal Television	A&E	$155,000

1995	*Melrose Place*	Spelling Television	E!	$200,000
	Picket Fences	20th Television	FX	$190,000
	Lois & Clark: The New Adventures of Superman	Warner Bros.	TNT	$275,000
	Dr. Quinn, Medicine Woman	MTM Enterprises	The Family Channel	$250,000
	NYPD Blue	20th Television	FX	$400,000
1996	*Xena: Warrior Princess*	Universal Television	USA	$300,000
	Hercules: The Legendary Journeys	Universal Television	USA	$300,000
	Chicago Hope	20th Television	Lifetime	$475,000
	Homicide: Life on the Street	NBC Productions	Lifetime	$425,000
	The X-Files	20th Television	FX	$600,000
	Walker, Texas Ranger	Columbia TriStar	USA	$750,000
	ER	Warner Bros.	TNT	$1.2 million

Not all programs in syndication are sold for a fee. Less popular programming may be distributed by *barter*, in which the syndicator, instead of selling the show to a station, offers the show for free, with the caveat that the station give up its advertising time on other shows to the syndicator's advertisers. Barter syndication, in addition to the cost advantage, is popular because of its flexibility; a station can typically pick up a barter syndicated program for only a few weeks or months, without the long-term financial commitment of a traditional syndicated series, allowing the station to plug the show into its lineup to fill a hole in the schedule.

Types of Deals

Cash deals are when a distributor offers a syndicated program to the highest bidder. A cash plus deal is when the distributor retains advertising space to offset some of the cost for the program. The station gets the program for a little less in exchange for some ad space for the producer.

Barter deals are usually for new untested shows or older shows. In this type of deal, distributors get a fraction of the advertisement revenue in exchange for their program. For example, in a 7/5 deal the producer gets seven minutes of advertising time, leaving five minutes for the station to insert local as well as national advertisements.

Radio Syndication

Radio syndication generally works the same way as television syndication, except that radio stations usually are not organized into strict affiliate-only networks. Radio networks generally are only distributors of radio shows, and individual stations (though often owned by large conglomerates) decide which shows to carry from a wide variety of networks and independent radio providers. As a result, radio networks such as WestwoodOne or Premiere Networks, despite their influence in broadcasting, are not as recognized among the general public as television networks like CBS or ABC (many of these distributors ally themselves with television networks; WestwoodOne, for instance, is allied with NBC, while Premiere is allied with Fox). Some examples of widely syndicated commercial broadcasting music programs include weekly countdowns like Rick Dees' *Weekly Top 40*, the *American Top 40*, *American Country Countdown* with Kix Brooks, *Canada's*

Top 20 Countdown, the *Canadian Hit 30 Countdown* and the nightly program, *Delilah*, heard on many U.S. stations.

Syndication is particularly popular in talk radio. While syndicated music shows (with the exception of some evening and overnight shows such as *Delilah* mentioned above) tend to air once a week and are mostly recorded, most popular talk radio programs are syndicated daily and are broadcast live. Also, with relatively few 24-hour live talk radio networks (though this, in recent times, has been changing), most radio stations are free to assemble their own lineup of talk show hosts as they so choose. Examples of syndicated talk programs are Premiere Networks' *The Bob & Tom Show*, Dial Global's *The Jim Bohannon Show*, and the self-syndicated *The Dave Ramsey Show* (more recently, talk networks such as Talk Radio Network have been marketing and packaging all-day lineups, marking a departure from the syndication model; as such, popular shows such as Cumulus Media Networks' *The Savage Nation* and Premiere's *The Rush Limbaugh Show* now air as part of a broader network lineup in many markets, particularly on Premiere owned-and-operated stations, though they continue to be syndicated to non-network stations as well). Talk syndication tends to be more prevalent because voice tracking, a practice used by many music stations to have disc jockeys host multiple supposedly local shows at once, is not feasible with live talk radio.

National Public Radio, Public Radio International, and American Public Media all sell programming to local member stations in the U.S., most of which are subsidized through the Corporation for Public Broadcasting but operated by private nonprofit organizations, universities, state or local governments. This is in contrast to centralized public radio networks in other countries (such as Canada's CBC and the United Kingdom's BBC) that own and operate all of their stations as arms of the national government and run them as a strict network (from 1948 to 2013, the United States had a strict anti-propaganda law, the Smith–Mundt Act, that prohibited broadcasting government-owned networks such as Voice of America to American audiences. The law was mostly repealed in 2013, but distribution of VOA or other federally produced radio programming is still rare). Two independently produced, non-commercial syndicated programs, heard on hundreds of community radio and indie radio stations, are *Alternative Radio* and *Democracy Now!*. Some (in fact, most) radio programs are also offered on a barter system usually at no charge to the radio station. The system is used for live programming or preproduced programs and include a mixture of ad time sold by the program producer as well as time set aside for the radio station to sell.

History

Before radio networks matured in the United States, some early radio shows were reproduced on transcription disks and mailed to individual stations. An example of syndication using this method was RadiOzark Enterprises, Inc. based in Springfield, Missouri, co-owned with KWTO. The Assembly of God, with national headquarters in Springfield, sponsored a half-hour program on the station called *Sermons in Song*. RadiOzark began transcribing the show for other stations in the 1940s, and eventually 200 stations carried the program. The company later produced country music programs starring among others, Smiley Burnette, George Morgan, Bill Ring and Tennessee Ernie Ford (260 15-minute episodes of *The Tennessee Ernie Show* were distributed), and more than 1,200 U.S. and Canadian stations aired the programs. Many syndicated radio programs were distributed through the U.S. mail or another delivery service, although the medium changed as technology developed, going from transcription disks to phonograph records, tape recordings, cassette tapes and eventually CDs. Many smaller weekend programs still use this method to this day, though with the rise of the Internet, many stations have since opted to distribute programs via CD-quality MP3s through FTP downloads.

It was not until the advent of satellite communications in the 1980s that live syndication became popular (though it could be transmitted through network lines, it was not particularly common because of cost, network congestion and quality issues). Since then, most syndicated radio programs are distributed using satellite subcarrier audio technology. Shortly after satellite networks such as RKO, Transtar and SMN began, the Fairness Doctrine was repealed, which is credited with helping Rush Limbaugh become the first national talk radio superstar. At the same time, the FCC began issuing more FM radio licenses to suburban and rural areas in the late 1980s, which allowed more room for music stations on the FM dial; radio formats such as country music that were traditionally AM fixtures even after most pop and rock music moved to FM were now moving to FM as well, leaving much more room for talk formats on the AM dial. As the 1990s went on, Dr. Laura and Howard Stern began their national shows, rising to become national icons. The Telecommunications Act of 1996, which led to significant concentration of media ownership, facilitated the rapid deployment of both existing and new syndicated programs in the late 1990s, putting syndication on par with, and eventually surpassing, the network radio format.

After the September 11, 2001 terrorist attacks, syndicated talk radio saw a notably rapid rise in popularity, as networks rushed new national shows into syndication to meet the demand for discussion of national issues. Many of these, such as Laura Ingraham, Bill O'Reilly, Sean Hannity and Glenn Beck, were mostly supportive of the actions of the Republican-led government; a few others, such as Alex Jones, were openly critical of the government's actions and motives. After the Democrats took control in the late 2000s, the gap between the two styles narrowed due to the mutual opposition of both camps to the government's actions, which allowed Jones greater clearance on stations.

In contrast to conservative talk radio, which has predominantly been driven by syndication, progressive talk radio has almost always been a network-driven model. The incompatibility of conservative and progressive ideologies and the lack of syndicated progressive hosts required solutions that could produce all-day programming to individual stations. It was not until Air America Radio launched in 2004 that progressive talk would become viable; though it failed several years later, Dial Global now carries a network slate that is carried on most progressive talk stations. Sports radio is likewise mostly a network phenomenon, partially because the irregular nature of sports pre-emptions makes having a full-time network to be able to cut into and join in progress at any time highly convenient. Syndicated radio is not as popular in other parts of the world. Canada has a few independently syndicated shows, but the bulk of syndicated content there comes from the United States, and the sum total of syndicated programming is far less than most American stations, as Canadian stations rely more heavily on local content. Most other countries still follow the network radio model.

International Syndication

Syndication also applies to international markets. Same language countries often syndicate programs to each other – such as programs from the United Kingdom being syndicated to Australia and vice versa. Another example would be programs from the United Kingdom, Mexico, Brazil, and Argentina being syndicated to local television stations in the United States, and programs from the United States being syndicated elsewhere in the world. One of the best-known internationally syndicated television series has been *The Muppet Show*, which was produced by Grade's English ITV franchise company ATV at Elstree Studios in Hertfordshire, and was shown around the world, including the United States, where it aired in syndication (including the owned-and-operated stations of CBS), and Canada, where CBC Television aired the show. The 1970s was a time when many British comedies, including *The Benny Hill Show* and *Monty Python's Flying Circus* were syndicated to the United States and worldwide. Many soaps and long-running series are also successfully syndicated around the globe.

The hit television show *CSI* earned $1.6 million per episode in its first cycle in cable syndication. There were many different versions of the show making it an international success. It was already popular in the U.S., so becoming a success internationally as well as within the U.S. made syndication sensible. Whether a series is produced in the U.S. or not is based on the economic value and potential viability of its sales internationally with the possibility of syndication.

Economic factors that influence production outside the U.S. play a major role in deciding if a television show will be syndicated, internally and internationally. International syndication has sustained a growing of prosperity and monetary value amongst the distributors who sell to them. Due to a rise in competition, syndicators have upheld high standards for different countries to buy the rights to distribute shows. During the 1990s poor ratings were popular amongst syndicated shows, but distributors still made it possible for international competition to happen and buy U.S. shows. Colombian, Brazilian, Mexican and Venezuelan telenovelas are programmed throughout the Portuguese and Spanish-speaking world, and in many parts of India, China and Europe, while Turkish television drama is broadcast in the Balkans, some other European countries, Western and Central Asia and North Africa.

U.S.-style Syndication Internationally

Because of the structural differences discussed above, there are presently very few areas where a true U.S.-style syndication model operates, whereby programs are sold on a per-area basis (within a single country) to local or regional stations with differing (or no) network affiliations. Canada was historically one of the few exceptions. Until the mid-1990s, television stations in Canada, like those in the U.S., were typically run as separate local operations, with a small number of moderately sized ownership groups such as Baton, CanWest, WIC, and CHUM. Those stations that were affiliated with a national network, i.e. CBC or CTV, did not always receive a full schedule of programming from that network.

At this time, it was not uncommon for U.S. syndicators to treat Canada as an extension of their domestic syndication operations, for both their first-run and off-network offerings. This is still the case for American radio programs; Canadian radio networks are not assembled as rigidly into networks (except for the CBC's radio division). However, an alternate form of first-run syndication was performed by some domestic broadcasters: as the Canadian rights to U.S. primetime series were often acquired by individual station groups (as opposed to full-fledged national networks), they would in turn resell local rights for those programs to stations in areas where they did not operate.

Since the late 1990s, as most stations have been consolidated into national networks consisting almost entirely of owned-and-operated stations and with full-day network schedules, both types of syndication have largely disappeared from the Canadian broadcast landscape. Programs that are sold in syndication in the U.S. are now generally sold to Canadian media groups to air across all their properties, with per-market sales now being very rare (the minor exception being the few remaining independent stations that exist in Canada, such as CHCH-DT in Hamilton, Ontario). *The Oprah Winfrey Show* appears to have been the last significant holdout to this model (prior to its 2011 conclusion), having aired primarily on CTV stations, but in some markets airing instead on a Global station, and even some CBC affiliates.

Regional Syndication

There are three key reasons why a radio station will decide to pick up a syndicated show – the program is unique and difficult to replicate content, has a decent ratings track record, and whether or not it has a celebrity host. New developing radio programs are generally able to claim one of these attributes, but not all three. Regional syndication attempts to replace these benchmark attributes with other benefits that are generally recognized by the industry as also being important. Given the financial downturn within the industry, the need for quality cost effective locally relevant programming is greater than ever before. Programs that offer regionally specific content while providing the economic benefits of syndication can be especially appealing to potential affiliates. Regional syndication can also be more attractive to area advertisers who share a common regional trading area versus assembling a radio network of stations that hopscotch across the United States.

Broadcast Programming

Broadcast programming is the practice of organizing and or ordering of broadcast media programs (Internet, television, radio, etc.) in a daily, weekly, monthly, quarterly or season-long schedule.

Modern broadcasters use broadcast automation to regularly change the scheduling of their programs to build an audience for a new show, retain that audience, or compete with other broadcasters' programs. In the United Kingdom, this is known as TV listings.

Television scheduling strategies are employed to give programs the best possible chance of attracting and retaining an audience. They are used to deliver programs to audiences when they are most likely to want to watch them and deliver audiences to advertisers in the composition that makes their advertising most likely to be effective. Digitally based broadcast programming mechanisms are known as electronic program guides (EPG).

At a micro level, scheduling is the minute planning of the transmission; what to broadcast and when, ensuring an adequate or maximum utilization of airtime.

Programming History

With the beginning of scheduled television in 1936, television programming was initially only concerned with filling a few hours each evening – the hours now known as prime time. Over time, though, television began to be seen during the day time and late at night, as well on the weekends. As air time increased so did the demand for new material. With the exception of sports television, variety programs became much more important in prime time.

Scheduling Strategies

Block Programming

Block programming occurs when the television network schedules similar programs back-to-back. The concept is to provide similar programming to retain viewership.

Bridging

Bridging is being used when a station tries to prevent the audience from changing channels during a junction point - the main evening breaks where all channels stop programs and shift gear. This is achieved in a number of ways including: having a program already underway and something compelling happening at a junction point, running a program late so that people 'hang around' and miss the start of other programs, or television advertising the next program during the credits of the previous.

Crossprogramming

Crossprogramming involves the interconnection of two shows. This is achieved by extending a storyline over two episodes of two different programs.

Counterprogramming

Counterprogramming is the practice of offering television programs to attract an audience from another television station airing a major event. It is also referred when programmers offer something different from the rival's program as an alternative, to increase the audience size. Is used when a time period is filled with a program whose appeal is different from the opponent program because it is a different genre or appeals to a different demographic.

Dayparting

Dayparting is the practice of dividing the day into several parts, during each of which a different type of radio programming or television programming appropriate for that time is aired. Daytime television programs are most often geared toward a particular demographic, and what the target audience typically engages in at that time.

- Sign-on
- Early morning news
- Early morning
- Late morning
- Daytime television

- Early fringe
- Lunchtime news
- Early afternoon
- Late afternoon
- Early evening
- Evening news
- Prime time
- Late-night news
- Late night television
- Graveyard slot
- Sign-off (closedown)
- Late fringe
- Post late-fringe

Hammocking

Hammocking is a technique used by broadcasters whereby an unpopular program is scheduled between two popular programs in the hope that viewers will watch it. Public television use this as a way of promoting serious but valuable content.

Hotswitching

In hotswitching, the programmers eliminate any sort of commercial break when one program ends and another begins; this immediately hooks the audience into watching the next program without a chance to change the television channel between programs.

Spoiling

Spoiling tactics are used to grab audience share, when broadcasters have similar products going head to head. In such cases broadcasters may jostle in getting a slightly earlier airing date or time, in the hope that once viewers have become committed to a program they will not switch channels.

Stacking

Stacking is a technique used to develop audience flow by grouping together programs with similar appeals to "Sweep" the viewer along from one program to the next.

Stripping

Stripping is running a syndicated television series every day of the week. It is commonly restricted to describing the airing of shows which were weekly in their first run; *The West Wing* could be stripped, but not *Jeopardy!*, as the latter is already a daily show. Shows that are syndicated in this way generally have to have run for several seasons (the rule of thumb is usually 100 episodes) in order to have enough episodes to run without significant repeats.

Tentpoling

In tent pole programming, the programmers bank on a well-known series having so much audience appeal that they can place two unknown series on either side, and it is the strength of the central program that will draw viewers to the two other shows.

Theming

Another strategem is having special theme days, such as for a holiday, or theme weeks such as Discovery Channel's *Shark Week*.

Time Slot

A show's time slot or place in the schedule could be crucial to its success or failure. It may affect casting; for example, ABC replaced Robert Lansing's character on *Twelve O'Clock High* because the show moved from 10 pm to 7:30 pm. Promising new series would often be premiered behind hits to help build an audience. Conversely, failing shows could be consigned to unfavorable times, such as the Friday night death slot.

Scheduling Strategies

A typical scheduling strategy used in Argentinian radio and television is called "pase" (Spanish for a "pass" as in a player passing the ball to another player of the same team). A few minutes before the end of a live broadcast show, followed by another live broadcast show, people from both programmes will share some air time together. This may be used for people from the starting programme to anticipate its contents of the day, or to participate in an ongoing discussion in the previous show, or simply for an entirely independent debate or chat that will not be furthered after the "pase". On the radio, where newscasts are usually broadcast every thirty minutes, often in coincidence with the end of a show, the "pase" may take some minutes before the news, and sometimes some minutes afterwards, too.

Alternatively, if there is no "pase", light jokes or comments can be made in a show involving people of the following show, so that some viewers or listeners might be interested in hearing what the reply will be.

Also, when a station has a new show starting, or if it needs to boost its ratings, part of its cast will be featured in other programmes in the same station, inserted in the dynamics of the programme they are in. For example, they will participate in game shows, be interviewed by the journalists of the station, make cameos in a series, substitute for the usual staff of other shows in their habitual functions, etc. Additionally, hosts of live programmes may mention repeatedly the new show and its time slot, trying to encourage their own viewers to watch it.

References

- Vogel, Harold (2011). "Television-programming accounting". Entertainment Industry Economics: A Guide for Financial Analysis (Eighth ed.). Cambridge University Press. p. 213. ISBN 978-1-107-00309-5.
- Meehan, Eileen R. (2005). Why TV is not our fault: television programming, viewers, and who's really in control. Rowman & Littlefield. ISBN 0-7425-2486-8.
- Brown, Maggie (September 23, 2012). "BBC pilots Tuesday night slot as it takes on ITV in the battle of the costume dramas". The Guardian. Retrieved December 5, 2014.
- Linke, Benjamin (2016), Public Financing of Public Service Broadcasting and its Qualification as State Aid, Peter Lang, ISBN 978-3-631-66568-8.
- Price, Monroe Edwin; Raboy, Marc (2003), Public service broadcasting in transition: a documentary reader (PDF), Kluwer Law International, ISBN 90-411-2212-5.
- Nebeker, Frederik (2009). Dawn of the Electronic Age: Electrical Technologies in the Shaping of the Modern World, 1914 to 1945. John Wiley & Sons. pp. 14–15. ISBN 0470409746.
- Banerjee, Indrajit; Seneviratne, Kalinga, eds. (2006), Public service broadcasting in the age of globalization, Asian Media Information and Communication Centre, ISBN 981-4136-01-8
- Stilson, Janet (January 26, 2014). "Binge Viewing, Cord Cutting and Streaming Platforms Are All the Rage at NATPE 'The syndicated model is broken'". AdWeek. Mediabistro Holdings. Retrieved June 25, 2015.
- Boardman, Madeline (27 April 2015). "Daytime Emmys 2015 Complete Winners List: Soaps, Talk Shows Win Big". Us Weekly. Retrieved 12 August 2015.
- Bibel, Sara (January 8, 2015). "'Celebrity Name Game' Renewed for Season 2 by Fremantle & Debmar-Mercury". TV By the Numbers (Press release). Zap2it. Retrieved May 24, 2015.
- Uribe, R., Buzeta, C. and Hurtado, D. (2011). "Looking for the audiences: The effect of using partial counterprogramming and a friendlier style of news presentation". INNOVAR 21 (42): 151–159. Retrieved 29 April 2014.
- Plunkett, John (April 3, 2013). "The Voice v Britain's Got Talent: scheduling wars recommence". The Guardian. Retrieved December 5, 2014.

5

An Integrated Study of Artmedia

All the materials and tools that are used by a composer, artist and designer to create an art are known as artmedia. Some of the significant topics studied in relation to artmedia are new media art and interactive media. The topics elaborated in this chapter will help in gaining a better perspective about the artmedia.

Artmedia, *Seminar and Laboratory of the Aesthetics of Media and Communication*, was one of the first scientific projects concerning the relationship between art, technology, philosophy and aesthetics. It was founded in 1985 at the University of Salerno. For over two decades, until 2009, dozens of projects, studies, exhibitions and conferences on new technologies made Artmedia a reference point for many internationally renowned scholars and artists, and contributed to the growing cultural interest in the aesthetics of media, the aesthetics of networks, and their ethical and anthropological implications.

Beginnings and International Events

Since the late 1970s, a permanent *Seminar of the Aesthetics of Media and Communication* has been directed by its founder Mario Costa at the University of Salerno. The basic principles of the aesthetics of technological communication were identified and conceptualized in 1983. A conference on "Technological Imaginary", held in 1984 at the Museo del Sannio in Benevento, discussed the issue of the new relationship between art and technology and the consequent need to re-evaluate aesthetics, warning that "all our future existence will be played at the crossroads between technology and imaginary".

The comprehensive relationship between art and technoscience, technology, and philosophy has also been the theoretical subject of the ten international "Artmedia" conferences which were held in Salerno and Paris between 1985 and 2008. Particularly relevant were conferences held in Paris between 2002 and 2008, which took place at the Ecole Normale Supérieure, the Bibliotheque Nationale de France (BNF) and the Institut National d'Histoire de l 'Art (INHA), with the partnership of the Société Française d'Esthétique, the Université du Québec à Montréal, the University of Toronto, the Universidade de São Paulo, the Université de Paris 1 Sorbonne, and the U.S. magazine Leonardo.

Continuous Debate Between Artists and Theorists

Artmedia wanted to gather theorists and artists from all over the world and encourage both joint and complementary work, beginning with the need to give attention to theoretical and artistic practices and developing both together. These also contributed towards spreading the spirit of the project, both in a number of festivals and shows, and through their own artworks and research.

Derrick de Kerckhove, René Berger and Mario Costa, Artmedia IV (1992)

Maurizio Bolognini, Richard Kriesche, Mario Costa and Eduardo Kac, Artmedia VII (1999)

Theorists who worked with Artmedia and participated in its activities included Bernard Stiegler, René Berger, Abraham Moles, Derrick De Kerckhove, Pierre Levy, Gillo Dorfles, Paul Virilio, Frank Popper, Roger Malina, Daniel Charles, José Jiménez, Anne Cauquelin, Edgar Morin, Thierry de Duve, Catherine Millet, Filiberto Menna, Andreas Broeckmann, Rudolf zur Lippe, Edmond Couchot, Dominique Chateau, Yannick Geffroy, Philippe Queau, Arlindo Machado, Tetsuo Kogawa, and Bernard Teyssedre.

Artists included Fred Forest, Roy Ascott, Takahiko Iimura, Maurizio Bolognini, Tom Klinkowstein, Tom Sherman, Eduardo Kac, Enzo Minarelli, James Dashow, Peter D'Agostino, Mit Mitropoulos, Shawn Brixey, Bruno Di Bello, Antoni Muntadas, Orlan, Kit Galloway, David Rokeby, Miguel Chevalier, Norman White, Richard Kriesche, Olivier Auber, Caterina Davinio and Casey Reas.

The questions raised in various projects promoted by Artmedia, in a continuous dialogue between artists and theorists, led to discussions on topics including *Aesthetics of Communication and the anthropology of the future* (1985), *Global aesthetic communication* (1986), *Electronic performativity and the art system* (1990), *Neo-technological arts between aesthetics and communication* (1992), *Aesthetic research and technology* (1995), *Developments in aesthetics: change or mutation?* (1999), *From the Aesthetics of Communication to Net art* (2002), and *Ethics, aesthetics and techno-communication. The future of meaning* (2008).

All Artmedia symposiums have been followed by many publications. For the two held in Paris, a complete video recording is also available, and can be viewed at the Institut National de l'Audiovisuel.

An assessment of 25 years of Artmedia activity was made into a seminar on *The aesthetic object of the future*, held at the University of Salerno in 2009. The Artmedia project produced a large number of publications and documents that are being catalogued, with a view to their proper placement and use.

Key Areas of Investigation

- Electronic music
- Photochemical versus digital photography
- Aesthetics of radio
- Electroacoustic poetry
- Electronic writing and poetry
- Video art
- Generative art and software art
- Computer art
- Aesthetics of networks
- Net art
- Aesthetics of virtual
- Telerobotics and remote interactivity
- Aesthetics of (technological) flux versus aesthetics of form

Proceedings and Catalogs

Artmedia I (1985)

- Mario Costa (ed.) (1985), *Artmedia*, Salerno: Opera Universitaria di Salerno (Catalog, pp. 206).

Artmedia II (1986)

- Mario Costa (ed.) (1986), *Artmedia, II Convegno Internazionale di Estetica della comunicazione*, Salerno: Università di Salerno (Catalog, pp. 80).

Artmedia III (1990)

- Mario Costa (ed.) (1990), *Artmedia. Terzo Convegno Internazionale di Estetica dei Media e della Comunicazione. Catalogo*, Salerno: Università degli Studi di Salerno (Catalog, pp. 80).

- Mario Costa (ed.) (1990), *Artmedia. Terzo Convegno Internazionale di Estetica dei Media e della Comunicazione. Atti*, Salerno: Università degli Studi di Salerno (Proceedings, pp. 96).

Artmedia IV (1992)

- Mario Costa (ed.) (1992), *Nuovi media e sperimentazione d'artista*, Naples: Edizioni Scientifiche Italiane (including Artmedia IV Proceedings, pp. 1–156).

Artmedia V (1995)

- Università degli Studi di Salerno, Comune di Salerno (1995), *Quinto Convegno Internazionale di Estetica dei Media e della Comunicazione*, Salerno (maquette).

Artmedia VI (1997)

- Università degli Studi di Salerno, Fondazione Filiberto Menna (1997), *Artmedia VI*, Salerno (maquette).

Artmedia VII (1999)

- Mario Costa (ed.) (1999), *Artmedia VII, Settimo Convegno Internazionale di Estetica dei Media e della Comunicazione*, Salerno: Università degli Studi di Salerno (Catalog, pp. 60).

Artmedia VIII (2002)

- *Dossier Artmedia VIII*, in "Ligeia", Paris, 2002, pp. 21–245 (CNRF journal, including Artmedia VIII Proceedings).
- Mario Costa (ed.) (2004), *New Technologies: Roy Ascott, Maurizio Bolognini, Fred Forest, Richard Kriesche, Mit Mitropoulos*, Salerno: Artmedia, Museo del Sannio (Catalog, pp. 64).

Artmedia IX (2005)

- Mario Costa (ed.) (2005), *Phenomenology of New Tech Arts*, Salerno: Università di Salerno (Catalog, pp. 56).

Artmedia X (2008)

- Mario Costa, Fred Forest (eds) (2011), *Ethique, esthétique, communication technologique dans l'art contemporain ou le destin du sens*, Paris: Institut National Audiovisuel, Editions L'Harmattan (including Artmedia X Proceedings).

New Media Art

New media art is a genre that encompasses artworks created with new media technologies, including digital art, computer graphics, computer animation, virtual art, Internet art, interactive art, video games, computer robotics, 3D printing, cyborg art and art as biotechnology. The term differentiates itself by its resulting cultural objects and social events, which can be seen in opposition to those deriving from old visual arts (i.e. traditional painting, sculpture, etc.). This concern with medium is a key feature of much contemporary art and indeed many art schools and major universities now offer majors in "New Genres" or "New Media" and a growing number of graduate programs have emerged internationally. New Media Art often involves interaction between artist and observer or between observers and the artwork, which responds to them. Yet, as several theorists and curators have noted, such forms of interaction, social exchange, participation, and transformation do not distinguish new media art but rather serve as a common ground that has parallels in other strands of contemporary art practice. Such insights emphasize the forms of cultural practice that arise concurrently with emerging technological platforms, and question the focus on technological media, per se.

Newskool ASCII Screenshot with the words "Closed Society II"

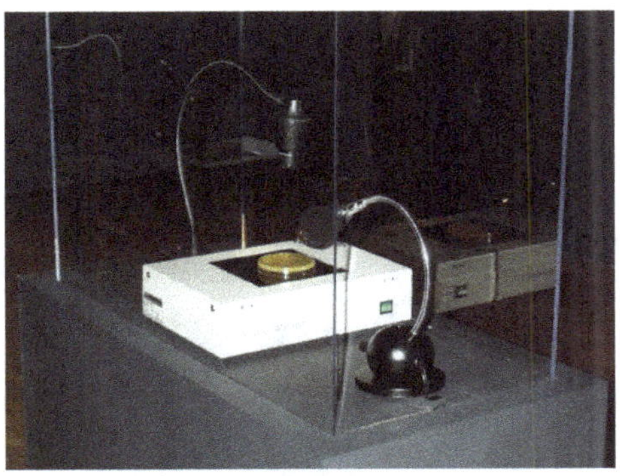
Eduardo Kac's installation "Genesis" Ars Electronica 1999

10.000 moving cities, Marc Lee, 2013, National Museum of Modern and Contemporary Art Seoul, Korea

New Media concerns are often derived from the telecommunications, mass media and digital electronic modes of delivering the artworks involve, with practices ranging from conceptual to virtual art, performance to installation.

History

The origins of new media art can be traced to the moving photographic inventions of the late 19th century such as the zoetrope (1834), the praxinoscope (1877) and Eadweard Muybridge's zoopraxiscope (1879). From the 1920s through the 1950s, various forms of kinetic and light art, from Thomas Wilfred's 'Lumia' (1919) and 'Clavilux' light organs to Jean Tinguely's self-destructing sculpture 'Homage to New York' (1960) can be seen as progenitors of new media art.

In 1958 Wolf Vostell becomes the first artist who incorporates a television set into one of his works. The *Black Room Cycle*. This installation is part of the collection of the Berlinische Galerie.

During the 1960s the development of then new technologies of video produced the new media art experiments of Nam June Paik, and Wolf Vostell with the installation *6 TV Dé-coll/age* in 1963 at the Smolin Gallery in New York. A. Michael Noll, and multimedia performances of E.A.T., Fluxus and Happening. In 1983, Roy Ascott introduced the concept of "distributed authorship" in his worldwide telematic project La Plissure du Texte for Frank Popper's "Electra" at the Musée d'Art Moderne de la Ville de Paris . The development of computer graphics at the end of the 1980s and real time technologies then in the 1990s combined with the spreading of the Web and the Internet favored the emergence of new and various forms of interactivity art by Lynn Hershman Leeson, David Rokeby, Ken Rinaldo, Perry Hoberman; telematic art by Roy Ascott; Internet art by Vuk Ćosić, Jodi; virtual and immersive art by Jeffrey Shaw, Maurice Benayoun and large scale urban installation by Rafael Lozano-Hemmer.

World Skin (1997), Maurice Benayoun's Virtual Reality Interactive Installation

Simultaneously advances in biotechnology have also allowed artists like Eduardo Kac to begin exploring DNA and genetics as a new art medium.

New Media Art influences on new media art have been the theories developed around hypertext, databases, and networks. Important thinkers in this regard have been Vannevar Bush and Theodor Nelson, whereas comparable ideas can be found in the literary works of Jorge Luis Borges, Italo Calvino, and Julio Cortázar. These elements have been especially revolutionary for the field of narrative and anti-narrative studies, leading explorations into areas such as non-linear and interactive narratives.

Themes

In the book *New Media Art,* Mark Tribe and Reena Jana named several themes that contemporary new media art addresses, including computer art, collaboration, identity, appropriation, open sourcing, telepresence, surveillance, corporate parody, as well as intervention and hacktivism. In the book *Postdigitale*, Maurizio Bolognini suggested that new media artists have one common denominator, which is a self-referential relationship with the new technologies, the result of finding oneself inside an epoch-making transformation determined by technological development. Nevertheless, new media art does not appear as a set of homogeneous practices, but as a complex field converging around three main elements: 1) the art system, 2) scientific and industrial research, and 3) political-cultural media activism. There are significant differences between scientist-artists, activist-artists and technological artists closer to the art system, who not only have different training and technocultures, but have different artistic production. This should be taken into account in examining the several themes addressed by new media art.

Non-linearity can be seen as an important topic to new media art by artists developing interactive, generative, collaborative, immersive artworks like Jeffrey Shaw or Maurice Benayoun who explored the term as an approach to looking at varying forms of digital projects where the content relays on the user's experience. This is a key concept since people acquired the notion that they were conditioned to view everything in a linear and clear-cut fashion. Now, art is stepping out of that form and allowing for people to build their own experiences with the piece. Non-linearity describes a project that escape from the conventional linear narrative coming from novels, theater plays and movies. Non-linear art usually requires audience participation or at least, the fact that the "visitor" is taken into consideration by the representation, altering the displayed content. The participatory aspect of new media art, which for some artists has become integral, emerged from Allan Kaprow's *Happenings* and became with Internet, a significant component of contemporary art. Art is not produced as a completed object submitted to the audience appreciation, it is a process in permanent mutation.

The inter-connectivity and interactivity of the internet, as well as the fight between corporate interests, governmental interests, and public interests that gave birth to the web today, fascinate and inspire a lot of current new media art.

Many new media art projects also work with themes like politics and social consciousness, allowing for social activism through the interactive nature of the media. New media art includes "explorations of code and user interface; interrogations of archives, databases, and networks; production via automated scraping, filtering, cloning, and recombinatory techniques; applications of user-generated content (UGC) layers; crowdsourcing ideas on social- media platforms; narrowcasting digital selves on "free" websites that claim copyright; and provocative performances that implicate audiences as participants."

One of the key themes in new media art is to create visual views of databases. Pioneers in this area include Lisa Strausfeld and Martin Wattenberg. Database aesthetics holds at least two attractions to new media artists: formally, as a new variation on non-linear narratives; and politically as a means to subvert what is fast becoming a form of control and authority.

The emergence of 3D printing has introduced a new bridge to new media art, joining the virtual and the physical worlds. The rise of this technology has allowed artists to blend the computational base of new media art with the traditional physical form of sculpture. A pioneer in this field was artist Jonty Hurwitz who created the first known anamorphosis sculpture using this technique.

Themes

G.H. Hovagimyan "A Soapopera for iMacs"

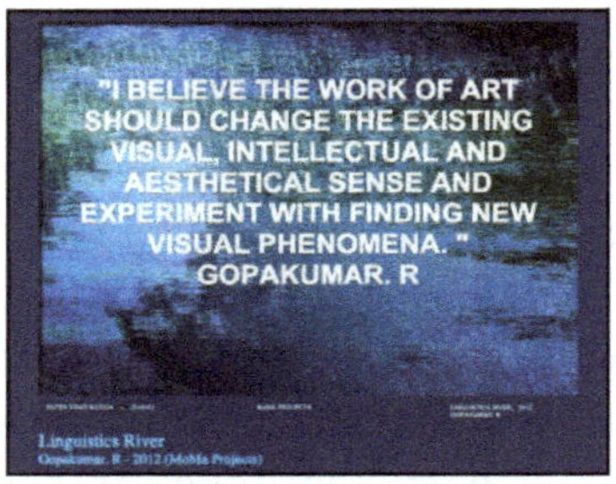

Gopakumar R. P. Linguistics River, Internet art

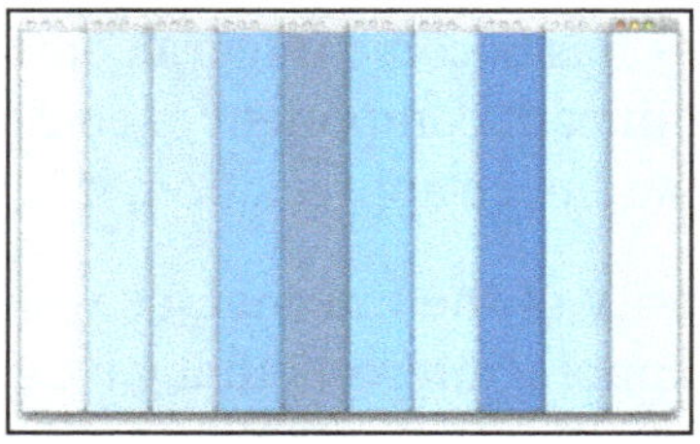

Michael Demers, 2009. *Color Field Paintings (Browser).*

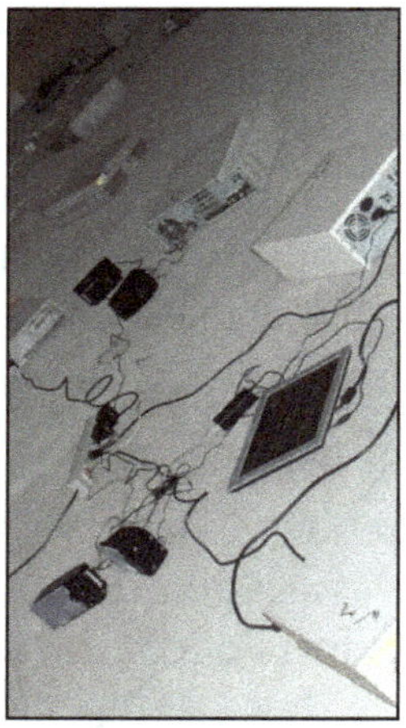

Maurizio Bolognini's programmed machines (*Computer sigillati* series, 1992): hundreds of computers have been producing endless flows of random images.

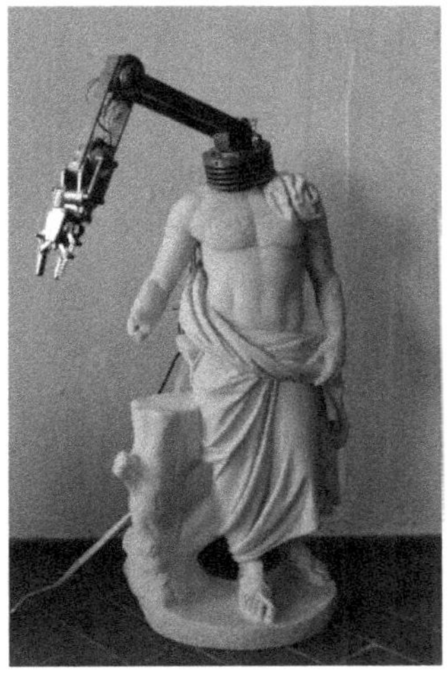

Genco Gulan "Hello, 2015. Sculpture with a Robotic Arm."

Presentation and Preservation

As the technologies used to deliver works of new media art such as film, tapes, web browsers, software and operating systems become obsolete, New Media art faces serious issues around the challenge to preserve artwork beyond the time of its contemporary production. Currently, research projects into New media art preservation are underway to improve the preservation and documentation of the fragile media arts heritage (DOCAM - Documentation and Conservation of the Media Arts Heritage).

Methods of preservation exist, including the translation of a work from an obsolete medium into a related new medium, the digital archiving of media, and the use of emulators to preserve work dependent on obsolete software or operating system environ-ments.

Education

In New Media programs, students are able to get acquainted with the newest forms of creation and communication. New Media students learn to identify what is or isn't "new" about certain technologies. Science and the market will always present new tools and platforms for artists and designers. Students learn how to sort through new emerging technological platforms and place them in a larger context of sensation, communication, production, and consumption.

When obtaining a bachelor's degree in New Media, students will primarily work through practice of building experiences that utilize new and old technologies and narrative. Through the construction of projects in various media, they acquire technical skills, practice vocabularies of critique and analysis, and gain familiarity with historical and contemporary precedents. New media studies lets students create and manipulate new technologies. The nature of New Media Art provides an opportunity for students to expand the art field in new directions, however they see fit.

In the United States, many Bachelor's and Master's level programs exist with concentrations on Media Art, New Media, Media Design, Digital Media and Interactive Arts.

Leading Art Theorists and Historians

Leading art theorists and historians in this field include Roy Ascott, Maurice Benayoun, Christine Buci-Glucksmann, Jack Burnham, Mario Costa, Edmond Couchot, Fred Forest, Oliver Grau, Margot Lovejoy, Dominique Moulon, Robert C. Morgan, Joseph Nechvatal, Christiane Paul, Catherine Perret, Frank Popper, and Edward A. Shanken.

Interactive Media

Interactive media normally refers to products and services on digital computer-based systems which respond to the user's actions by presenting content such as text, moving image, animation, video, audio, and video games.

Definition

Interactive media is a method of communication in which the output from the media comes from the input of the users. Interactive media works with the user's participation. The media still has the same purpose but the user's input adds interaction and brings interesting features to the system for better enjoyment.

Development

The analogue videodisc developed by NV Philips was the pioneering technology for interactive media. Additionally, there are several elements that encouraged the development of interactive media including the following:

- The laser disc technology was first invented in 1958. It enabled the user to access high-quality analogue images on the computer screen. This increased the ability of interactive video systems.
- The concept of the graphical user interface (GUI), which was developed in the 1970s, popularized by Apple Computer, Inc. was essentially about visual metaphors, intuitive feel and sharing information on the virtual desktop. Additional power was the only thing needed to move into multimedia.
- The sharp fall in hardware costs and the unprecedented rise in the computer speed and memory transformed the personal computer into an affordable machine capable of combining audio and color video in advanced ways.
- Another element is the release of Windows 3.0 in 1990 by Microsoft into the mainstream IBM clone world. It accelerated the acceptance of GUI as the standard mechanism for communicating with small computer systems.
- The development by NV Philips of optical digital technologies built around the compact disk (CD) in 1979 is also another leading element in the interactive media development as it raised the issue of developing interactive media.

All of the prior elements contributed in the development of the main hardware and software systems used in interactive media.

Terminology

Though the word *media* is plural, the term is often used as a singular noun.

Interactive media is related to the concepts interaction design, new media, interactivity, human computer interaction, cyberculture, digital culture, interactive design, and includes augmented reality.

An essential feature of interactivity is that it is mutual: user and machine each take an active role. Most interactive computing systems are for some human purpose and interact with humans in human contexts. Manovich complains that 'In relation to computer-based media, the concept of interactivity is a tautology. .... Therefore, to call computer media "interactive" is meaningless – it simply means stating the most basic fact about computers.'. Nevertheless, the te- rm is useful to denote an identifiable body of practices and technologies.

Interactive media are an instance of a computational method influenced by the sciences of cybernetics, autopoiesis and system theories, and challenging notions of reason and cognition, perception and memory, emotions and affection.

Any form of interface between the end user/audience and the medium may be considered interactive. Interactive media is not limited to electronic media or digital media. Board games, pop-up books, gamebooks, flip books and constellation wheels are all examples of printed interactive media. Books with a simple table of contents or index may be considered interactive due to the non-linear control mechanism in the medium, but are usually considered non-interactive since the majority of the user experience is non-interactive reading.

Advantages

Effects on Learning

Interactive media is helpful in the following four development dimensions in which young children learn: social and emotional, language development, cognitive and general knowledge, and approaches toward learning. Using computers and educational computer software in a learning environment helps children increase communication skills and their attitudes about learning. Children who use educational computer software are often found using more complex speech patterns and higher levels of verbal communication. A study found that basic interactive books that simply read a story aloud and highlighted words and phrases as they were spoken were beneficial for children with lower reading abilities. Children have different styles of learning, and interactive media helps children with visual, verbal, auditory, and tactile learning styles.

Intuitive Understanding

Interactive media makes technology more intuitive to use. Interactive products such as smartphones, iPad's/iPod's, interactive whiteboards and websites are all easy to use. The easy usage of these products encourages consumers to experiment with their products rather than reading instruction manuals.

Relationships

Interactive media promotes dialogic communication. This form of communication allows senders and receivers to build long term trust and cooperation. This plays a critical role in building relationships. Organizations also use interactive media to go further than basic marketing and develop more positive behavioral relationships.

Types

Distributed Interactive Media

The media which allows several geographically remote users to interact synchronously with the media application/system is known as Distributed Interactive Media. Some common examples of this type of Media include Online Gaming, Distributed Virtual Environment, Whiteboards which are used for interactive conferences and many more.

Examples

A couple of basic examples of interactive media are video games and websites. Websites, especially social networking websites provide the interactive use of text and graphics to its users, who interact with each other in various ways such as chatting, playing online games, sharing posts that may include their thoughts and/or pictures and so forth. Video games are also one of the common examples of Interactive Media as the players make use of the joystick/controller to interactively respond to the actions and changes taking place on the game screen generated by the game application, which in turn reacts to the response of the players through the joystick/controller.

Technologies for Implementation

Interactive media can be implemented in a wide variety of platforms and applications encompassing virtually all areas of technology. Some examples include mobile platforms such as touch screen smartphones and tablets, was well as other interactive mediums that are created exclusively to solve a unique problem or set of problems. Interactive media is not limited to a certain field of IT, it instead encompasses any technology that supplies for movie parts or feedback based on the users actions. This can include javascript and AJAX utilization in web pages, but can further be extended to any programming languages that share the same or similar functionality. One of the most recent innovations to supply for interactivity to solve a problem the plagues individuals on a daily bases is Delta Airlines "Photon Shower." This device was developed from Delta's collaboration with Professor Russell Foster of Cambridge University. The device is designed to reduce the effect of jet lag on customers that often take long flights across time zones. The systems interactivity is evident because of the way in which it solves this commonplace problem.. By observing what time zones a person has crossed and matching those to the basic known sleep cycles of the individual, the machine is able to predict when a persons body is expecting light, and when it is expecting darkness. It then bombards the individual with the appropriate light source variations for the time, as well as an instructional card to inform them of what times their body expects light and what times it expects darkness.Growth of interactive media continues to advance today, with the advent of more and more powerful machines the limit to what can be input and manipulated on a display in real time is become virtually non-existent.

References

- Soler-Adillon, Joan (2015-12-21). "The intangible material of interactive art: agency, behavior and emergence". Artnodes. 0 (16). doi:10.7238/a.v0i16.2744. ISSN 1695-5951.
- Dale Hudson and Patricia R. Zimmermann. (2015). Thinking Through Digital Media Transnational Environments and Locative Places. New York: Palgrave Macmillan. P. 1. ISBN 978-1137433626
- Maurizio Bolognini, "De l'interaction à la démocratie. Vers un art génératif post-digital" / "From interactivity to democracy. Towards a post-digital generative art", in Ethique, esthétique, communication technologique, Edition L'Harmattan. Paris, 2011, pp. 229-239.
- See Mario Costa, Fred Forest (eds) (2011), Ethique, esthétique, communication technologique dans l'art contemporain ou le destin du sens, Paris: Institut National Audiovisuel, Editions L'Harmattan, and Dossier Artmedia VIII, in "Ligeia", Paris, 2002.
- Information Processing Society of Japan. "LINKS-1 Computer Graphics System-Computer Museum". Retrieved 15 June 2015.
- Maurizio Bolognini, "From interactivity to democracy. Towards a post-digital generative art", Artmedia X Proceedings. Paris, 2010.
- Robinson, Stuart. "The Disadvantages and Advantages of Interactive Media." EHow. Demand Media, 10 May 2011. Web. 23 Nov. 2014.
- DeYeso, Jennifer. "The Effect of Interactive and Traditional Media on Relationship Building." Slideshare. LinkedIn Corporation, 25 Apr. 2012. Web. 23 Nov. 2014.
- Catricalà, Valentino (2015). Media Art. Toward a new Definition of Arts in the Age of Technology. Gli Ori. ISBN 978- 88-7336-564-8.
- Dix, Alan; Finlay, Janet; Abowd, Gregory D.; Beale, Russell (2004). Human-computer interaction. 3rd edn. Pearson Education. p. xvi. ISBN 9780130461094.
- Jon Peddie: The History of Visual Magic in Computers: How Beautiful Images are Made in CAD, 3D, VR and AR, Springer, 2013, p. 101, ISBN 978-1447149316

6

Impact of Digital Media

Digital and social media have a significant impact on various sectors such as business, education and health. This chapter has been carefully written to provide an easy understanding of the impact of digital media on these sectors as well as the impact of social media.

Impact of Digital Media on Business

It is important to know the effects of digital media. This influences business on a large scale. In fact, the impact of the same on the traditional market has been profound and pervasive. The world of digital marketing unleashes the doors and help the person with the right opportunity to feel and get connected with business at the most. When you can see the output of the business online you feel enticed and interested to work hard for the cause of business in and out. The digital sphere of business is vast. It helps you demonstrate your products and services on net.

Reaching to the Wide Audience

It is true to know that digital media influences business at the most. This is the most affordable method to reach to the wide range of audience. Advertising things online is less expensive than printing things to make people know the details. There are several buyers and other interested people who move online to know the details of the intended service and solutions. Running a single print or a newspaper can be comparatively costlier. Online you can reach the targeted demography though the intended online advertisement. Things are simple and you can make use of the arrangement for the enhancement in the sales graph.

Impact of Digital Marketing

As it is evident, that mode of digital media influences business. If you have the variety more it becomes easy to access the marketing outlets with the best of might. Digital marketing will help you with the right set of options and opportunities. There are options like email campaigns, social media, search engine optimization, content marketing, banner ads and the rest. These are all online functional specifications and this helps in making the process smooth and simple. This way you can indeed make things known to the better part of the audience.

Putting up with the Ads

The arrangement of digital media influences business. Online people have the best chance to see your ads. This way, people come to know more about your specialties. Swiping the finger and clicking the mouse helps in revealing things at the best. The latest affairs and things are on the list are perfectly portrayed online. You can rely on online gossips and news and get to know the latest offerings with the best of sincerity and dedication. Online you can talk about things you are selling. This will give people an idea what you are dealing in.

Advantage of Digital Form of Marketing

The whereabouts of the digital media influences business. For the same, it is important that you know about the benefits of the digital marketing. In fact, digital marketing can influence businesses of all shapes and sizes. This gives an access to smart marketing. Just like television and print advertising this is the personalized form of marketing that you can cherish. The prime advantage of the form of marketing is that you can reach the target audience in the measurable and the cost effective manner. Other advantages of digital marketing include increase of the brand loyalty and driving of the online sales.

Making use of the Marketing Website

There are several benefits of digital marketing. With the same you can get to know that digital media influences business. If you hold a website it will allow you to look for the new markets and the kind of global training mainly in case of small investments. You should plan the digital marketing campaign in the right order to reach the targeted audience, at the lowest cost. This you can do by making use of the traditional and the conventional form of marketing. The digital form of marketing is perfect and authentic. It helps you make people aware of your professional presence.

Best Result of Digital Marketing

There is much to know about the concept of digital media influences business. This comes with the trackable and the measurable result. It is apt that you measure the online marketing with the usage of the web analytics and also by making use of the online metric tools. This will help in establishing the effectiveness of the campaign. This way, you can collect the data of how the consumers are making the best use of your website in response to the advertisement. It is easy to set up the web analytics to show the amount of money you can earn by making use of the tactics.

Linking the Website with the Customers

One can easily understand that digital media influences business. In case the database of the customer is linked with the website, you can greet the customers once they enter the site to know the details of the offer. The more people will buy from you, the more you can refine the profile of the customers. This will help them market things with the best of intention.

Getting Involved with Social Media

You can easily get involved with the social media and manage things with the right method and intention. This is how you can look for the relevance of digital media influences business. Here, you have the provision of building the kind of customer loyalty, and you can even create the best reputation for the sort of easy engagement. Digital marketing can even help you create the engaging sort of campaigns by making use of various rich media contents. As part of the internet base the campaigns can get the social currency. This is passed from one user to the other, and the system has become viral.

Right Influence of Digital Marketing

The effects of digital media influences business. This you can understand from the improved conversion rates. In case, you are holding a website you customers are few clicks away from you. In the manner, they can complete the purchase process with the least hassle. In the manner of buying things you don't have to make a phone call or visit the shop. The transaction you can complete immediately and seamlessly. In the way, digital marketing can add up more to the amount of sales.

The Positive Impact of Digital Media on Business

Thoughts of your traditional marketing efforts may be swirling through your head. This is probably inevitable, especially if you've already formed a successful merger of traditional and digital marketing tactics. In this case, you already know what digital media can do for your business. Some of the primary effects digital media can have on a business include:

- Digital media can give a business boundless reach. There's a good reason digital media is known as "the great equalizer"; who's to know whether that vibrant website with the provocative pictures and compelling content emanates from a two-person operation or a 2,000-person operation? The customer won't know, and the customer could reside five blocks away or 5,000 miles away. Of course, not every small-business owner wants a global customer base. But with digital media, it's there for the taking. As Brandon Gaille puts it: "You can target TV viewers, for example, or radio program listeners or magazine readers. Direct mail can reach a specific zip code or neighborhood. Digital marketing, however, can reach an entire globe."
- Digital media can be a money-saver – at least if you believe that you have to spend a little money to save money. Compared with what you may have been spending on traditional marketing methods, even pay-for-click ads (otherwise known as paid search) are relatively affordable. Meanwhile, traffic from organic searches can stream your way for free, though you will have to make a "sweat equity" investment in content to see results. The same is true for email campaigns, search engine optimization (SEO) and social media. For businesses facing lean financial times – and what business doesn't? – an integrated digital media strategy can do more than save money; it can save a business that is fighting to survive.* Digital media can ingratiate a business with its customers. Owners of brick-and-mortar stores might argue that building customer relationships through superior service is a concept as old as time itself. They have a point. But there is no doubt that inbound marketing affords a small-business owner many ways to flaunt that service – namely, through blogs, case studies, ebooks, videos and webinars. Building relationships through these channels can instill customer loyalty and fuel word-of-mouth. The essence of marketing hasn't changed, but digital marketing has multiplied the channels exponentially.
- Digital media can deliver fast results and sales. It ought to. People want information fast. They'll rarely scroll beyond the second page of an organic search. They'll ditch a website that takes more than a few seconds to load. And more and more, they're searching while they're on the go, spawning a digital domain known as mobile marketing. In addition to appealing to consumers' need for speed, digital media can deliver fast sales returns. If you've grown accustomed to your marketing team likening a marketing tactic to a "seed" – as in planting a seed – digital media can help a business reap a quick and bountiful harvest.

- Digital marketing allows a business to respond to customers and make any adjustments quickly. It's an obvious offshoot to the inherent speediness of digital media; a small-business owner can nip a problem in the bud and respond in an equally speedy manner to questions, gripes, complaints, rants and lawsuit threats. Meanwhile, a complimentary anecdote or compelling customer success story can be used as the cornerstone of a short-term marketing campaign. From a devil's advocate point of view, digital media should all but eliminate the "I wish I knew" excuse from a business owner's repertoire. Consumers have demonstrated that they're more than happy to share their experiences through inbound marketing, email and social media in particular. And a business owner who adds regular online customer satisfaction surveys to the mix should remain "in the know." In this way, too, digital media holds the potential of doing more than insulating a business from ruin; it can save it from this fate, too.

The Negative Impact of Digital Media on Business

Naturally, digital media is far from a perfect vehicle. No means of mass communication is. Digital media scores some negatives among small-business owners because:

- Digital media can sweep up a business in "media fatigue." Consumers are bombarded with thousands of messages a day – a consequence that is largely their own doing. They could, after all, simply put down or shut off their smartphones. But this means they are also more discerning about what they do take the time to read as well as what they choose to ignore.* Digital media can be a time drain on a business. Social Media Today reports that more than 60 percent of marketers spend at least six hours a day on digital marketing. This is time you may not be able to allocate, forcing some tough choices. Even if you forego paid digital ads, the sweat equity investment can be unrelenting and considerable.

- Digital media can devolve into a damage-control operation. This is the most virulent complaint of small-business owners, who grow understandably perplexed by the scammers, spammers, trolls and "reviewers" whose sole purpose seems to be stirring up trouble. "Going viral" was usually considered a good thing for businesses five years ago. It can strike fear in the hearts of small-business owners today.

- Digital media can expose a business to copycats. Since digital marketing campaigns are so "out there," it also makes them easy to replicate and even copy – right down to the same offer with similar wording against a familiar background shot. Many professional writers have dismantled their online writing portfolios to thwart plagiarists. Small-business owners don't have this luxury and must remain vigilant about marketing mooches.

- This last negative can breed a peculiar feeling of vulnerability and loss of control in some small-business owners. Unlike a print ad that's undeniably yours, a radio ad that includes your voice or an ageless brochure that you've been mailing to customers for years, putting so much information "out there," online, to a global audience, may prompt you to wonder, "Who's really reading all this information and what are they going to do with it?"

Impact of Digital Media on Education

Individual Abilities in Processing Information

A shift is happening in schools towards online education and the change is still accelerating. This pressures schools to provide students with proper digital equipment, but it also provides media designers a challenge regarding how to design educational material in the best possible way. There are three relevant issues to learning: technological, cognitive and communication abilities. Technological abilities refer to issues related to different devices and platforms, cognitive abilities refer to individual preferences in processing information and communication abilities which will become more important as education is shifting away from traditional teaching methods towards more group work with the teacher acting as a coach.

Technological Abilities

Technological abilities are the starting point, as one must possess technological skills to be able to use a variety of different technologies and platforms. Research on building technological abilities for children at home has focused previously primarily on computers as a technological tool. Nowadays children have a variety of handheld devices (such as smart phones, handheld games), computers, tablets, television, interactive books, games consoles, DVD players, as well as cameras and MP3 players at home. There are many opportunities for children to get engaged with a number of technological tools according to individual interest and opportunity. Some parents actively teach their children to use different technological tools, but in many cases learning occurs as children follow the way their parents or siblings use different tools. Plowman et al. discovered that preschool children typically have acquired basic levels of competence in acquiring operational skills, extending knowledge of the world, developing dispositions to learn and understanding its cultural role by the time they start school. Children possess sufficient technological abilities when going to school, but the challenge for teachers is to keep up to date with technological progress and to utilize that technology to promote learning.

Cognitive/Learning Abilities

When technological abilities can be taken for granted the focus shifts to cognitive/ learning abilities as the design of various platforms plays a crucial role for individuals' understanding of the presented material. The shift in teaching from printed material to online education brings about new challenges, as students can browse online material in a different manner than if they were reading a book, and this poses challenges also to the design of the content. It has been argued that navigation through websites mimics the associative nature of human memory and information processing (structural isomorphism) and thereby suggesting Web superiority over printed material. Conflicting evidence does exist, as some research has shown that hypermedia increases cognitive load and produces disorientation, implying that the Web would be less effective for learning than would print. Researchers compared learning from either printed material or a website and found no differences in learning. Additional findings related to learning from a website also suggests that cognitive load does inhibit learning, as noted previously, but another finding was that high Web expertise facilitates it. In the case of cognitive overload one process or more will suffer at the expense of the other, and therefore it is essential to understand how individuals process and make meaning for incoming information.

Content of the educational online material is essential in preventing cognitive overload and in providing the content in a way that everyone is able to grasp the information. A lot of effort has been made to design educational material in the best possible way, but there is still little guidance from cognitive style or learning style researchers for the practitioner to do this. Clarifying style theory, including both cognitive styles and learning styles, and making better use of it in professional practice should be a common goal. Cognitive style research reflects the work of experimental psychologists investigating the area of individual differences in cognition and perception, whereas learning style research focuses on the process-based issues related to meeting individual differences in the classroom environment. Distinction between cognitive styles and learning styles is difficult, as the terms have been used interchangeably, according to many sources (e.g., Sternberg and Grigorenko, but more recent research has shown that they are separate dimensions.

The term 'cognitive style' was originally used by Allport, and it has been described as a person's typical or habitual mode of problem solving, thinking, perceiving and remembering. Overall, cognitive style refers to an individual's way of processing and organizing information; Messick identified nineteen cognitive styles altogether. The two main streams are the wholist-analytic dimension, broadly referring to whether individuals tend to process information in wholes or in parts, and the verbalizer-visualizer dimension, referring to individuals' preference to use either verbal or visual material in processing information. Verbalizer-imager cognitive style has been widely used in learning studies to discover whether verbalizers should be taught with textual material and visualizers with visuals to enhance learning, but the results have been contradictory. Recent studies by researchers attempted to clarify and revise the visualizer-verbalizer dimension, as they discovered the existence of two different types of visualizers, namely object visualizers (2D) and spatial visualizers (3D). Their revised cognitive style includes three dimensions dividing individuals as 2D visualizers, 3D visualizers or verbalizers.

The main differences in visualizers are that object (2D) visualizers use imagery to construct high-quality images of the shapes and objects, and they tend to encode images globally as a single perceptual unit, which they process holistically, whereas spatial (3D) visualizers use imagery to represent and transform spatial relations and tend to encode and process images analytically, part by part, using spatial relations to arrange and analyse the components. Spatial visualizers don't seem to keep a lot of pictorial details in their images in order to develop efficient spatial transformation abilities, while object visualizers tend to develop an ability to maintain a lot of pictorial details in their images, which impedes effective spatial transformations. Although these dimensions are relatively independent on structural and functional levels, in many real life tasks these three systems collaborate; there is also evidence of interferences and trade-offs between them. These also might be cases where verbal and spatial processing interferes, as, e.g., in physics or mathematics, verbal and spatial processing might serve as alternative strategies to approach the same issue. In order not to overload working memory one chooses the strategy in which one is more efficient. Altogether R have said that "in addition to being a useful instrument in providing vocational guidance, the OSIVQ [their cognitive style dimension test] could be a useful tool for educators in the development of efficiently targeted teaching methods and a choice of instructional educational materials."

Cognitive styles can be considered to be adaptive control mechanisms without individual awareness, whereas learning styles involve a conscious choice of alternatives (Learning styles on the other hand can be considered from an individual's perspective of "how I learn", or they can automatically be linked with various stages in the learning cycle. Online learning provides the possibility of making conscious choices when browsing through the material; one possibility is that individuals tend to make decisions based on what kind of content is easiest for them to understand. It has been shown that online courses held at the university had higher drop-out rates when visualizations were absent, leading to the conclusion that educational material needs to contain a lot of visualizations. This is true to some extent, but Hegarty and reserchers have shown that, for example, object visualizers have difficulty interpreting scientific graphs as abstract schematic representations and instead interpret them literally as pictures. This shows that there is a true need to design versatile content in order to provide individuals the possibility to select the content they feel most familiar with.

Communication Abilities

The third important aspect is communication abilities, as the needs for communication are increasing and altering in nature. Face-to-face communication changes as teachers are becoming more coaches and group work increases, causing the need for efficient face-to-face communication to increase. Children are already engaged in online communication with their friends utilizing various channels, e.g., Facebook or WhatsApp, which is mostly social communication. Motivational reasons to get engaged in social communication depend on an individual's basic needs, which in this case are related to autonomy and relatedness. The use of social media in education has been experimented with, but as it was compulsory for students, it did not work, even though they use it when they are not in school. The reason for this is that, when intrinsically motivated people are controlled by extrinsic factors, they lose interest.

Formal and Informal Education

Informal education consists of all learning activities happening outside formal education environments. It can be defined as "the sum of activities that comprise the time individuals are not in the formal classroom in the presence of a teacher". Informal education captures a great number of different environments under its definition.

Internet

For the purpose of this research, the Internet as a tool and platform is regarded as the key game changer, both for formal and informal education. Disruptive new technologies such as the Internet not only change the way we access information, but they also affect the way we think. The Internet has become mundane for twenty-first century society; however, it should be noted how such a technology has changed the way humans solve problems and impacts how they process information. Search engines especially, as trivial as they seem, particularly to digital natives, influence our thinking, as they provide personalized data. Further, search engines such as Google that are structured by various machine learning methods such as algorithms, represent an ultimate external memory which have in a short time revolutionized our problem solving process.

In addition to the Internet changing the way data is gathered and processed, it also impacts how it is shared. Traditional formal education was and is based on books, which are a type of technology that is dependent of the social context of use. At its core, learning is a social process which can be facilitated by the Internet (ibid). With the Internet, learning is transforming from mere information searching to new, more sophisticated forms of information processing. The students' technological skills, attitudes, beliefs and preferences that are largely constructed outside of formal education "may greatly influence how they learn and how they perceive learning supported by new technologies". By studying the technological abilities of individuals in formal and informal educational environments, researchers aim for predictions on how technologies should and will impact human learning (ibid). Currently, the main trend in scholarly research emphasizes the social character of learning. The Internet has great potential to influence learning via online communities and collaboration.

Online Education

Online education is the form of education provided by entities, educational institutions and companies through platforms based on online technologies. The last years have witnessed the fast-growing success of these platforms. Formal online education consists of courses delivered on learning platforms and provided by universities. In this context, the objective is to obtain certificates and recognition in terms of credits as the outcome of the course.

Computer-based learning has its roots in the early 1960's when a team of psychologists at Stanford University began the first experimentations of computer-based learning. Computer-based learning was developed during the 1970's and 1980's. After the advent of the Internet, the Open University in Britain and the University of British Columbia were the first institutions of higher education to implement online means of delivering learning activities and distance learning. This was one of the revolutions of the Internet: the advent of education for everyone. In its first days, online education provided by universities consisted of the creation of online curricula and websites related to the classical courses held at these universities. A university course on the Internet was taught for the first time in 1994 at the University of Pennsylvania. This was the beginning of a new educational paradigm, leading to the birth of the MOOCs, massive open online courses. The MOOCs deliver freely accessible multimedia documents useful for teaching purposes related to the material of the course. In addition to the conception of distance learning, the MOOCs integrate students into an online community. This community creates a virtual classroom for students, where discussions and peer confrontation take place.

According to a survey the social impact of online courses among deans and graduates of 1,055 colleges in United States has received good feedback. The majority (51 percent) of college presidents think online courses provide the same value. More than three-quarters of college deans (77 percent) report that their institutions now offer online courses. Fifty percent of college presidents predict that ten years from now most of their students will take classes online. Twenty-three percent of graduates report that they have taken a class online. Among all students who have taken a class online, 39 percent say the format's educational value is equal to that of a course taken in a classroom.

Top American universities, such as MIT, Princeton University and Stanford University, have launched their Mooc programs. Even if they offer free courses for a global audience, these do not lead to university credits. Along with top universities, many private entities have emerged, like Codecademy, Coursera, Curriki, edX, Khan Academy, Learnstreet, Udacity and Udemy. In order to understand their common features, we describe some of them.

Khan Academy is a non-profit organization whose website offers users several learning activities and multimedia educational content. The aim of Khan Academy is to deliver free education and create a global classroom. It offers thousands of courses (not held at any school or college) at a variety of levels (from primary school to college) in several languages. The website features videos of the courses (about 4,000 on YouTube) and exercise activities on the related material. Since Khan Academy is non-profit, the business model is based on private donations.

Coursera is a profit organization providing online enrolment in college courses. Coursera has forged partnerships with many top universities worldwide in order to feature current courses held in these universities. Only in a few cases do courses offered on Coursera's website lead to college credits. The courses are featured through videos, and (complete automatically graded) tests and assignments are submitted electronically. The website also serves as a social platform (very similar to a discussion forum), where students might ask and answer questions about the material. The business model of Coursera is based on fees coming from certificates and other agreements with the partner universities. Coursera has already reached one million registered students, though only a fraction of them are active.

Coursera had students registered in 196 countries. The highest proportions are in United States (38 percent), Brazil (6 percent), India (5 percent) and China (4 percent). Udacity is a for-profit company with the same structure and educational offers as Coursera, although Udacity is completely focused on computer science and related fields. Udacity has reached 739,000 students coming from 209 countries: from United States (42 percent), India (7 percent), Britain (5 percent) and Germany (4 percent).

LearnStreet offers a platform to learn to program software online. Learnstreet offers beginner courses on Javascript or Python, and students can practice coding in the browser, exploring video tutorials, using a library of Code Garage projects, where they can use existing code to build more involved programs. Currently the offerings are free and are funded by the venture capital firm Khosla Ventures. Learnstreet also plans to introduce placement services for connecting users with the many in-demand technology jobs in Silicon Valley.

From the analysis of all these platforms, we deduce that one of their main common features is the personalization of the study path. Indeed, the courses provided by these platforms are divided into different short modules, coherently organized into single short videos. Depending on their own backgrounds, skills and interests, students can choose which part is worth listening to or which part is worth watching again. They might ask and answer questions in the online community of the platform. This is a step toward the creation of a global classroom.

As we have already noticed, these platforms offer the backdrop for courses taken by thousands of students from all corners of the world. One issue faced by these education providers is to manage to grade thousands of tests and homework in order to certificate and grade students' performance. The trend is to use self- and peer-grading, which are very close to teacher-grading.

Microlearning

Microlearning deals with relatively small learning units and short-term-focused activities. These learning activities last from a few seconds to fifteen minutes or more. The learning activities typically provide subsequent meaning that can continue over multiple events and over a longer period of time. Some people use micro learning explicitly for learning, while many others do related activities just for fun or for other purposes. Examples of microlearning activities are:

- Reading blogs and following feeds.
- Participating in short message service (SMS) news quizzes.
- Noticing employer's screensaver campaign on a personal computer.
- Writing and tagging blog postings.
- Making social bookmarks.

Microlearning typically takes place in different digital media environments. A typical characteristic of these environments is that they 'push' information to the learners, reducing the need from learners to actively seek information.

But how will microlearning impact education? Microlearning has proven to play an important role in knowledge creation. People are learning by collecting, observing and combining data. Through microlearning, these activities happen all the time: following an RSS feed is about collecting and observing. Adding tags to blog posts is about combining information. Often these simple tasks are part of routines that happen from one day to another. On a yearly level, these activities can add up to hundreds of hours. Many media technologies allow this information to be documented and structured. Whenever the social aspect is there, which it almost always is, others can contribute to the microlearning process, making it an even richer learning experience. Research has found that when properly used, microlearning can increase students' engagement in the learning process.

Microlearning has proven to be highly successful in corporate and other professional training. For example, the support of anytime–anywhere access to learning resources is one relevant property of microlearning that definitely should be adopted in formal learning. This is a strong signal of how digital media is influencing current education.

It is worth noting also that microlearning comes with some negative impacts. The use of media services can lead to increased distraction. This means that pupils may use less time studying, because they use so much time on social media. Some studies confirm that the use of social media has a negative impact on students' grades. Similarily, it has been found that other areas of digital media such as games and television have a negative impact on students' grades.

Social Media

One form of microlearning, social media, is characterized as a user-generated platform in which consumers mainly discuss with one another. In 2013, 87 percent of sixteen-to-twenty-four-year-old Finnish consumers had been using social platforms during a period of three months. Such statistics suggest that the social media consumption of the generation of digital natives likely will increase.

Different social media platforms, such as weblogs, allow students to interact with and learn from one another. "Peers can be a powerful resource for children's learning, if activities are structured to promote productive interactions". Social media enables collaboration, enhances the connections to the real world and is therefore a great addition to learning tools (ibid). Social media platforms, such as Facebook and Twitter, have been increasingly scrutinized for their potential to impact both formal and informal education. In one such study, teenagers who had been using social media such as Bebo or MySpace predominantly were found to create new accounts and shift platforms to Facebook as they were preparing for their university studies "Their move to university was associated with Facebook emerging as the dominant SNS".

The study of researchers as well as peers such as have however found that with the current abilities and associations of students related to social media platforms, the potential seen in their usage is primarily seen as informal. As researchers describes:

First year undergraduate students generally thought the use of Facebook was most importantly for social purposes, secondarily for informal learning purposes (i.e., for student-to-student interactions about academic work-related matters) but definitely not for formal teaching purposes (i.e., between staff and student and involving formal assessment).

If teachers want to use social media for educational purposes, according to students, they should avoid some clear mistakes, such as considering YouTube videos to be pointless. Also, students "criticized failed attempts to use social media when teachers do not provide feedback or interact with them during the process" (ibid). Therefore, it is no surprise that Bruckman suggests that we should emphasize those technologies that promote creativity and students' thinking.

Questions such as 'Does the use of Facebook vary with disciplinary background, social capital, ethnicity and access to computing facilities?' and 'How might these digital inequalities then impact educational achievement and development of social networks in everyday lives?' are still left unanswered. Despite the fact that studies have shown only poor experimentation of social media for formal teaching purposes, the evidence from successful informal experiments suggests a potential for change.

Games

Any form of play or sport which is played according to some rules and evaluated by skills, strength and/or luck in a competitive environment, is termed as a game. The use of games in education holds great promise, as many aspects of educational experiences are closely related to a game. Students have a series of assignments for which they are rewarded with grades. Due to this fact, evidence proves that games have the potential to support education in a variety of contexts, from primary and secondary schools to universities and adult education.

The idea of learning through games is associated with the fact that students learn in different ways and that they learn many things outside the schools, often via access to digital media and online community or social media. This type of learning outside the school matters a great deal to a student's ability to learn in school; therefore, games could be one way to attract some students' attention inside the schools.

One tremendous benefit of games is that they promote cognitive skills. One such skill is called 'situated cognition' or 'learning by doing' (meaning teaching a concept in the environment where students can practically demonstrate that knowledge). Research has shown that the use of situated cognition for education purposes promotes learning, students learn faster, retain knowledge longer and transfer that knowledge to the real world. Another thing that games do very well is promote systems thinking, for example, Simcity.

Games like Simcity and similar others help to understand the system behind the interface and think of the game not as a set of discrete items but as a system. We learn how to interact with different items assuming that these are part of the whole not just single or separated items. This is the type of thinking expected from education, however is not seen in any of the educational experiences so far. Another way that games are very effective is that games promote collaboration (which also often called as 21st century learning skill).

World of Warcrafts is one of such multi-player online role playing games build on this concept where thousands of people work together. Sociologists and educators consider this game as an excellent example of collective intelligence and social negotiation of skills. People working together to solve a problem, that could not be solved individually. These types of skills set are highly required to solve real world problems, for example shortage of oil, energy crisis, hunger and poverty. A further well studied benefit of games is that they develop problem-solving skills. Dave Jonassen argues that the heart of a good instructional problem has two key characteristics. One it has a goal that requires to generate new knowledge in order to solve the problem. The other part is the value to the learner in solving that problem. However, schools include the first part sometimes but never consider the second part. Finally, another important aspect of games is that these introduce engagement.

Many people have misperceptions about what actually this engagement means in terms of games (e.g., it is about fun, entertainment and/or motivation). It is actually a cognitive effort required to solve a problem. More intuitively the engagement is a combination of problem solving and optimizing the challenge. In other words, it is an example of individualized instruction.

Although there are many benefits that games offer in educational experiences, there exist key challenges. One of the challenges is the feasibility and applicability of games in classrooms. Games are the disruptive technologies meaning that they expect us to operate in the same way they are designed to be operative. For instance, when we talk about situated cognition or authentic learning we have to recognize that we have 30 kids, say, in the classrooms and situated cognition would mean field trips or lab experiments after every hour of the day. Similarly when we discuss about systems thinking and collective intelligence, in our current educational model it is regarded as cheating. The educational experiences emphasize in doing own work and generally do not allow communicating and collaborating with others in the classrooms especially during the examination. A further challenge is the concern about competition, rewards and incentives. Usually the parents are worried with the notion that when the games do not progress, their children get addicted and the only thing children would like to do is to get better and better. Another challenge is the training of teachers. Learning through games modifies the role of teachers from instructor to coach. Teachers require a special set of skills and training in how to use games to teach students.

Impact of Digital Media on Health

At first glance, it may seem like a surprising notion that social media can affect your health. When we consider how much time people spend engaging on sites such as Facebook, Twitter, Instagram and others, however, it really makes sense.

Anything that takes up large amounts of your time, including work, watching TV, exercising or driving, has some impact on your health. The simple answer is that it can be both. Fortunately, there are ways to help reduce its harmful effects while maximizing the benefits.

Ways that Social Media Impacts your Health

There are a number of ways that social media can have an influence on your health:

- Addiction to social media: People who are addicted to social media may experience negative side effects such as eye strain, social withdrawal or lack of sleep.
- Stress: If you spend your time researching problems or arguing with people, you may experience stress, which can have a negative impact on your health.
- Emotional connections: Social media can help you connect with more people and stay in touch with those with whom you're already close. Connecting with people has proven health benefits.
- Information: You can find a large amount of health-related information on social media. This can be quite helpful. On the other hand, if you take random advice without doing proper research, it can also be harmful.

As these points illustrate, there's no simple answer to whether social media is good or bad for you. Because it's such a pervasive influence on modern life, it has many positive and negative effects.

Social Media Addiction

Social media addiction is a real phenomenon. As more people carry around smartphones and other devices wherever they go, it becomes harder to escape the internet. And people increasingly spend their online time on social media sites such as Facebook, Twitter and Instagram.

For people who are addicted to these sites, it can have a harmful effect on their lives and even their health. Any addiction is potentially harmful if it saps your energy away from other activities, such as work, physical activity and offline relationships. There are various ways that social media addiction harms your mental health.

Emotional Impact

People use social media for many things, such as socializing, finding and sharing information, shopping and simply as a diversion. Some of these activities are fairly neutral while others may cause strong emotions.

Positive connections with people are important for your mental and even physical health. There's plenty of evidence that social isolation is associated with a shorter life span, not to mention a diminished quality of life. While interacting with people on social media is not enough, and not a substitute for live interactions, it can be beneficial nonetheless.

Seniors and those who are disabled, who may have limited mobility, can use social media to connect in ways that they otherwise could not. Elderly people can talk to their grandkids. Someone stationed overseas in the military can talk to his or her spouse back home. Friends who live in different states can chat online. These are just a few of the ways that social media can improve people's lives.

On the other hand, social media can cause stress and other negative emotions. The issue of cyber-bullying is a good example of this. There are also people who are attached to trolling or arguing about everything from politics to sports. If interacting on social media causes stress, it's not good for your health.

Impact on Physical Health

Social media can directly impact physical health. This is usually associated with the way you use it. For example:

- Carpal Tunnel Syndrome: If you do too much keying, you may experience problems that affect your hands or wrists. There are also specific problems associated with keying on mobile phones, which can strain the tendons of your fingers. These problems aren't all caused by social media. It can just as easily be caused by having to type term papers for school or reports at work.
- Eye problems: You can get eyestrain from staring at screens for too long.
- Fatigue: This is another symptom of overusing social media. If you're staying up too late posting on Twitter of Facebook, you may be losing valuable sleep.
- Lack of exercise: Social media can cut into time you might otherwise be spending outdoors or exercising.
- Distraction: One of the most dangerous potential consequences of social media addiction is driving while being distracted. As recent stories have confirmed, you can even get hurt texting and walking.

The above are harmful effects that aren't caused by social media per se, but by overdoing it or being online or texting while you should be concentrating on something else. Some of these, of course, also apply to activities other than social media, such as texting on the phone, writing emails or browsing internet sites.

Accessing Health Information

There are innumerable places to get health information online. If you're active on Facebook, you probably have friends who post their favorite health advice. You may subscribe to the pages or tweets of celebrity doctors or people who have created diets. You could learn about a potential therapy, cure or drug that's truly helpful for you or someone you care about.

On the other hand, if you accept everything you see on social media uncritically, you could end up taking bad advice. You should never mistake a tweet or Facebook post as expert opinion. Even if it's given by a qualified expert, that person hasn't examined you.

Staying Healthy on Social Media

When used consciously and in moderation, social media can have a positive impact on your life and even your health:

- Use social media at certain scheduled times. Don't let it interfere with your work, studies or offline relationships.

- If you have difficulty getting off social media, try productivity apps that limit your access to certain sites. If you have a serious addiction problem, seek professional help.
- Use social media to research health issues, but always consult with your own doctor before taking any advice.
- Stay off social media and any communications platforms while driving or doing anything else that's potentially hazardous.
- Stay positive. Don't waste time arguing with people online.

Impact of Social Media

A social media is an online platform which people use to build social networks or social relations with other people who share similar personal or career interests, activities, backgrounds or real-life connections. The impact of social networks on young people is significant. It is becoming increasingly clear that social networks have become part of people's lives. Many adolescent people are using their laptops, tablet computers and smart phones to check Tweets and status updates from their friends and family. Due to the advancement in technology, people are pressured to accept different lifestyles. Social networking sites can assist young people to become more socially capable. Social media is a web-based form of data communication. Social media platforms allow users to have conversations, share information and create web content. Social media has different forms, together with blogs, micro-blogs, wikis, social networking sites, photo-sharing sites, instant messaging, video-sharing sites, podcasts, widgets, virtual worlds, and more. Billions of people around the world use social media to share information and make connections.

On an individual level, social media allow us to communicate with our friends and relatives, gain knowledge of new things, develop your interests, and be entertained. On a professional level, we can make use of social media to expand or broaden our knowledge in a particular field and build our professional network by connecting with other professionals in our industry. At the business level, social media allows us to have a conversation with our audience, gain customer feedback, and elevate your brand.

Social Media is an innovative idea with a very brilliant opportunity with additional scope for advancements. With the advancement of social media many organizations are making use of this medium to better their practices. With the use of social networking we can advertise or communicate in a more efficient way. Likewise people don't have to rely on the media or TV to get their daily dose of news it can all be obtained from a social networking site. People can track or get information from all over the world.

Popular Social Media Sites

Facebook

This is the largest social media network on the Internet, both in terms of total number of users and name recognition. Facebook came into existence on February 4, 2004, Facebook has within 12 years managed to collect more than 1.59 billion monthly active users and this automatically makes it one of the best mediums for connecting people from all over the world with your business. It is predictable that more than 1 million small and medium-sized businesses use the platform to advertise their business.

Twitter

We might be thinking that restrictive our posts to 140 characters is no way to advertise our business, but we will be shocked to know that this social media stage has more than 320 million active monthly users who can build use of the 140 character limit to pass on information. Businesses can use Twitter to interact with prospective clients, answer questions, release latest news and at the same time use the targeted ads with specific audiences. Twitter was founded on March 21, 2006, and has its headquarters in San Francisco, California.

Google+

Google+ is one of the popular social media sites in these days. Its SEO value alone makes it a must-use tool for any small business. Google+ was propelled on December 15, 2011, and has joined the major alliances enlisting 418 dynamic million clients as of December 2015.

YouTube

YouTube is the biggest and most well-known video-based online networking site — was established on February 14, 2005, by three previous PayPal workers. It was later purchased by Google in November 2006 for $1.65 billion. YouTube has more than 1 billion site guests for every month and is the second most well-known internet searcher behind Google.

Pinterest

Pinterest is commonly a beginner in the online networking field. This stage comprises of computerized announcement sheets where organizations can stick their substance. Pinterest reported September 2015 that it had obtained 100 million clients. Private ventures whose intended interest group is for the most part comprised of ladies should put resources into Pinterest as the greater parts of its guests are ladies.

Instagram

Instagram is a visual online networking stage. The site has more than 400 million dynamic clients and is possessed by Facebook. A significant number of its clients utilize it to post data about travel, form, sustenance, workmanship and comparable subjects. The stage is likewise recognized by its remarkable channels together with video and photograph altering highlights. Right around 95 percent of Instagram clients additionally utilize Facebook.

Tumblr

Tumblr is a standout amongst the most hard to utilize informal communication stages, but at the same time it's a standout amongst the most fascinating locales. The stage permits a few diverse post groups, including cite posts, talk posts, video and photograph posts and in addition sound posts, so you are never constrained in the kind of substance that you can share. Like Twitter, reblogging, which is more similar to retweeting, is speedy and simple. The long range informal communication site was established by David Karp in February 2007 and at present has more than 200 million sites.

Flickr

Flickr, articulated "Glint," is an online picture and video facilitating stage that was made by the then Vancouver construct Ludicorp in light of February 10, 2004, and later obtained by Yahoo in 2005. The stage is well known with clients who share and install photos. Flickr had more than 112 million clients and had its impression in more than 63 nations. Million of photographs are shared day by day on Flickr.

Reddit

This is social news and excitement organizing site where enlisted clients can submit substance, for example, coordinate connections and content posts. Clients are likewise ready to arrange and decide their position on the site's pages by voting entries up or down. Entries with the best votes show up in the best classification or primary page.

Snapchat

Snapchat is a image informing application training item that was made by Reggie Brown, Evan Spiegel and Bobby Murphy when they were understudies at Stanford University. The application was authoritatively discharged in September 2011, and inside a limited ability to focus time they have become hugely enrolling a normal of 100 million every day dynamic clients as of May 2015. More than 18 percent of every social medium client utilizes Snapchat.

WhatsApp

WhatsApp Messenger is a cross-platform instant messaging client for smartphones, PCs and tablets. This application needs Internet connection to send images, texts, documents, audio and video messages to other users that have the app installed on their devices. Launched in January 2010, WhatsApp Inc. was purchased by Facebook on February 19, 2004, for about $19.3 billion. Today, more than 1 billion persons make use of the administration to speak with their companions, friends and family and even clients.

BizSugar

BizSugar is a person to person communication stage and specialty asset for entrepreneurs, business visionaries and directors. The site was made in 2007 by DBH Communications, Inc., a supplier of honor winning business distributions, and later obtained by Small Business Trends LLC, in 2009. The stage enables clients to share recordings, articles, blog entries, podcast among other substance. It additionally enables clients to view and vote on entries by different individuals.

Delicious

This site was established by Peter Gadjokov and Joshua Schachter in 2003 and obtained in 2005 by Yahoo. Before the finish of 2008, Delicious guaranteed that it had bookmarked 180 million URLs and procured more than 5.3 million clients. In January this year, Delicious Media said that it had obtained the administration.

Impact of Social Media on Medical and Health

Social media provide Health Care Professionals with tools to share information and to promote health behaviors, to engage with the public, and to educate and interact with patients, students, and colleagues. HCPs can use social media to potentially improve health outcomes, develop a professional network, increase personal awareness of news and discoveries, motivate patients, and provide health information to the community.

Physicians most frequently join online websites where they can read news articles, listen to experts, research medical advancements, discuss with colleagues concerning patient issues, and network. They can explore and share ideas, discuss practice management challenges, make referrals, disseminate their research, market their practices, or engage in health advocacy. A large number of physicians also use social media to converse directly with patients to enhance clinical care. It is clear that social media is having a distinct consequence on healthcare systems, and that its impact is relevant both in the developed and developing worlds. Healthcare consultants provide improved healthcare to a larger number of citizens, while clients are able to use it to empower themselves, their families and their communities.

Positive Effects of Social Media on Health

- Sharing of Doctors prescriptions to friends, relatives and colleagues.
- Consulting Doctors online anywhere and anytime.
- Sharing Suggestions among friends, relatives and colleagues about various diseases and its symptoms.
- Access to information in developing regions.
- Support and mutual accountability on online health forums.
- Support for health-related causes.
- Helping health services to prioritize critical cases.
- Increased accountability to consumers.
- More data available to health researchers.

Negative Effects of Social Media on Health

- Incorrect self-diagnosis.
- Potential breach of privacy.

Impact of Social Media on Business

Social Media is the new buzz sector in promoting that incorporates business, associations and brands which make news, influence companions, to make relations and make groups. Business utilize web-based social networking to upgrade an association's execution in different ways, for example, to achieve business targets, expanding yearly offers of the association. Web-based social networking gives the advantage as a correspondence stage that encourages two way communications between an organization and their stock holders. Business can be advanced through different long range informal communication destinations. A considerable group of the organization advances their business by giving promotion on the online networking with a specific end goal to draw in greatest clients. Clients can associate and collaborate with business on a more individual level by utilizing online networking. Many organizations with the use of social media can make their strategy to promote their Business.

Positive Effect of Social Media on Business

- With the use of Social Media, It is better to understand the customer requirements.
- Social Media helps in promoting the Business all over the World.
- Social Media builds deals and client maintenance through standard connection and auspicious client benefit.
- Social Media provides rich customer experiences.
- With Social media monitoring you can gain key information about your competitors.
- With the help of social media, Sharing contents about the Business faster and easier.
- Social networking sites helps to make new customers by providing various facilities.
- It helps to increase market insight and expand out beyond your rivals with online networking.
- It also helps to increase awareness among customers for better understanding of products.

Negative Effect of Social Media on Business

- In business, Social Media isn't totally hazard free in light of the fact that a significant number of the fans and supporters are allowed to post their feeling on a specific association; the negative remark can lead the association to disappointment.
- Negative customer reviews are harmful.
- Highly time consuming.
- The web is crowded with more and more content.
- A mistake made on social media is hard to rectify.
- Many of the substantial association have succumbed to the programmers.
- The wrong online brand system can fate an organization, and put at a tremendous viral social drawback.

- Getting included with Social Media is extremely time consuming. As an association you ought to appoint a man to dependably support your pages and profile with noteworthy substance.
- Most organizations experience issues measuring the consequences of web-based social networking promoting.

Impact of Social Media on Education

Social networking technologies also allow one to share a thought with anotherIt helps a man toward one side of the world to interface and trade thoughts with a man at the other side. With the use of social media students can easily communicate or share information quickly with each other through various social networking sites like Facebook, Orkut, and Instagram etc.

Positive Effect of Social Media on Education

One can adopt its benefits to gain positive results in education:

- Socializing: An important part of growing up, is to socialize and make friends. Why this is important? It is because, it allows the children to exchange ideas and learn new things. This will invariably result in them becoming more confident in life.
- Sharing knowledge: It provides an easy and an effective way in which students can share knowledge. Students can simply access the information, study, transform (if needed) and share. Hence, the flow of knowledge becomes smooth.
- Updating oneself: They will have the capacity to know new things as and when it happens. This causes them refresh their own particular information base.
- Learning from various sources: The long range interpersonal communication advances are worked in such a way, to the point that understudies will have the capacity to pick the gathering, movement or the individual they would need to take after for every day refreshes. The ways of learning is plenty.
- Being Prepared: The social networking technologies are all about showcasing the trends that run around the world. Students can setup a plan of what might be expected out of them in the future by observing the changes that are being updated, shared, discussed or spoken about on the social networking sites.
- Sharing what they feel or think: Students frequently don't get the right stage to share their feelings. Through social networking technologies they are given an option to sound their thoughts. If students were permitted to share what they think and feel, it becomes simple for them to decide what is good and what is bad:
    - Social media gives a path to the understudies to adequately achieve each other with respect to class wanders, group assignments or for help on homework assignments.
    - Many of the understudies who don't take an intrigue reliably in class may feel that they can express their musings effectively via web-based networking media.

  - Teachers may post via web-based networking media about class exercises, school occasions, and homework assignments which will be exceptionally valuable to them.
  - It is seen that web-based social networking advertising has been developing in profession alternative. Web-based social networking advertising plans youthful specialists to end up noticeably fruitful advertisers.
  - The access of web-based social networking gives the chance to instructors to show great computerized citizenship and the utilization of Internet for profitability.

Negative Effect of Social Media on Education

- Reduced learning and research capabilities: Students are depending more on the information reachable easily on these social networking sites and the web. This reduces their learning and research capabilities.
- Reduction in real human contact: The additional time the students spend on these online networking destinations, the less time they will go through associating face to face with others. This decreases their relational abilities. They won't have the capacity to convey and mingle adequately face to face with others. The businesses are getting increasingly unsatisfied with the relational abilities of the new graduates because of this reason. The compelling relational abilities are critical to achievement in reality.
- Reduces command over language use age and creative writing skills: Students generally utilize slang words or abbreviated types of words on long range interpersonal communication locales. They begin depending on the PC language structure and spelling check highlights. This decreases their charge over the dialect and their experimental writing abilities.
- Time wastage: Students, while seeking and concentrate on the web, get pulled in to utilizing online networking locales and once in a while they overlook why they are using internet. Sometimes students are not able to deliver their work in the specified time frame as their time wastes.
- Low grades: Students get low evaluations in school because of absence of the coveted data and composing abilities.
- Loss of motivation in students: The student's motivational level lessens because of the utilization of these long range interpersonal communication locales. They depend on the virtual condition as opposed to increasing reasonable learning from this present reality.
- Effect on health: The unnecessary use of these sites has an effect on the mental as well as physical health. Students do not take their meals on time and take proper rest. The abuse of these destinations once a day has many adverse impacts on the physical and psychological wellness of students making them lazy and unmotivated to make contact with the general population face to face. The guardians should check and adjust on their kids when they utilize the web. They ought to be suspicious whether they are utilizing it for fitting time period or not. The companions and educators ought to likewise enable understudies to make them mindful of the negative impacts and clarify what they are losing in reality by adhering to these long range interpersonal communication locales.

Impact of Social Media on Society

As we all are well aware of social media to facilitate a massive impact on our society. Some social media destinations have changed the way where individuals convey and mingle on the web. Person to person communication destinations render the open door for individuals to reconnect with their old companions, partners and mates. Person to person communication destinations render the opportunities for individuals to reconnect with their old companions, partners and mates. It additionally causes individuals to influence new companions, to share content, pictures, sounds, recordings among them. Web-based social networking moreover changes the life style of society.

Positive Effect of Social Media on Society

- Connectivity: The first and foremost benefit of the social media is connectivity. People from anywhere can connect with anyone. Regardless of the location and religion. The prettiness of social media is that you can attach with anyone to learn and share your thoughts.
- Education: Social networking provide various benefits to the students and teachers. It is very easy to educate from others who are experts and professionals via the social media. One can follow anyone to learn from him/her and enhance his knowledge about any field. Regardless of our location and education background we can educate ourself, without paying for it.
- Help: You can impart your issues to the group to get help and energy. Regardless of whether it is helping in term of cash or in term of advices, you can get it from the group you are associated with.
- Information and Updates: The primary favorable position of the web-based social networking is that you refresh yourself from the most recent happenings around on the planet. More often than not, Television and print media nowadays are one-sided and does not pass on the genuine message. With the assistance of web-based social networking you can get the actualities and genuine data by doing some exploration.
- Advertising: We can promote our business to the largest audience. The whole world is open for you, and can promote to them. It will help in increase the profits and achieves the targets of Business.
- Noble Cause: Social media can also be used for the noble causes. The public is making use of social media for contribution for needy people and it can be a quick way to help such people.
- Helps in Building Communities: Since our world has different religions and beliefs, so people of different communities can connect to discuss and share related stuffs.
    - Conventional marketing mediums such as the radio, TV commercials and print ads are completely obsolete now and demand for thousands of dollars. With the use of social media the businesses can connect with their targeted customers for free, the only cost is energy and time.
    - The increasing popularity of social sites like Twitter, Facebook and LinkedIn, social

networks has gained attention as the most viable communication choice for the bloggers, article writers and content creators.

- These long range informal communication destinations have opened the open door for every one of the bloggers to associate with their well-informed customers to share your ability and articles your viewers will share your articles, blog or expertise in their social circle which further enhance your networks of the followers.
- Students and experts are competent to share and exchange information with like-minded people and can ask for the input and opinion on a particular topic.
- Social Media helps to meet people who have not met outside the social media forums.
- Social Media helps to share ideas beyond geographical boundaries.
- It provides open opportunity for all writers and bloggers to connect with their clients.
- It unites people on a huge platform for the achievement of specific goals. This brings positive change in the society.

Negative Effect of Social Media on Society

- Cyber Harassing: The greater parts of the youngsters have progressed toward becoming casualties of the digital bulling over the past. Since anyone can make a phony record and do anything without being tailed, it has ended up being exceptionally straightforward for anyone to spook on the Internet. Dangers, terrorizing messages and bits of gossip can be sent to the majority to make inconvenience and uproar in the general public.
- Hacking: Personal information and security can be hacked and shared on the Internet. Some twitter and Facebook accounts have been hacked in the past and the programmer had posted materials that have influenced the person's lives.
- Addiction: The addictive piece of the online networking is awful and can exasperate individual lives also. It can likewise squander individual's time that could have been used by profitable tasks and exercises.
- Fraud and Scams: Several cases are available where people have committed fraud and scams through the online networking.
- Reputation: Social media can without much of a stretch destroy somebody's notoriety just by making a false story and spreading over the online networking.
    - It prompts fixation. Spending endless hours on the social destinations can occupy the concentration and consideration from a specific errand. They principally depend on innovation and the web as opposed to taking in the down to earth information and skill of the regular day to day existence.
    - Kids can be extraordinarily influenced by these person to person communication locales on the off chance that they are permitted to utilize them. The reason is that occasionally individuals share photographs via web-based networking media that contains savagery and sex, which can harm the conduct of children and youngsters.

- Another drawback of the web-based social networking is that the client shares excessively data which may posture dangers to them. Indeed, even with the tight security settings your own data may spill on the social locales. Downloading your recordings or pictures and copying your status is a simple assignment and should be possible inside couple of snaps.

Impact of Social Media on Kid and Teens

Media today has a huge influence on teenagers. Be it television, computers, video games, social networking sites – it hugely impacts all aspects of a teen's life. Everything is not bad with the media. If used in right way, media can transform lives of the youth from good to better. This post highlights both positive and negative media influence on teens.

Positive Effect of Social Media on Kid and Teens Help Develop Awareness

Most teens live a sheltered life. But with exposure to various media outlets, they can develop awareness about society and the world. With news channels, magazines, social networking sites blaring about world happenings, youth can understand that there is more to the world than just what is happening in the 'hood.

- Help develop social skills: Many teens are socially awkward. Social Media also gives them the probability to develop their social circle and develop new friendships. Other benefits include social confidence, heightened literacy in the media, and more social support. Social media diversifies teen's social skills, which in turn helps them navigate successfully through modern society.
- Inspire them: When our teen watches an action flick, don't just despair about the violence. With a minute control on teens, they can use the movie as encouragement, motivation and inspiration. Maybe our teen will decide to take up martial arts training, all thanks to a Bruce Lee movie. Mostly youngsters give the impression of being celebrities, and when a celebrity tells them to stay off drugs, they just might listen.
- Help develop reading and writing skills: When a celebrity talks of her favorite book, a teenager might be tempted to grab a book too.

Positive Effect of Social Media on Kid and Teens

- Distorted body image: The world is full of perfect people today. With the use of Photoshop the images are everywhere and lead to distorted body image among a number of teenagers. Anorexia and bulimia are a fall out of this body image crisis.
- Risky sexual behavior: Young people are simply finding their sexuality. It is exceptionally typical for them to be occupied with everything sexual. However, the measure of sex in media today can make an adolescent befuddled. Sex without duty – that is by all accounts the message being radiated at adolescents. This can prompt untrustworthy sexual conduct and undesirable pregnancies.
- Score low in school: Teens who watch too much television have lower scores in exams. During a study it is mentioned that persons with high degree scores watch less television

in their childhood and teenage. Another study reveals that different media affects school work differently. The media today is powerful and omnipresent. You just can't escape its tentacles. And you don't need to! Retain this information in mind, media is presently a tool and like any other tool, how you use it depends on you.

Handling Influence of Social Media on youth and Teens

Here are some ways to handle the influence of social media on teenagers:

- Check out the music, movies, TV shows, games and celebrities your child likes. Once we know what is interesting to them, we can spot the pictures and messages that are influencing them.
- It is quite easy for our teens to watch YouTube videos on mobiles so that we may not know what he is watching. Parents must try monitoring the teenager on what he is watching on TV or the internet and try to discuss some limits and rules.
- One of the best ways to help the teens navigate the influences on media is to talk about messages. For instance, if the teen love girls, we can talk to them about female friendships, life choices, self-esteem and sexuality.
- Monitoring teen's choices does not mean we ban them from watching media. It is just making them aware of the negative influences.
- We should also choose to ban some apps, shows and games. Explain why we are doing so.
- We can also encourage our teen to interpret media by putting forward some questions they can ask. Pick out a TV ad or a magazine and ask the teen: who's behind it, what is their motivation, how does it make them feel, what they needs from it, and so on.
- We can do the same with our teen's role model. Encourage our teen to ask him like why does they like that celebrity, does they follow him in real life, what values of the celebrity interest our teens and so on.

References

- Impact-of-digital-media-on-business: sourceessay.com, Retrieved 18, April 2020
- Positive-negative-impact-digital-media-business-20910: smallbusiness.chron.com, Retrieved 29, January 2020
- How-Will-Digital-Media-Impact-Education-280529197, researchgate.net, Retrieved 02, August 2020
- Can-social-media-affect-health: sysomos.com , Retrieved 10, March 2020
- A-Study-on-Positive-and-Negative-Effects-of-Social-Media-on-Society- 323903323: researchgate.net, Retrieved 20, June 2020

Permissions

All chapters in this book are published with permission under the Creative Commons Attribution Share Alike License or equivalent. Every chapter published in this book has been scrutinized by our experts. Their significance has been extensively debated. The topics covered herein carry significant information for a comprehensive understanding. They may even be implemented as practical applications or may be referred to as a beginning point for further studies.

We would like to thank the editorial team for lending their expertise to make the book truly unique. They have played a crucial role in the development of this book. Without their invaluable contributions this book wouldn't have been possible. They have made vital efforts to compile up to date information on the varied aspects of this subject to make this book a valuable addition to the collection of many professionals and students.

This book was conceptualized with the vision of imparting up-to-date and integrated information in this field. To ensure the same, a matchless editorial board was set up. Every individual on the board went through rigorous rounds of assessment to prove their worth. After which they invested a large part of their time researching and compiling the most relevant data for our readers.

The editorial board has been involved in producing this book since its inception. They have spent rigorous hours researching and exploring the diverse topics which have resulted in the successful publishing of this book. They have passed on their knowledge of decades through this book. To expedite this challenging task, the publisher supported the team at every step. A small team of assistant editors was also appointed to further simplify the editing procedure and attain best results for the readers.

Apart from the editorial board, the designing team has also invested a significant amount of their time in understanding the subject and creating the most relevant covers. They scrutinized every image to scout for the most suitable representation of the subject and create an appropriate cover for the book.

The publishing team has been an ardent support to the editorial, designing and production team. Their endless efforts to recruit the best for this project, has resulted in the accomplishment of this book. They are a veteran in the field of academics and their pool of knowledge is as vast as their experience in printing. Their expertise and guidance has proved useful at every step. Their uncompromising quality standards have made this book an exceptional effort. Their encouragement from time to time has been an inspiration for everyone.

The publisher and the editorial board hope that this book will prove to be a valuable piece of knowledge for students, practitioners and scholars across the globe.

Index

www.ingramcontent.com/pod-product-compliance
Lightning Source LLC
LaVergne TN
LVHW080725210926
848485LV00003B/519